Troubleshooting, Maintaining and Upgrading PCs

S Nugus
S Harris

D1402694

NCC Blackwell

MANCHESTER • OXFORD

British Library Cataloguing in Publication Data

Nugus, S. (Sue), *1957* –
Harris, S. (Steve), *1966* –
    Troubleshooting, Maintaining and Upgrading PCs
I.   Title II. Harris, Steve
    658.4′038′0285

    ISBN 1-85554-164-5

First published in 1992 by:

NCC Blackwell Limited, 108 Cowley Road, Oxford OX4 1JF, England.

Editorial Office, The National Computing Centre Limited, Oxford Road, Manchester M1 7ED, England.

Typeset in 10pt Palatino by TechTrans Ltd, Kidmore End, Reading, RG4 9AY; and printed by

ISBN 1-85554-164-5

Contents

Introduction   7

1   Personal Computer Configurations   9
   Generic categories of personal computers   9
   Key components of a PC   11
   The systems unit box   11
   The disk drives   13
   The keyboard   16
   The display unit   17
   The printer   20
   Other system components   21
   Bringing it all together   22
   Configuration charts   24
   Summary   28

2   Preparing To Investigate   29
   Tools and techniques for system disassembly   29
   Getting to know the personal computer   32
   Disassembling a personal computer   33
   What can be seen?   34
   Dismantling individual components   36
   Reassembling the system   38
   Summary   38

3   The Motherboard   39
   What is the motherboard?   39
   The microprocessor   41
   The maths co-processor   45
   Connector slots   45
   Support circuitry   46
   Random access memory (RAM)   48
   Read only memory (ROM)   50
   System comparison   51
   The crystal   51
   DIP switches   52
   Summary   54

4   Maximising Memory Usage   **55**

The limitations imposed by DOS   55
Modern operating environments   57
Summary   59

5   Troubleshooting Component Faults   **61**

Introduction   61
A structured approach   61
Routine checks   66
Problem reports and fault logs   67
Hand control to the troubleshooter   70
Heat and moisture   70
Diagnose a particular peripheral or unit   73
The power supply   73
Disk drives   75
System board   83
Display unit   85
Keyboard   85
Summary   88

6   Software Diagnostics   **89**

What is the role of software diagnostics?   89
How a computer system begins to work?   90
Diagnostics software   92
Diagnostic software for other systems   95
Other software for the troubleshooter   95
Summary   105

7   Preventative Maintenance   **107**

What does preventative maintenance involve?   107
Factors affecting computer reliability   107
The user   107
Heat/cold   108
Dust/ash   110
Power   111
Corrosion or rusting   114
Magnetism   115
Disk drive maintenance   116
Floppy disk care   120
Summary   121

8   Installing Optional Devices   **123**

Introduction   123
Option cards   123
Hardware devices   133
Integrated circuits   136
Summary   143

9   Using DOS For System Control   **145**

Why is software a troubleshooting issue?   145

Preparing the hard disk 145
Making and changing directories 149
Configuring the system within DOS 152
CONFIG.SYS 153
The AUTOEXEC.BAT file 158
Modifying the software configuration 160
Batch processing 160
EDLIN 161
Batch files for menus. 162
Summary 165

10 Debug **167**
What can Debug be used for? 167
Debug commands 168
A worked example using Debug 170
Summary 175

11 Hardware, Software and Data Security **177**
Introduction 177
Protecting the hardware 178
Protecting the software 179
Protecting the data 179
Analysing requirements 180
Security methods 183
Selecting a system 184
A summary of popular security products 186
Summary 186

12 Internal Control Of Your Software **187**
Introduction 187
Forms of software theft 187
Possible consequences 189
Combatting software theft 189
Summary 194

13 Computer Networks **195**
What is a computer network? 195
What constitutes a local area network? 196
Network components 197
Types of LAN 198
Hardware requirements 201
Popular local area networks 201
The cost of a LAN 204
Installing and using a LAN 204
Possible LAN installation problems 207
LAN diagnostics and maintenance 209
Diagnostics 209
The network manager 215
Maintenance 216
Summary 218

14 The Computer Virus   **219**
  What is a computer virus?   219
  Types of virus   220
  Methods of infection   221
  Recognising a virus   224
  Some popular virus programs and their effects   225
  Viruses in the network environment   228
  Preventing and curing a virus attack   229
  PC virus countermeasures   233
  How much should you worry?   234

15 Troubleshooting Case Situations   **237**
  Problem situations   237
  Suggested solutions   241
  Summary   250

16 How to Introduce PC Support into Your Organisation Effectively   **251**
  The importance of PC support   251
  Summary   252

Appendices
  1 Glossary   253
  2 Bibliography and reading list   265
  3 Board layouts   267
  4 IBM Error Messages   273

Index   **285**

Introduction

One of the latest issues in personal computing is how PC users can better control the personal computer environment in which they work. It is no longer satisfactory to depend solely on engineers to diagnose and fix problems, as maintenance contracts can be costly and the down-time incurred whilst waiting for repairs cannot be tolerated. As PC configurations become more complex, so the necessity for PC users to understand more about how their system functions increases.

The ability of individuals to master their computers has come about because general attitudes to computers have changed as they have affected a greater and greater part of our working life. Only a few years ago the inside of a personal computer was considered to be completely taboo or off limits. Anyone who opened the systems box on his/her own was considered crazy or stupid, or perhaps both. After all, it was full of printed circuit boards, semiconductors, microprocessors and other highly technical, if not downright mysterious and intimidating things. Thus when anything went wrong you had to have an expert come and see it.

This arrangement can work well, especially for the experts, who are often called out to fix quite trivial problems and paid significant fees. In fact many of the so-called experts are not all that expert. The high demand for people in the spectacularly fast growing personal computer industry has meant that frequently insufficient training is given to technical support people, and that if a person fixing your machine has three or four years experience then you are very lucky. Of course, the reality is that you don't need to have highly skilled or experienced people fix a personal computer. In fact you yourself, with a bit of preparation, ie reading a book, buying a few inexpensive tools and a bit of patience can actually do quite a lot. It is also useful to talk to other users and to your supplier. If you do call an engineer make sure that you watch what he/she is doing and ask him/her as many questions as you can.

When personal computers cease to function correctly it is invariably due to one or more of the following three types of problems:

- The user does not know how to operate the system and thus is getting a different result to what he/she is expecting. This leads to a fault which is often referred to as finger trouble.

- The software and the hardware have not been correctly configured, or there is a conflict between the two and thus there is a mismatch which has to be resolved.

- A component has failed. As personal computers are actually very reliable this is perhaps the least probable cause of a problem. Nonetheless component failure does occur and must be rectified.

The purpose of *Troubleshooting, Maintaining and Upgrading PCs* is to examine and investigate these categories of problem, leading to a discussion of the techniques and methods required for remedial action. However, before an in-depth investigation of such situations can be carried out, it is necessary provide some background information, and to introduce you to the components of your machine. How the components function and how they are inter-dependent on each other is discussed and detailed instructions as to how to dismantle a computer are supplied. Later chapters cover the issues associated with system configuration, in particular how new systems can be initialised, how option cards and add-in devices can be installed etc.

The book is not intended to train you to be an engineer, but rather to help you familiarise yourself with the inside of a personal computer and to learn how to look after the welfare of the machine. If problems do arise, how to identify these, and in some cases how to rectify them will be explained. If, as in many cases, an experienced engineer is required to fix a fault, it is hoped that after reading this book you will be able to properly brief the experts in order that the correct repair may be made as speedily as possible.

Finally, before embarking on the journey to becoming a troubleshooter a word of caution is appropriate. PC troubleshooting is recommended to users because it will reduce the inconvenience caused by minor faults and speed up rectification of such problems. Doing your own troubleshooting will also reduce corporate bills for maintenance and option board installations. However, there is a definite risk associated with troubleshooting. This risk is not only one of damaging the equipment, but also of possible harm to the you, primarily due to electric shock. Therefore throughout this book, the reader is regularly reminded to ensure that the system being worked on is switched off and disconnected from the main supply.

In short the troubleshooter must always place his/her safety first. The second concern is to not damage the equipment, and finally the speedy repair and installation of the system.

1 Personal Computer Configurations

1.1 GENERIC CATEGORIES OF PERSONAL COMPUTERS

The term PC is very broadly applied, and is used to describe anything from the oldest, slowest IBM PC, to the most modern, high-tech file server. Thus before examining the nature of the personal computer configuration, it is worthwhile considering the different categories of PC that are available.

1.1.1 THE IBM PC

The original IBM PC was released in 1980, and featured the Intel 8088 microprocessor. It set the trend that the rest of the industry has since followed. Early models were equipped only with a cassette drive for permanent data storage, offered no graphics capabilities, and were aimed mainly at the specialist and educational market. Further developments provided floppy disks and increased the quality of the screen display, but the fundamental electronics of the computer remained the same.

1.1.2 THE IBM PC/XT

A great enhancement on the original PC, the XT provided a hard disk and a slightly modified micro processor in the form of the Intel 8086. Other improvements included an increased number of peripheral slots, and the capacity for up to 512K of on-board memory, although it was still only supplied with 256K.

1.1.3 IBM PC COMPATIBLES

Soon after the release of the IBM PC a large number of manufacturers designed systems to look and function like the IBM, although they were sold at much lower prices. Far Eastern companies were among the first to realise the potential of the PC compatible market, and are still a major force in the computer industry.

Whilst the compatibles looked and operated much the same as the IBM PC, internally they were slightly different. In many cases they offered increased performance over the original, either in terms of speed of processing, or in terms of the facilities and features they offered.

When it became clear that MS-DOS was to be the primary operating system for personal computers, the other large manufacturers such as DEC, Wang, Olivetti, Hewlett Packard etc, all produced IBM PC compatible machines.

1.1.4   THE IBM PC/AT

AT stands for advanced technology, and the PC/AT, as it became known, was a significant enhancement over the standard PC and its compatibles. The AT uses the Intel 80286 microprocessor, which although offering a superior set of facilities, still retained compatibility with the original PC. The AT is noticeably faster than the PC/XT, and is supplied as standard with a hard disk and high-density floppy.

1.1.5   AT COMPATIBLES

The advent of the AT opened the gates for the compatible market. The competition for improvements in performance whilst retaining basic compatibility led to a surge of different systems becoming available. Many of these systems provided features that were not available with the true IBM system, such as 3½ inch floppy disk drives, very high quality display standards etc.

1.1.6   386 SYSTEMS

The next development from the AT was the production of computers based around the 80386 chip. This microprocessor was considerably more powerful than its predecessor, the 80286, and was capable of functioning at increased speeds. However, at this point IBM did not have a machine based on the chip, so there was little or no standardisation. As a result, the majority of the systems are very similar to 80286 based AT compatibles.

1.1.7   THE IBM PS/2

The Personal System/2 was IBM's answer to the 80386-based AT compatible. Using a slightly different design, it made better use of the features of the 386 chip, whilst still allowing standard PC software to be used.

1.1.8   486 SYSTEMS

The production of the 80486 chip lead to another boom in high-performance compatible systems, primarily for use in networks, CAD, DTP and other power-hungry applications. IBM followed with a 486-based PS/2 machine when the original bugs in the chip had been ironed out.

1.1.9   PS/1

At this point IBM had no cheap entry-level system, so decided to introduce the PS/1. This uses some of the design concepts of the PS/2, but uses the 80286 processor, and offers relatively little in the way of other features.

1.1.10   THE CURRENT STATE OF THE MARKET

There are today a variety of machines in the marketplace that are, to a greater or lesser extent, compatible with the original IBM PC. By this is meant that they will run software that would run on a PC. Most offer many more features and facilities than the original system, and all operate at much greater speeds.

However, from a troubleshooting point of view there is a great diversity of hardware that will be encountered. Some is relatively simple and standardised, whilst other devices are state-of-the-art. Fortunately they can all be classified as one or other of the key components of the PC, and it is these classifications that the following sections examine.

1.2 KEY COMPONENTS OF A PC

The remainder of this chapter focuses on the hardware components that make up a personal computer configuration. Every effort has been made to provide information that will be relevant to users of a wide range of different personal computer models.

There are five key modules that comprise a basic PC configuration. These are the:

- main system unit, containing the microprocessor chip and control circuitry
- screen or monitor
- keyboard
- disks
- printing device.

The way in which the hardware components of a computer are packaged is largely a function of the marketing strategy of the vendor. The original IBM PC configuration was comprised of four separate devices, namely the system box which also contains the disk drives, a screen, keyboard and printer. The Compaq and Toshiba portables, to mention only two of the many vendors, have the system unit, disk drives, screen and keyboard all in one box, with only the printer as a separate device. The Panasonic portable even has a built-in printer and therefore the five hardware components are in one system box. Irrespective of the way in which the components are packaged and presented, they are fundamentally separate units, and thus can be considered as totally independent components.

1.3 THE SYSTEMS UNIT BOX

The systems unit houses the main printed circuit board, often referred to as the *motherboard*, a power supply unit, the disk drives and their associated controller. Other controllers for the printer and the display, to mention only two possibilities, will also be found in the systems unit. These extra controllers are usually referred to as *option boards*, and are directly connected to the motherboard. The systems unit also contains a speaker for sound output and a number of control switches and indicator lights.

In most cases the systems unit plugs directly into a main electric socket via a suitable connector on the rear panel. The power supplied to the system is usually controlled by an ON/OFF switch which may be located on the right side of the unit towards the back, on the back panel, or on the front of the box. Also on the rear of the box there will be a number of ports, plugs and connectors. The number and design of these depends upon the type of option boards which have been installed. The weight of the systems unit varies substantially depending upon the number and type of disk drives installed, as well the number and type of option cards.

There are several computers that differ substantially from the above in terms of system unit configuration. The following list illustrates some of the main variations that may be encountered:

- Whilst the Amstrad PC is a desktop machine, it houses the power supply in the monitor casing. The aim of this design is twofold; first, the weight of the systems unit is minimised, but more importantly there is less heat generated within the box when it is operating. This in turn minimises heat-related problems.

- The majority of laptop computers, including Toshiba, Zenith, Bondwell, Sharp etc, have a substantially more compact, and therefore lighter system unit. These tend to house motherboard, keyboard, disks and screen, but make little or no provision for option boards to be fitted. Additionally, they are more difficult to disassemble due to the tight packing of the components within the box itself.

- One of the system designs that is becoming popular is the notebook computer. These are extremely small, compact, lightweight computers that are designed to be carried in a briefcase or document wallet. Typically they measure no more than 30cm wide, 20cm deep and 5cm high. However, these physical dimensions mean that there is no room for expansion at all within the unit, and furthermore there is no room for a power supply. Thus the majority of these systems run on a two or three hour battery, which must be regularly recharged using an external charger.

Owing to the sophisticated nature of laptop and notebook computers, it is recommended that users take extreme care when disassembling these systems. In fact many manufacturers use special fixings which prevent users from taking these computers apart, as the reassembly of the machines is a very delicate operation indeed.

1.3.1   THE MOTHERBOARD

The motherboard, which may also be referred to as the system board, backplane or planar, is the main circuit board of the computer. It houses the microprocessor, memory, peripheral ports and control circuitry. The detail of this key component is discussed in Chapter 3, but in terms of PC configurations the motherboard will have certain characteristics depending on the type of microprocessor and disk drive technology supported by the system.

1.3.2   THE POWER SUPPLY

The power supply consists of a metal box, which for desktop systems will be approximately 6 inches × 4 inches × 3 inches, with a socket to allow connection to the mains supply, and a high voltage output which allows another device (typically a monitor) to be powered from the same supply. The high voltage connector is normally found next to the mains socket, on the rear panel of the machine.

The remainder of the outputs from the power supply are used inside the systems unit to give power to the motherboard, disk drives and other components. They will be in the form of groups of coloured wires terminated in small plastic connectors. The number of wires/connectors and the voltages that they carry will vary between different supplies. However, in general there will be at least two connectors offering +5Vdc, two at +12Vdc, four at Ground (0Vdc), one at -5Vdc and one at -12Vdc. There may also be logic outputs, such as an indicator that the power supply is delivering an acceptable voltage. Figure 1.1 is a table of typical power supply specifications.

Certain power supplies have an extra input connection which must be grounded before the power supply will work. This is to allow security measures to be built in to the PC, such as the provision of a lock to secure the system from unauthorised use.

Power supplies in laptop systems are generally of the same designs as their larger counterparts, but are physically smaller. They tend to have a limited range of output voltages and therefore less wires/connectors. External power supplies for notebook computers are housed in a plastic case, and usually generate a single output voltage.

Input Requirements – Mains Supply

Voltage (Vac)			Frequency (Hz)	Current (A)
Nominal	Minimum	Maximum	+/–3Hz	Maximum
120	90	137	50/60	4.10 @ 90Vac
220	180	259	50/60	1.75 @ 180Vac

Output Specifications

System Configuration	Wattage (W or VA)
PC, Twin floppy, minimal additions	70W – 100W
PC, Twin floppy, several cards	80W – 120W
PC XT, minimal additions	80W – 120W
PC XT, several cards	100W – 140W
PC AT, minimal additions	100W – 140W
PC AT, several cards	120W – 180W
386 system, minimal additions	140W – 200W
386 system, several cards	175W – 225W

Figure 1.1   Typical power supply requirements

1.4 THE DISK DRIVES

Personal computers are supplied with a variety of disk drive options, from no disk drives at all to a combination of several floppy and hard drives. Although it is generally regarded as essential for standalone PCs to have some kind of disk drive, it is becoming increasingly common to have diskless workstations in the network environment, or to limit systems to a single floppy disk. Many of the new notebook computers also depend on downloading data to an external disk drive. In high security installations, hard disk only systems are a possibility in order to minimise the introduction of viruses and unauthorised software onto the system.

Early models were sold with the option of not using a disk at all, but using a tape cassette. Whilst this is no longer the case, it is still possible to find personal computers with only one floppy disk. Such a machine would not be practical for business use as there would be continual difficulties, as most software requires the system to have at least two floppy drives in order to work. Even the process of copying of disks for backup purposes is significantly more time-consuming and error-prone with such systems.

Most business computers have a hard disk and one or more floppy drives. Floppy disk drives may either be of the traditional 5¼ inch standard, or the more modern 3½ inch type. The 3½ inch disks are becoming increasingly popular because they are more compact and more robust, and therefore more reliable. In addition to their physical size, floppy disks are also specified in terms of *density*, which determines how much data they can store. Modern disks can be double density or high density. Double density disks store 360KB and 720KB of data for 5¼ inch and 3½ inch types respectively, whilst the high density counterparts store 1.2MB and 1.44MB. A new development that has appeared with recent IBM PS/2 systems is the 2.88MB 3½ inch floppy, and disks with capacities of this order will become the standard for such systems. The disk drives may be located either one on top of the other or side by side, depending on the layout of the system box.

The hard disk drive is a superior form of data storage to the floppy. Sometimes referred to as Winchester drives, this type of drive has a disk made of a non-flexible material sealed into the drive unit. Although in most cases the actual disk is 5¼ inches or less in diameter, it has much greater capacity than any floppy disk, as well as having a very much faster data retrieval speed. Hard disk technology is very reliable. One of the reasons for this is that they are supplied in a sealed air tight cabinet. The capacity varies from as small as 10 megabytes to several gigabytes. The speed of the disk is also variable, with the hard disk supplied with an IBM PC/XT retrieving data at an average speed of 85 milliseconds (ms), whilst more modern disks function at speeds of 18ms or less.

In order to use a hard or floppy disk it is necessary to have an appropriate controller card installed in the computer. This must support the appropriate technology used by the device (see below), as well as providing appropriate connections and cables for everything to be connected. Modern disk controllers are often hybrid designs, allowing two hard disks and anything up to four floppies to be controlled by a single card.

1.4.1   HARD DISK TECHNOLOGIES

There are a number of further definitions encountered when dealing with hard disk drives. These relate to the techniques that are used for storing data on the disk, and whilst the technicalities are not relevant from a user's point of view, the differences do affect the operations and usage of the devices. The terms that are most often used include:

- FM
- MFM
- RLL
- SCSI
- ESDI
- IDE

1.4.2   FM – FREQUENCY MODULATION

Frequency modulation was the original technique employed by disk drive manufacturers for storing data onto disks. FM encoding implies that data is stored in standard density. On floppies this meant that 160KB or 180KB of data could be stored on a 5¼ inch disk. FM encoding was rarely used for hard disks as it was soon superseded by MFM.

The relevance of FM is that it forms the basis for MFM and RLL techniques, and whilst it is almost never encountered in its original form, it still exerts a great influence on the design of current devices.

1.4.3   MFM – MODIFIED FREQUENCY MODULATION

MFM encoding was derived directly from FM, and is the equivalent of double density storage. That is to say 5¼ inch floppy disks using MFM encoding will store 360KB of data, and 3½ inch disks will store 720K of data.

MFM encoding is also used on hard disks, and typically offers 20MB, 40MB or 80MB of storage depending on the particular model in use. MFM is reliable and devices are available that work with most PC systems. However, there is a distinct upper limit to the disk storage capacity that can be achieved with MFM techniques if the devices are to remain reliable and inexpensive. To exceed this limit, it is necessary to use other encoding methods.

1.4.4 RLL – RUN LENGTH LIMITED

RLL encoding allows a disk drive of a given specification to store approximately 50 percent more data than its MFM equivalent. Thus RLL devices may offer 30MB, 60MB or 120MB of storage.

The drawback to RLL is that the actual storage device must be manufactured to closer tolerances than if MFM encoding was used. Thus RLL devices are more expensive than MFM devices. A second drawback is that there is still an upper limit to the storage capacity of the device, albeit 50 percent more than the MFM limit.

1.4.5 SCSI – SMALL COMPUTER SYSTEMS INTERFACE

Unlike MFM, SCSI is not a disk interface, but a systems-level interface. Up to eight controllers can be connected to a single SCSI system, and all can talk to each other. This means that a SCSI interface can be used to support one or more disk controllers, a serial port, a scanner card and so on.

A further benefit offered by the SCSI interface is that it supports large capacity disk drives. Thus SCSI devices are available that offer capacities of 330MB, 650MB and greater, and in ideal circumstances they access this data approximately four times as quickly as an RLL device.

The popularity of the SCSI interface has been further enhanced by the recent adoption of the interface by IBM for use in their PS/2 systems. However, as with all modern developments, the cost of SCSI devices is considerably greater than MFM or RLL drives.

1.4.6 ESDI – ENHANCED SMALL DEVICE INTERFACE

ESDI is a hard disk and tape drive interface that was established as a standard for high performance disk drives by the Maxtor Corporation in 1983. The ESDI interface includes advanced commands that enable the controller to read the drives capacity parameters directly from the drive. It also supports a fast transfer rate which makes it attractive for high capacity drives.

1.4.7 IDE – INTELLIGENT DRIVE ELECTRONICS

The IDE interface is the most modern of those discussed, and is especially popular with laptop computers. The principle behind the IDE design is that the electronic circuitry situated on the drive is designed to interface (almost) directly with the motherboard of the computer. Thus there is very little required in the way of controller cards etc.

This has the obvious advantage of minimising cost, as it is necessary to purchase only a disk drive, rather than the disk drive and controller card combination that is required with the other technologies. A hidden benefits is that there will be fewer compatibility problems with IDE devices because they follow a rigid standard.

The one problem that applies to all current IDE devices is that they are still limited in terms of maximum storage capacity. The largest IDE drives offer 300MB of storage, and although there are prototypes of even larger devices, it still seems unlikely that IDE will challenge the ESDI and SCSI technologies for the very high capacity drives.

1.4.8 DISK DRIVE CONFIGURATION

Most PCs, ATs and compatibles will be supplied with a one or two floppy disk drives, and normally one hard disk drive. However, it is quite possible to install up to four floppy disks, and two hard disks into any system, and these may be any combination of 3½ and 5¼ inch floppies and any capacity hard disk.

1.4.9 OTHER STORAGE OPTIONS

Various other storage media are available for PC type systems. These include demountable hard disks such as the Bernoulli box and the Tandon DataPac, as well as CD-ROMs and tape streamers. However, the technologies behind these devices still have not stabilised sufficiently for the troubleshooter to consider fault diagnosis and remedy.

1.5 THE KEYBOARD

Personal computer keyboards vary greatly in design between different models. For desktop computers the keyboard will usually be a detachable device, connected to the systems unit by a coiled cable, whilst for laptop and notebook systems the keyboard is likely to be built in to the main box.

1.5.1 KEYBOARD LAYOUT

The layout of the keyboard also varies considerably. For desktop machines there are two main options:

- the standard keyboard, as supplied with the IBM PC and compatibles, which consists of 84 keys. This has:
  - a standard typewriter layout of alphanumeric keys
  - a number of special keys marked Ctrl, Alt, Esc etc
  - a numeric keypad containing the digits 0 to 9 as well as mathematical operators, insert, delete and enter keys. These double as cursor movement keys, and therefore have arrows marked on them as well as numbers.
  - a block of *function* keys marked F1 through F10, which may be allocated by application programs for special uses and commands. These are usually situated to the left of the alphanumeric keys.
- the enhanced keyboard, as supplied with the IBM PC/AT and compatibles, which consists of 102 keys. This design of keyboard uses primarily the same layout as the standard 84 key design, but has a number of enhanced features:
  - in addition to the Ctrl, Alt and Esc keys, the enhanced keyboard also has keys marked AltGr, Pause, PrintScreen etc
  - the enhanced layout provides 10 extra keys dedicated to cursor movement, although the numeric keypad still functions in this capacity if desired
  - rather than providing just 10 function keys, the enhanced layout provides 12, which are usually situated above the alphanumeric keys.

Not unexpectedly, because of the technical differences between the two keyboard layouts, it is not possible to interchange them. Thus the enhanced keyboard will not work on PC systems, and the standard keyboard will not work on AT type systems.

Laptop and notebook computer keyboards are usually slightly simplified versions of the above designs. For example the Toshiba T5100 uses a keyboard of 82 keys, which includes cursor control keys but no numeric keyboard, although the T5200 uses a full 102 key layout, providing all the facilities associated with a powerful computer system.

Irrespective of the layout, the keyboard can be used to generate all 128 standard ASCII characters, as well as the special symbols, shapes and control characters provided within the 256 character set used by IBM PCs and compatibles. Holding a key down for more than about half a second causes the character to be repeated quickly, thus allowing streams of identical characters to be easily generated. Additionally, a buffer is provided in the keyboard which allows the operator to enter characters faster than they can be processed by the computer and displayed on the screen.

1.5.2 INTERNATIONAL KEYBOARDS

A further complication to the keyboard layout is the fact that there are keyboards available for different language options. These keyboards provide any special characters that may be required by the appropriate language, as well as accents and punctuation symbols. Each type of keyboard must be matched with a special DOS utility before the system will recognise the special layout.

The layout of the alphanumeric keys on these keyboards is often quite different to the standard UK or US keyboard. For example, the UK layout has the top row of alphabetic keys as QWERTY (this term is often used to describe the standard layout). However, the French keyboard has the top row as AZERTY.

1.5.3 OTHER KEYBOARD OPTIONS

Other keyboards are available for specific tasks or systems. For example, a special device known as the *3270 keyboard equivalent* is used when the PC is acting as a terminal to an IBM mainframe system. Similarly, Wang provide a special keyboard with extra keys that allow the Wang menu system to be more easily used. However, these devices are non-standard and when a problem occurs it will be necessary for the user to have an appropriate technical manual to hand before any remedial work is commenced.

1.6 THE DISPLAY UNIT

There is an extremely large range of display units, or monitors as they are more commonly known, on the market today. These will however fall into one of two broad categories; *monochrome* screens or *colour* screens. Most monochrome display units, and all colour display units will include a graphics capability. Most monitors can be powered directly from the high voltage output of the systems unit box, and will normally incorporate their own, independent on/off switch.

Monochrome screens come in a wide range of colours, and there is much debate as to which is preferable. Popular colours are green on black, amber on black and white on black. Some of the more advanced displays are switchable to display black on green, black on amber, or black on white, which some users find preferable. Monochrome monitors are available in many different standards, from the very simple text-only displays supplied with the original IBM PC, to modern high-tech displays for graphics and desktop publishing, some of which are over 27 inches corner to corner. Monochrome monitors usually have brightness and contrast controls, but little else.

The variation in the design of colour screens is even greater than that of monochrome devices. The simplest colour screen is capable of displaying four colours at a fairly low resolution. The more expensive monitors can display over 65,000 colours at very fine resolutions. In fact the most modern monitors actually exceed the quality of television sets. However, they are far from cheap. Controls on colour monitors include brightness, contrast, colour, as well as vertical and horizontal positioning and synchronisation.

1.6.1   DISPLAY QUALITY

The quality of the image produced on the monitor is not only dependent on the actual monitor itself, but also on the video card installed in the system unit. Video cards are specified in terms of the graphics standard that they support, which may be one of the following:

- MDA
- Hercules
- CGA
- MCGA
- EGA
- VGA
- SVGA
- XGA

In addition to the above standards, there are a number of manufacturer specific display standards. These are primarily developed for particular applications such as DTP or CAD, and are not yet widespread.

1.6.1.1   MDA – Monochrome Display Adapter

This was the first video standard for the IBM, and supplied text-only images. Crude graphic images could be created using the extended ASCII character set, but this was very different to the pixel graphics used by other display standards. Thus there was no way graphics could be produced on the screen.

1.6.1.2   Hercules

The Hercules video adapter was one of the first third-party video cards available for the IBM, and remains to this day a viable alternative to EGA and VGA. Whilst it provides only a monochrome display, it does offer a very high resolution (720*348 pixels) for graphics. Thus it is suitable for CAD and DTP applications. Furthermore it has the advantage of being relatively inexpensive, as it is a well established technology.

1.6.1.3   CGA – Colour Graphics Adapter

The CGA was, for a long time, the standard display supplied with PCs and compatibles. It offers a four colour graphics display in a medium resolution (320*200 pixels maximum).

There were some problems with early CGA displays as they were not properly compatible with the IBM PC, which lead to fuzzy or snowy displays with certain software.

1.6.1.4 MCGA – Multi-Colour Graphics Adapter

The MCGA is the CGA equivalent for PS/2 systems. However, rather than four colours, the MCGA offers 16. In other aspects, including resolution, it is similar to CGA.

1.6.1.5 EGA – Enhanced Graphics Adapter

This was the first video adapter to really offer high-resolution colour graphics. It supports up to 16 colours at resolutions of up to 640*350 pixels, a vast improvement on the CGA that preceded it. Although still widely used on PCs today, EGA was not good enough for graphically orientated applications such as DTP.

1.6.1.6 VGA – Variable Graphics Array

The VGA standard is a significant improvement over its predecessor (EGA). VGA offers 256 colours at resolutions of up to 640*480 pixels. This is actually very close to the quality offered by television sets. One of the problems of VGA is that of performance; it is normally necessary to install 512K of display memory on the VGA card if full use is to be made of its features.

1.6.1.7 SVGA – Super VGA

This is an enhanced form of VGA card, offering 256 colours at resolutions of up to 1024*768 pixels. Displays produced by SVGA cards are truly eye-catching! However, SVGA cards are produced by many different manufacturers, and tend to have more compatibility problems than other standards.

1.6.1.8 XGA – eXtended Graphics Adapter

XGA is the current state of the art in video standards. It is supplied with top of the range PS/2 systems, and offers 256 colours at a resolution of 1024*768. Furthermore, many of the graphics operations are carried out in hardware rather than software. Thus XGA displays offer much greater performance than any of their predecessors.

1.6.2 MATCHING DISPLAY CARD AND MONITOR

When selecting a display card, it is essential to match it with an appropriate monitor. Most cards specify that they must be connected to a monitor with a bandwidth of XXKHz, and similarly most monitors are specified in terms of having a YYKHz bandwidth. Certain display cards, notably SVGA and XGA, require that they are connected to a *multi-sync* monitor. This simply means that the monitor is capable of several bandwidths, and can be switched under software control.

It is not surprising that monitors supporting the more advanced standards are expensive, and those offering multi-sync capabilities are even more so. However, the quality offered by the more advanced displays will very often more than offset the extra cost.

1.6.3 GREY SCALE IMAGING

One final point to note in conjunction with monitors relates to the use of monochrome monitors with EGA, VGA, SVGA and XGA cards. When these devices are connected to monochrome monitors they cannot display colours, so instead they display varying shades of grey or shades of the principle colour on the screen. Whilst in theory the display could consist of up to 256 different shades, in practice the human eye can only distinguish between 37. Therefore there is no point in purchasing a high-spec, 256 colour card if it is being used solely with a monochrome monitor; it will look exactly the same as a less expensive, simpler one.

1.7   THE PRINTER

A wide variety of printers are available. These range from slow and inexpensive dot matrix printers, to fast, high quality, and very expensive laser printers. The following are among the more common categories of printer:

1.7.1   DOT MATRIX

The most common printer used with IBM PC compatible computers is still the dot matrix. This type of printer has improved substantially over the last few years from a low quality so called graphics printer which could not produce quality type, but which could produce an acceptable bar chart, to the Letter Quality (LQ) dot matrix printers which are standard today. The LQ printer is capable of functioning in two modes. In draft mode this printer will generate approximately 100 lines per minute, whereas in LQ mode only 15 to 50 characters per second will be generated. These inexpensive printers have caused the downfall of the once standard daisywheel and spinwriter printers.

1.7.2   DAISYWHEEL AND SPINWRITER

The daisywheel and spinwriter printers use impact technology similar to standard electric typewriters. These printers are noisy, inflexible, and incapable of producing any form of graphics. Most organisations have already abandoned these devices in favour of more modern dot matrix and laser printers. However, they do offer extremely high quality print for correspondence etc.

1.7.3   INK JET PRINTERS

Ink spray printing technology has been miniaturised and promoted by one major manufacturer, although it has not yet captured the imagination of the marketplace. It has the advantage of offering multiple colours, but has suffered from performance problems in the past. Ink jet technology is likely to compete with the low end of the laser printer market in terms of quality and price.

1.7.4   LASER PRINTERS

Laser printing is the current state of the art in printers. The price of a laser printer has been reduced by 75 percent in the last three years, and most major printer manufacturers seem to agree that the price will continue to fall in the future.

There are in fact two distinct families of laser printers. The first is typified by the Hewlett-Packard LaserJet type machines. These printers are based on a *page composition language* (PCL) that allows text and graphics to be combined to produce very high quality output. However, in PCL machines, the majority of the composition work that is required to produce the finished image must be performed by the computer. Thus these devices tend to be simpler, less expensive, and slower than their counterparts.

The second family of laser printers are known as Postscript printers. Postscript is a special programming language developed by Adobe systems, which is of particular use in printing. However, rather than relying on the host computer to perform the composition process, all Postscript printers have a processor and associated circuitry built into them that allow the printer to do the work. Thus the host computer simply transfers the raw data to the printer using the Postscript language, and the printer does the rest. Therefore Postscript devices are more flexible, faster and more costly.

1.7.5 PRINTER CONNECTIONS

Most printers are connected to the parallel port of the system unit. This connection is relatively simple and requires no special software set-up on the part of the user. However, there are some printers, in particular those using the Postscript language, that need to be connected to the serial port, and these require certain commands to be issued from DOS before they will work correctly.

1.8 OTHER SYSTEM COMPONENTS

In addition to the key components discussed so far, a personal computer may have a number of other peripherals connected to it. These typically perform specific tasks, and may not be required by all users. Examples include the following:

1.8.1 MOUSE

The mouse is a secondary input device, and is extensively used in graphical user environments such as GEM and Windows. The mouse is also essential when working with CAD and DTP systems.

It typically consists of a small plastic box, shaped to fit the human hand, with two buttons on top and a ball projecting beneath. As the mouse is moved the ball rotates, and this rotation is measured by the computer and translated into the movement of a pointer on the screen

1.8.2 SCANNER

The scanner is a special device that allows images, drawings and photographs to be converted into an electronic form and stored in the computer. They can then be incorporated into documents, designs and drawings.

Scanners are generally expensive devices, and are required only for specific applications. Furthermore there is little standardisation of designs.

1.8.3 PLOTTER

The plotter is a special form of output device used primarily for graphics and CAD applications. They offer very accurate multiple-colour drawing ability, although all but the most expensive tend to be quite slow.

1.8.4 ANALOGUE I/O DEVICES

Analogue input/output devices allow the personal computer to be connected to peripherals such as sensors, electric motors, heating controllers, humidity controls and machine tools. The use of a PC in conjunction with such equipment allows the control and maintenance of these systems to be fully automated. Thus it is possible to program heating and air conditioning systems to be as efficient as possible, to program machine tools so that they can automatically produce engineered parts with no operator intervention etc. Such systems have limited applications in most organisations.

1.9   BRINGING IT ALL TOGETHER

Once all of the components of a PC have been brought together, they will be neatly packaged in a suitable case. The exact design of the case varies greatly between different manufacturers; some use pressed metal fabrications, whilst others use injection moulded plastic. In fact the quality of the case can add considerably to the overall cost of the system. For example, Compaq computers have long had an enviable reputation as being of extremely high build-quality, and have proved to be reliable in quite hostile environments. The main reason for this is the fact that whilst externally the system appears to be cased in plastic, there is an internal metal framework that protects all of the electronic and mechanical components from damage due to accidental knocks etc. In turn, this metal framework adds to the cost of the system due to the cost of materials, and the extra time that is required to fit all the components to such a frame.

From a troubleshooting point of view this can cause its own problems. First, the process of dismantling the computer takes considerably more time. Secondly, it will be necessary to acquire appropriate screwdrivers etc for all of the fixings used by the manufacturer. In the case of Compaq this can be difficult, as they use special fixings for holding delicate components such as the disk drives.

Thus it should be borne in mind that the external appearance of a computer system does not necessarily govern its internal construction. Figures 1.2 – 1.5 show examples of typical personal computer configurations, and whilst all appear relatively similar in many aspects, the internal constructions differ considerably, and in turn the performance, functionality and pricing of these systems varies greatly.

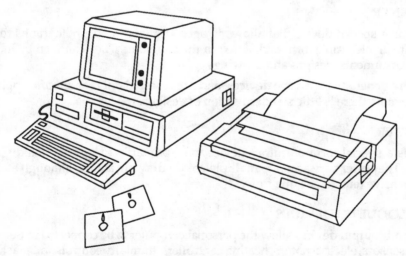

Figure 1.2   Typical IBM PC compatible computer

Figure 1.3   The Amstrad personal computer

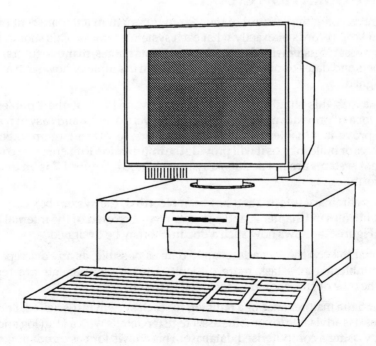

Figure 1.4   The IBM PS/2 Model 57 computer

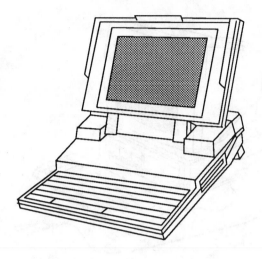

Figure 1.5   The Toshiba T5100 laptop computer

1.10   CONFIGURATION CHARTS

In order to retain on-going control of the PC environment in a department or firm it is important to keep records of exactly what each system contains. This should be held in the form of an asset register with details of components names, manufacturers, suppliers, serial numbers and dates of purchase. Figure 1.6 is an example of how such a document may be designed.

A chart such as this should be completed for every PC that the troubleshooter is responsible for as it provides useful information in a very concise and easy to read format. It will also prove invaluable if it becomes necessary to move large numbers of PCs between offices or buildings, as it will provide the information to ensure that components from different systems are not accidentally interchanged. Figure 1.7 is an example of a completed form.

Once the preliminary information has been recorded, the system box can be opened using the guidelines in Chapter 2, and a similar record created of the internal aspects of the system. Figure 1.8 shows how such a document may be designed.

It is essential to keep these charts as up to date as possible, as any discrepancies will make the troubleshooter's task more difficult. Thus if components are replaced or upgraded, the new details should be included in the charts.

In Chapter 5 the maintenance of a fault log for each system is discussed, and in larger organisations it is advisable to combine asset register details with a fault log and problem report facility using a computerised database. This allows for easy updating and cross-referencing of equipment within the organisation.

SYSTEM DESCRIPTION

Internal Reference Number: _____

		Date Purchased	Warranty Expires

Make and model of system box _____ _____ _____
    Serial number _____

Make and model of monitor _____ _____ _____
    Serial number _____

Make and model of keyboard _____ _____ _____
    Serial number _____

Is a printer attached?   Yes ☐   No ☐
    If yes - Make and model _____ _____ _____
    Serial number _____

Is a modem attached?   Yes ☐   No ☐
    If yes - Make and model _____ _____ _____
    Serial number _____

Is an external disk drive attached?   Yes ☐   No ☐
    If yes - Make and model _____ _____ _____
    Serial number _____

Is a mouse attached?   Yes ☐   No ☐
If yes - Make and model _____ _____ _____
    Serial number _____

Any other peripherals?   Yes ☐   No ☐
    Make and model _____ _____ _____
    Serial number _____

    Make and model _____ _____ _____
    Serial number _____

    Make and model _____ _____ _____
    Serial number _____

Version of DOS installed _____

Figure 1.6   A system configuration chart

SYSTEM DESCRIPTION

Internal Reference Number: ___MKT 019___

		Date Purchased	Warranty Expires
Make and model of system box	TANDON 386/20	09/91	09/92
Serial number	25897-4A		
Make and model of monitor	TAXAN VIKING I	12/91	12/92
Serial number	KG 3792/4		
Make and model of keyboard	TANDON	09/91	09/92
Serial number			

Is a printer attached?   Yes ☑   No ☐
  If yes - Make and model   OKI LASER 6   08/89 08/90
  Serial number   H-4927A-KV

Is a modem attached?   Yes ☐   No ☑
  If yes - Make and model
  Serial number

Is an external disk drive attached?   Yes ☑   No ☐
  If yes - Make and model   PFM 3.5
  Serial number   627-49682

Is a mouse attached?   Yes ☑   No ☐
  If yes - Make and model   MICROSOFT BUS   09/91   12/91
  Serial number

Any other peripherals?   Yes ☑   No ☐
  Make and model   MITSUBISHI SCANNER   12/91   06/92
  Serial number   724-148-X3

  Make and model
  Serial number

  Make and model
  Serial number

Version of DOS installed   TANDON DOS 3.3

Figure 1.7   A completed configuration chart

INTERNAL SYSTEM CONFIGURATION

Internal Reference Number: _____

Microprocessor chip number _____

   Speed Rating (MHz) _____

Make of ROM BIOS _____

   Date of manufacture _____

Is a maths co-processor installed?   Yes ☐   No ☐

   Type _____

   Speed Rating (MHz) _____

Amount of memory installed _____ MB

   Type (DIL,SIMM,SIPP) _____

   Bank 0 capacity _____

   Bank 1 capacity _____

   Bank 2 capacity _____

   Bank 3 capacity _____

Floppy disk drives   Size _____   Capacity _____

                        Size _____   Capacity _____

                        Size _____   Capacity _____

                        Size _____   Capacity _____

Hard disk drives   Type   Capacity

   Make and model _____   _____ _____

   Make and model _____   _____ _____

Option cards

   Make and model _____   _____

   Serial number _____

   Make and model _____   _____

   Serial number _____

   Make and model _____   _____

   Serial number _____

Power supply   Rating _____   Manufacturer _____

Figure 1.8   A record of internal configuration

1.11 SUMMARY

Computer systems are available in a wide variety of configurations, with vastly differing specifications and performances. However, the fundamental components are the same for all machines, whether they are PCs, ATs or the very latest PS/2s. It is important to understand the roles that each of these components play in the operation of the computer. Only when these basic functions are correctly understood will the more sophisticated details presented in later chapters be fully appreciated.

2   Preparing to Investigate

2.1 TOOLS AND TECHNIQUES FOR SYSTEM DISASSEMBLY

Chapter 1 discussed, in some detail, the categories of components that comprise a personal computer. Familiarity with these fundamental components of the system is essential before any troubleshooting can successfully be performed. However, as the components can vary so much between systems, the only certain way to identify the devices in a particular computer is to actually open the system unit and inspect the individual subsystems. Therefore this chapter describes the tools that are required to form the basis of a PC Support Toolkit, and how these tools can be used to dismantle a personal computer in order that the main components may be exposed and identified.

The toolkit that must be assembled will contain not only screwdrivers, pliers etc, but also reference material and software. Thus the term toolkit is used in its broadest sense.

2.1.1 APPROPRIATE MANUALS

All the manuals relating to the personal computer should be to hand. This includes user manuals, DOS manuals, repair manuals, technical support manuals and various software manuals. Depending on the number of option cards and peripherals attached to the computer, this could mean as many as six or seven separate manuals. It is not always easy to obtain the required hardware manuals, and users may have to be satisfied with textbooks of a more general nature.

HINT

PC user groups may be helpful in obtaining manuals, books and information about specific problems. Other members may have encountered similar circumstances themselves and have already found the solution.

2.1.2 A SELECTION OF SCREWDRIVERS

A variety of flat head and a cross-point screwdrivers will be required, ranging from the small delicate variety required for removing component screws, to the larger, stronger ones required for removing the chassis screws that hold the power supply and cover.

A set of jewellers screwdrivers will also be useful for performing adjustments and accessing certain small fittings. These are usually available in pre-packaged boxed sets.

HINT

Avoid metal handles, as if applied to live wiring the handle becomes live, and then you do too! Use screwdrivers with insulated plastic handles and a plastic sleeve along the blade.

2.1.3 PLIERS, WIRE CUTTERS AND WIRE STRIPPERS

Needle-nosed pliers are ideal for holding small nuts or wires, although flat pliers will not be so useful. When cutting or trimming wires, do not rely on the wire cutter part of pliers, but rather obtain a small wire cutter for this purpose.

Stripping the ends of wire can also prove difficult. Whilst this can be done with a pair of pliers, some cabling inside the personal computer is quite delicate and if wire strippers are available these will undoubtedly come in useful.

2.1.4 CHIP EXTRACTOR

This is an absolutely essential tool if chips are to be removed from the system. Computer chips have extremely delicate legs which are prone to bending and breaking. They must only be removed and replaced with the proper tool.

Similarly, the chip extractor insulates the chips from the static electricity that will undoubtedly build up on the users body and clothes. If this is discharged through certain chips, as may happen if they are inadvertently touched, then the chips may be damaged.

2.1.5 ANTI-STATIC WRIST BAND

Just as the chip extractor helps insulate the chips from the static buildup on the user, the anti-static wrist band insulates the rest of the computer circuitry.

The device consists of a small elasticated band which is fixed around the wrist of the user and attached to the metal chassis of the computer. Any static generated by the troubleshooter's body or clothes is instantly grounded to the case of the system, thereby negating any chance of damage being caused to the computer circuitry or components.

2.1.6 SOLDERING IRON

This piece of equipment may put some potential troubleshooters off, and indeed is only required by those who plan to build their own cables. Some chips are soldered to the computer boards in the system, but it is generally recommended that the manipulation of these be left to the experts.

2.1.7 OSCILLOSCOPE AND TEST METERS

These sophisticated pieces of test equipment will generally only be required by experienced troubleshooters, or those creating their own cables and interfaces.

An oscilloscope is a device that allows electrical signals to be viewed on a screen similar to a television. Two, three, or more signals may be viewed simultaneously, with the scaling and duration being variable for each signal independently of the others. Oscilloscopes are expensive and are not required by most troubleshooters.

A test meter is a much simpler device. It allows electrical current or voltage to be measured, either against a scale (an *analogue* meter) or numerically (a *digital* meter). Digital meters allow signals to be more accurately measured but are more expensive. An analogue meter is suitable for most situations that a troubleshooter will encounter. An important application for a test meter is in the construction and testing of cables, as they allow the constructor to determine which pins are connected at either end of the cable.

2.1.8 SOFTWARE

A range of software packages aid the identification of personal computer faults and the toolkit should include all or some of the following:

- a diagnostics disk appropriate to the systems for which the troubleshooter is responsible;
- any special terminators or loop-back cables that may be required by the software;
- a general purpose utility package such as Norton Utilities, PC Tools etc;
- a general purpose anti-virus product such as Dr Solomon's Anti-Virus Toolkit;
- a full copy of every version of DOS that is in use on any system.

2.1.9 OTHER USEFUL ADDITIONS

When dismantling a computer, every step that is taken should be recorded in writing, so that it can be retraced if necessary, and so that the procedure followed to remedy a fault is not forgotten when the fault occurs again. Therefore a pad of paper and some pencils and erasers are essential. Pencils are more useful than pens as they will not dry up if stored for a time, and also make drawing diagrams much easier.

A variety of cleaning implements will be useful. This should include lint-free cloths, cotton swabs and a suitable solvent. The simplest solvent to use for cleaning electrical contacts is ethyl alcohol. Alternatively methylated spirits can be used, or one of the proprietary cleaners specially designed for the job. When using the proprietary cleaners it is essential that the safety advice is followed and that adequate ventilation is provided.

> | WARNING |
>
> *It should be remembered that water should NEVER be used for cleaning or brought anywhere near a computer, as it facilitates the corrosion of contacts and component leads.*

Finally a collection of small containers will be useful for storing small screws and fixings during the dismantling and reassembly processes. Figures 2.1 and 2.2 illustrate some of the tools required.

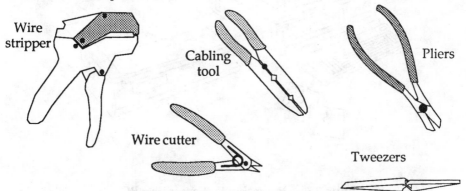

Figure 2.1   Some of the tools required for disassembly of a PC

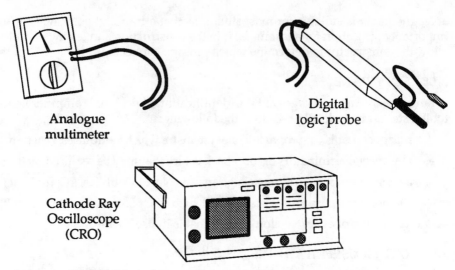

Analogue
multimeter

Digital
logic probe

Cathode Ray
Oscilloscope
(CRO)

Figure 2.2   An oscilloscope and test meters

2.2   GETTING TO KNOW THE PERSONAL COMPUTER

Before attempting to identify and possibly repair faults in a personal computer it is essential to be fully familiar with the system in terms of the various components and the role they play in the overall system. The best way to do this is to disassemble the computer in order that the motherboard (the main board that contains the elements that control the computer), may be exposed and the various parts identified.

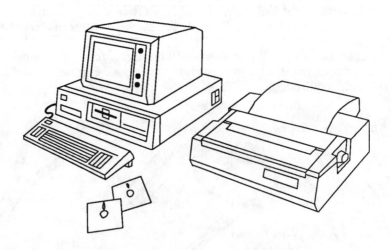

Figure 2.3   Preparing to dismantle a PC

2.3   DISASSEMBLING A PERSONAL COMPUTER

The personal computer market is such nowadays that the precise construction of a computer can vary enormously from one machine to the next. There are, however, some ground rules which apply to most systems and by following the steps itemised below readers should be able to successfully dismantle their computer in such a way that it will be easy to re-assemble after the exercise!

2.3.1   A CLEAR WORKING AREA

Ensure that the machine is on a table with sufficient space for the extracted parts to be safely placed. Have to hand a small container into which screws can be placed, and a piece of paper and pencil so that notes can be made of the steps necessary for re-assembly. Ensure that there is a good light source over the computer.

2.3.2   DISK CARE

Particularly in the case of hard disk computers it is important to stabilise the disk head before moving or dismantling the machine. This is usually achieved by running a program from DOS called PARK. To run this program, switch on the computer and access the DOS directory. Type PARK followed by Enter at the DOS prompt and an appropriate message should be displayed indicating that the disk head or heads have been locked. If this procedure does not work check with the Guide to Operations Manual before proceeding. Some modern systems, and especially laptops, have self parking disks, but this should be checked before proceeding.

> #### WARNING
> *There are different PARK programs for different systems, and it is important to ensure that you use the appropriate program for your disk.*

2.3.3   BREAK ALL POWER CONNECTIONS

Switch off the power and unplug the machine from the wall socket. Repeat this process for any attached devices such as a monitor or printer.

> #### WARNING
> *Never attempt to open a system without first disconnecting all mains power connections.*

2.3.4   DISCONNECT PERIPHERALS

Unplug the monitor, printer and other cabling from the computer. This might involve the use of a small screwdriver, depending on the type of attachment used – if a screwdriver is required it will normally be a flat blade type.

2.3.5   LOCATE THE FIXINGS

If the monitor is on top of the main computer box, remove it and position the box on the table in such a way that the fixings of the lid can be seen.

2.3.6   REMOVE THE SYSTEM UNIT LID

The lid of the box must be removed. On the original IBM PC series of computers, and many compatibles, this involves removing five large screws from the back panel of the box. However, systems differ considerably, and it may be found that the system has either a lift up lid which is simply released by pushing two buttons either side of the box, or is comprised of sliding plastic panels..

If it is necessary to remove screws, be sure to count them and make a note of the number and type of screw on paper before placing them into the screw container. If the lid of the box is screwed in place it is usually necessary to slide it forwards and then to slightly lift the cover over a rim at the front edge to free it from the system.

2.4 WHAT CAN BE SEEN?

At this point, precisely what is visible will largely be a function of the type of computer, but the general outline will be the same. Towards the back right of the box will be a large metallic box, probably with louvred vents in it. This is the power supply and fan unit, and is the component which gives the most weight to the computer. The power supply should not be tampered with by users and so should be treated as a sub-assembly. This means it can be replaced as a sealed unit, but it should never be dismantled.

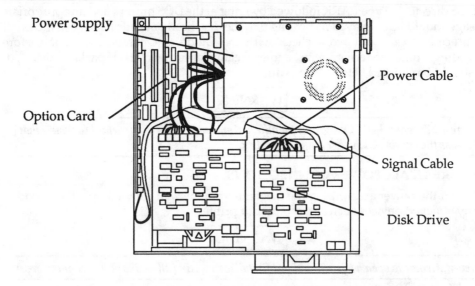

Figure 2.4   The layout of a typical system box

– In front of the power supply, at the front right of the machine are the disk drive chassis. Most computers will have at least two chassis which may be on top of each other or they may be side by side. Higher-spec models usually have four or more chassis. The disks in the chassis may be floppy disk drives or hard disk drives. It should be easy to identify which is which, as the floppy disk drive has an open mechanism whereas hard disks appear as sealed units and the actual drive assembly cannot be seen. Both types of disk drive are approximately the same size and are usually held in place in the chassis by screws on the sides of the drives. These may be flat or Phillips.

– Occupying the centre and left side of the box is the main system board or motherboard. This contains the microprocessor and a range of support circuitry, as well as the main system memory and a varying number of option cards. Figure 2.5 shows the layout of a typical 80386 system motherboard. Appendix 3 provides a range of motherboard diagrams for popular personal computer models.

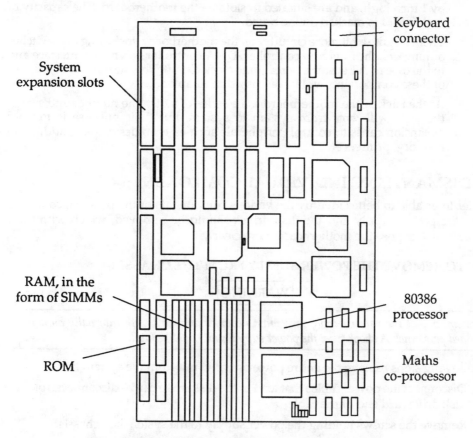

Figure 2.5   Typical IBM PC compatible motherboard

- The main microprocessor chip is usually either to the top right or middle right of the board and may easily be identified by its part number – 8088, 8086, 80286, 80386 or 80486. There may be an empty socket to the side of this chip which is reserved for the maths co-processor chip (8087, 80287, etc). 8088 and 8086 chips tend to be rectangular, whilst the later, larger chips are square.

- To the right of the processor area there will usually be a series of large connectors and in front of these will be a regular array of chips which form the system board memory. These chips will probably have numbers like 4164 or 41256. The last digits of this number (64 or 256 in this case) denote the capacity of the memory chip, in Kbits. As they are arranged into banks of 8 chips, each bank will thus have a capacity of 64KBytes or 256KBytes. Therefore, by counting the number of banks and the capacity of each, the overall memory size of the system can be determined.

- Some newer systems, such as the one shown in Figure 2.5, do not use traditional RAM chips (DIL chips as they are known), but rather opt for the more modern SIMM. SIMM stands for Single Inline Memory Module, and refers to the design of the small circuit board containing the memory chips. These are much more compact than traditional memory devices, and are capable of storing larger amounts of information. They are usually about 4 inches long by 1 inch high, and are situated in slots on the motherboard. The capacity of each SIMM is marked on the board.

- There is quite a bit more circuitry on the motherboard, including dip switches or jumpers, the interrupt controller, DMA controller, keyboard interface and in the case of AT systems, a real time clock circuit. The meaning and purpose of these components will be discussed in Chapter 3.

- At the back of the motherboard are a series of slots. The number and size of the slots will vary from system to system, but their purpose is to hold expansion cards to control peripherals such as graphics display, additional memory, printers etc.

2.5 DISMANTLING INDIVIDUAL COMPONENTS

In order to be able to better identify the various components of the personal computer system the power supply and the disk drives should be removed, which with most computers will expose the motherboard more clearly.

2.5.1 TO REMOVE THE POWER SUPPLY FROM THE CHASSIS

WARNING

Remember that the power supply unit must never be tampered with internally by non-trained personnel. A shock from the power supply unit could be fatal.

The following steps remove the entire power supply unit from the system box.

- Disconnect the power cables that lead to the disk drive card – disconnect from the disk drive card end of the cable.

- Remove the screws holding the power supply to the system box chassis.

- Ensure that no cables are still attached and carefully lift the power supply away from the chassis.

Figure 2.6 shows a power supply that has been removed from the system box.

2.5.2 TO REMOVE THE DISK DRIVES FROM THE CHASSIS

WARNING

If removing a hard disk do not attempt to dismantle the outer casing as the drive is sealed into this unit, and may only be opened in a completely dust free environment by trained personnel. An attempt to open a hard disk drive will immediately nullify any warranty, and will almost certainly result in the corruption of any data stored on that disk.

- In order to ensure that the correct cable is returned to the correct disk drive when

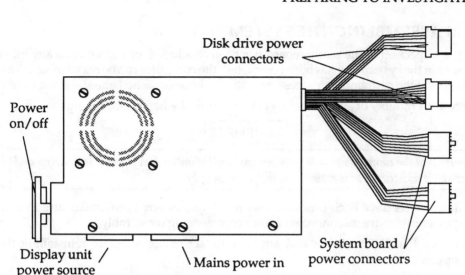

Figure 2.6   Power supply after removal

the disk drives are replaced, either mark the cables in some way with a pen or place a small sticky label on the cable to indicate whether it is the cable for Drive A or Drive B.

– Disconnect the disk drive cables from the back of each disk drive.

– Remove the screws holding the drives to the chassis. These tend to be located to the right of each drive.

– Gently remove the disk drives from the chassis.

2.5.3   TO REMOVE THE OPTION CARDS

It is likely that all or some of the option card slots on the motherboard contain cards which control peripherals such as printers, or modems, as well as colour graphics and additional memory. These may also be removed and whilst in most cases it does not matter which slot which card is placed in, there are exceptions to this rule so it is worth noting down, or marking each card so that they will be replaced in the same slots.

– Remove the Phillips screw which attaches the card to the rear of the system box.

– Ensure that there are no cables attached to the card. If there are, and there may be some very small cables which control the clock or the speaker of the computer, be sure to note exactly where they were positioned before removing them.

– The option card may now be lifted out of the slot. The fit is often quite tight and it may be quite stiff to remove. Be careful not to grip the card over the circuitry, but touch only the edges of the card.

The system box should now contain little more than the motherboard and the chassis for the disk drives.

Before proceeding to examine the motherboard in more detail, ensure that each component is placed safely on a table and that all screws are collected into a pot and are not loose on the table.

2.6   REASSEMBLING THE SYSTEM

Once the inspection of the motherboard has been concluded, or indeed once any other work within the system box has been completed, the computer can be reassembled. This is a reverse of the dismantling process, and should be approached one stage at a time.

There are a number of special factors to bear in mind when reassembling the system:

REMEMBER

Ensure that the components of the system are handled only when the user is wearing and anti-static wristband, or is earthed via the power supply.

– If any tests have been conducted with the system box open, make sure that all power cables are disconnected before commencing reassembly.

– Check that DIP switches and jumpers are set correctly before reinstalling the option cards etc.

– Always hold circuit boards by their edges; try to avoid touching the metallic tracks, as perspiration on the fingertips may exacerbate corrosion.

– Remember to refit cables the correct way round. The markings placed on the cables at the time of disassembly will assist in this process.

– Ensure that the power supply, disk drives, and all option cards are securely fixed during the reassembly process. Failure to observe this precaution will most likely result in hardware failure at a later date.

– Don't over-tighten screws and fixings, as it is possible to damage the components that they are holding in place. A firm but careful touch is required.

Once the system has been completely reassembled, and the system unit lid is in place, reconnect all external cabling and switch on. Check that the computer boots into DOS in the normal way, then if possible run a diagnostics utility that will check the integrity of the system. Chapter 6 covers such software in more detail.

2.7   SUMMARY

The process of dismantling a PC is one that many troubleshooters will have to repeat on a regular basis. The most important issue is familiarity with the computer system in question, as this will ensure that no steps are overlooked in the diagnosis of the problem.

When preparing to dismantle the system, a suitable working area should be cleared, preferably with a light source overhead. Appropriate tools should be collected together along with containers for screws or fixings which will be removed. Before starting to dismantle the unit a checklist should be prepared, and as much information as possible should be filled in. The system box can then be opened and the necessary units replaced or repaired. Further details should be entered on the checklist as they become available.

It should always be remembered that certain units are not serviceable except by trained technicians. This refers particularly to hard disk units and power supplies. If faults with these components are suspected then it will be necessary to engage a maintenance department or organisation to effect repairs. It is also important to check the warranty situation before attempting any investigative or repair work on a system.

3   The Motherboard

3.1   WHAT IS THE MOTHERBOARD?

The motherboard, or system board, of a personal computer houses the major components that constitute a working system, including printed circuit boards, chips and crystals, as well as wires, sockets and cables. This chapter explains the major components in some detail and enables the reader to identify the various parts on his/her own system.

Unfortunately, with the ever increasing number of IBM compatible computers in the market it is impossible to supply every variation on the layout of the motherboard. Figure 3.1 shows the motherboard for an IBM PC and Figure 3.2 shows the motherboard for an IBM PC/XT compatible. Figure 3.3 shows the motherboard of an IBM PC/AT computer, and Figure 3.4 shows the layout of a PC compatible computer that uses the 80386DX microprocessor.

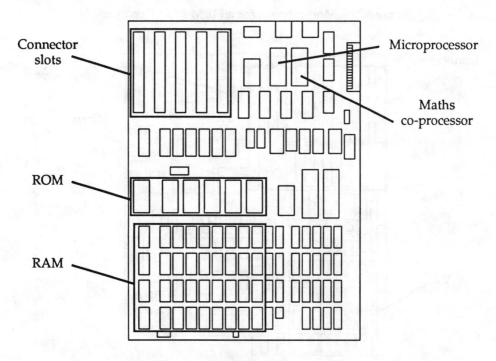

Figure 3.1   Motherboard layout for the IBM-PC

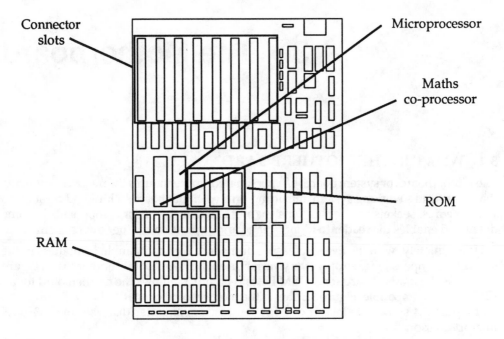

Figure 3.2   Motherboard for an IBM-PC/XT compatible

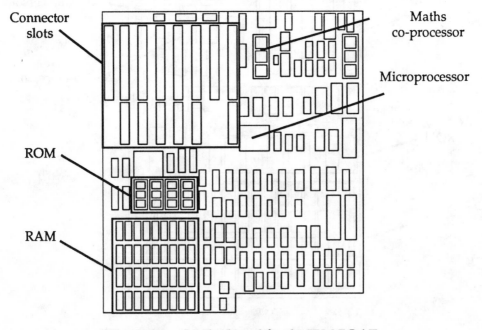

Figure 3.3   Motherboard for the IBM-PC AT

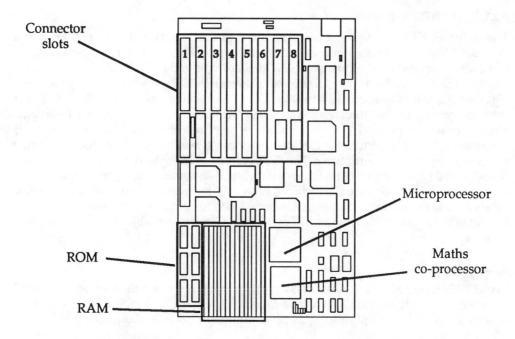

Figure 3.4   Motherboard for an 80386dx system

Readers should spend some time identifying the components described below on their own computers, especially if the layout does not compare exactly with any of the supplied diagrams. A diagram of the motherboard may be supplied in the user manual which should help with the identification process.

Providing the computer is a 100 percent IBM PC or IBM-AT compatible machine, the numbers of the chips should correspond with those mentioned in this chapter – only the precise location is likely to differ. Some 386 systems will also follow the same basic numbering system.

3.2 THE MICROPROCESSOR

The microprocessor is the central engine of the computer, and hence is referred to as the central processing unit (CPU). It is the device which has the ability to carry out instructions, ie to execute programs, and is sometimes described as the brain of the computer.

Most personal computer microprocessors today are manufactured by Intel and those most frequently encountered are the following:

Intel 8088	Intel 80386
Intel 8086	Intel 80486
Intel 80286	

The original IBM PC and XT computers use the Intel 8088 microprocessor, whilst the IBM-AT uses the Intel 80286 processor chip. Most IBM PC compatible computers use the Intel 8086 chip whilst the AT compatibles use the 80286. More recent systems, as well as some IBM PS/2 models, use the 80386 and 80486 processors.

3.2.1 THE 8088 AND 8086

The 8-bit 8080 CPU was the first processor used as a self-contained computer brain in a dedicated, standalone microcomputer. This chip was in the Altair/MITS which was a kit computer produced in Albuquerque, New Mexico in the mid 1970s. After much enhancement this chip was reintroduced some years later as the Zilog Z80 - a second generation eight-bit chip which utilised the same machine instructions as the Intel 8080. Looking for more processing power, Intel refined the 8080 architecture to accommodate 16-bit data chunks, enabling the CPU to cope with more complex instructions and to increase its execution speed. The result was the Intel 8088 which was adopted by IBM for its first generation of personal computers. The 8088 is an 8/16 bit hybrid chip, which has an 8 bit external data bus, and a 16 bit internal data bus. The next development of the 808 was the improved 8086 processor, which has both a 16 bit internal and external data bus. When the other major manufacturers developed IBM compatible computers, they tended to adopt the superior 8086 processor. The original Compaq portable PC is an example of such a system.

3.2.2 THE 80286

The 80286 chip used in the AT and compatible machines is a still more sophisticated member of the original family which is capable of mimicking a standard 8086 CPU in *Real Access Mode*, or supplying 16/24-bit computing power in *Protected Virtual Access Mode*.

Real Mode means that the 286's special features and special powers are in disguise, so that the computer is fully compatible with a standard PC. However, even when running in real mode, the 286 microprocessor is inherently much more powerful than an 8086 or 8088 chip because it can execute programs faster due to a more streamlined internal design requiring fewer clock cycles. For example, to multiply two numbers together with an 8088 processor takes about 120 clock cycles, but the same operation will only take 20 cycles with the 286 processor. Furthermore, the speed of each clock cycle is greater with the 286 chip than the 8088 or 8086. A standard PC uses a 4.77MHz clock which means that the clock that drives the microprocessor clicks 4.77 million times each second. With the 286, however, the clock speed will be 6 MHz or more. Bench tests have shown that an IBM-AT is approximately five to eight times faster than a standard IBM PC.

Protected Mode with the 80286 processor provides a series of features that can expand the number of programs the computer can be working on at one time. This is accomplished through four main facilities, namely *protection, extended memory, virtual memory* and *multi-tasking*. As many of the most popular PC programs assume they have exclusive use of the computer, they are not compatible with protected mode, and indeed the MS-DOS operating system was not designed with protected mode in mind. For these reasons protected mode is not widely used and the only real benefit gained by users of the 80286 microprocessor over the 8088 and 8086 chips is the faster speed of operation.

3.2.3 THE 80386

The 80386 chip is a true 32-bit processor, ie it allows 32 bits, or four bytes of data to be transferred simultaneously. In information terms this means that approximately four characters can be processed by a single command. This can be contrasted with the original 8088 chip that could only process one character at a time. In addition to this increase in processing capacity is the fact that a considerable amount of design effort has been put into the streamlining of the internal circuitry of the 80386 to improve its speed of operation. The combination of these two factors means that the 80386 is able to process data much more efficiently than its predecessors, thus greatly speeding up all operations.

The 80386 has also given computer designers much more flexibility in the way that their systems can be developed. It is compatible with all 80286 features, including protected mode. Additionally it allows the system configuration to be determined by software, thus reducing the complexity of the motherboard and negating the need for DIP switches and jumpers. These problematic components have been replaced by ROM or software driven configuration routines.

3.2.4 THE 80486

The 80486 is a more compact version of the 80386. However, Intel have also grouped several other chips onto the device in addition to the basic CPU. These include a floating-point arithmetic unit, a cache buffer and an associated controller. Externally the chip appears similar to the 80386, and has a 32 bit data bus. Its internal architecture is somewhat different, and is designed around a mixture of 32 bit and 64 bit data transfer connections. The use of the cache buffer means that fewer accesses will be required to the main memory of the system, as when using appropriate software most data that is required will already be in the cache area. The effect of this is that 1 486 system running at 25MHz will perform significantly better than a 386 system running at 33MHz. As the cost of computing is still exponentially high on systems with clock speeds in excess of 25MHz, the 486 processor is an attractive option for many users. Although the first 80486 powered systems ran at 25MHz, this speed was soon boosted to 33MHz, and in July 1991 Intel released the specifications for a 50MHz version of the 80486, which is ideal for high power applications such as computer aided design and file servers.

3.2.5 THE SX CHIPS

All of the chips discussed so far have been unrestricted versions, offering the maximum possible computing power and performance that their designers could offer. However, from the user's point of view there are a number of problems with this design philosophy:

- Every time a new processor is produced, new motherboards have to be designed to accommodate it

- As the microprocessors are state-of-the-art, they are very expensive, as are the appropriate supporting chips which are also required on the motherboard

- As soon as a new processor becomes available, software is generally upgraded to take advantage of the new features that it offers. Thus the software offers significantly lower performance when run on older systems.

These problems mean that to stay at the forefront of technology and use the most modern software it is necessary to buy brand new computer systems every 18 months or so. To alleviate this problem to some extent, Intel released some slightly restricted versions of the 80386 and 80486 chips, called the 80386sx and 80486sx respectively.

The 80386sx is internally identical to the full 386, or 80386dx as more correctly called. However, externally the 80386sx is restricted to a 16 bit data bus, and a 24 bit address bus. This in turn means that motherboards using the 386sx can be closely based on 286 systems (although they are NOT identical), and therefore are significantly cheaper than the true 80386dx systems. An additional benefit is that the cost of an 80386sx chip is much less than an 80386dx, and only slightly greater than that of an 80286. Thus overall, the 80386sx allows systems to be produced at a very economical price, whilst still retaining many of the advanced features of the 80386dx.

The 80486sx is designed in a slightly different way. Externally it appears to be the same as a true 80486dx, but internally there is a difference; it does not have the in-built maths co-processor that the true 80486dx has. Thus it is slightly restricted in terms of overall performance when compared to the original. However, for many applications the maths co-processor is little used. It is the in-built memory cache that accounts for a large proportion of the performance increase of the 486 over its predecessors, and the cache is present in the 486sx as well. Thus in this case the savings made are in terms of the cost of the microprocessor, which in its original form is quite expensive.

Both of the sx chips have speed ratings that are lower than their dx counterparts. This means that they run at a slower clock rate (typically 20 percent or so slower), but it also means that less expensive support circuitry is required on the motherboard. Therefore, there is a further reduction in the price of an sx based system compared to a dx based system. Figure 3.5 summarises the microprocessors that are used in personal computers.

Chip	Internal Data Bus	External Bus Data	Address	Speed Rating
8088	16 bit	8 bit	20 bit	4.77MHz
8086	16 bit	16 bit	20 bit	4.77MHz
80286	16 bit	16 bit	24 bit	6 – 12MHz
80386	32 bit	32 bit	32 bit	16 – 33MHz
80386sx	32 bit	16 bit	24 bit	16 – 25MHz
80486	32 bit	32 bit	32 bit	25 – 50MHz
80486sx	32 bit	32 bit	32 bit	20 – 33MHz

Figure 3.5   Comparison of popular microprocessors

It is in the microprocessor that the arithmetic/mathematical functions are executed and where the logical operations are performed. In fact microprocessors can perform the four basic arithmetic operations of addition, subtraction, division and multiplication. As well as performing arithmetic the microprocessor controls a variety of instructions referred to as *logic*. There are three main kinds of logic operation: *tests, conditional branches* and *repeats*. These operations are required many thousands of times every second, and so the performance of the microprocessor is the major determinant of the computing performance of the system.

One of the major differences between the various chips listed above is the speed at which they execute instructions. For a PC using the 8088 microprocessor, two numbers can be added together about one million times in a second. Two numbers can be multiplied together about 40,000 times in a second, and a conditional branch may be performed approximately half-million times in a second. On average a PC using the 8088 chip performs a quarter of a million instructions per second. In the case of a system using the 80286 microprocessor, adding two numbers may be performed two million times a second, or approximately twice as fast as an 8088 system; multiplying can be done about 300,000 times a second, or over seven times faster than in the 8088, and a conditional branch can be performed about 600,000 times each second, about five or six times the speed of the original IBM PC.

It is important to bear in mind when assessing these figures that even the simplest task that the computer is instructed to do involves hundred and thousands of individual detailed instructions being performed. Even so, since the computer can perform millions of instructions in seconds, tasks can be completed very quickly.

3.3 THE MATHS CO-PROCESSOR

On all but 80486dx systems, somewhere on the motherboard there will be an empty slot into which an optional 8087, 80287 or 80387 maths co-processor chip may be placed. This provides for high speed numeric processing whereby the main microprocessor offloads appropriate number-crunching onto the special circuits of the 87 chip. However, this is only possible when the software in use is compatible with the presence of an 87 chip. In fact there are two categories of programs that use the 87 chip, those which require its presence, such as certain versions of AutoCAD, and those which are able to take advantage of it, such as Lotus 1-2-3 or Framework. Maths co-processor circuitry is built into the 80486 chip when it is manufactured, although there is an 80487 chip available for use with the 80486sx.

On PC and XT systems the socket for the 8087 is usually located immediately to the right of the microprocessor. On ATs and compatibles this may not be so, and in fact the chip could be located anywhere on the motherboard. The situation is further confused by the fact that 80287 co-processors are not necessarily the same shape as the 80286 chip, and therefore the sockets can look very different, although in most systems the circuit board is printed with the appropriate chip number to aid identification.

Whilst the 80X87 chips predominate as maths co-processors, they are by no means the only ones available. For example, there is a Weitek device that takes the place of an 80387, offering similar functionality. However, in order to use a non-standard maths co-processor, it is necessary to use software that specifically supports it.

3.4 CONNECTOR SLOTS

At the rear of the motherboard there are a number of connector slots. These slots are used to connect option cards to the motherboard, which give the system integration flexibility and expandability. Through these connector slots extra memory or additional devices are added.

The slots are numbered J1 (slot 1) through J5 (Slot 5) from left to right on the original IBM PC. There are eight connector slots on the IBM PC/XT, numbered J1 through J8. On the PC and XT (and all PC/XT compatibles) these slots are 8-bit slots, following the ISA (Industry Standard Architecture) design standard which was used by IBM on these early machines.

The PC/AT also has eight slots, although six of these are 16-bit slots allowing more advanced devices to be connected. These slots also follow the ISA design, but obviously have more connectors.

PC, XT and AT compatible machines have varying numbers of slots, typically between six and nine. These may be a mixture of 8-bit and 16-bit slots. The exceptions to this are portable and laptop computers, which may have only one, or sometimes no expansion slots at all. In order to add devices to these systems it is usually necessary to purchase a special interface box into which the cards are placed.

IBM's PS/2 systems have varying numbers of slots, although rather than use the ISA design they have adopted a new standard called the MCA (Micro Channel Architecture). The MCA interface is more flexible than the ISA, and allows devices to interface more easily with the computer.

One of the problems with MCA is that the design is owned by IBM, and in order for third-party companies to use it in their machines they must pay a royalty. For this reason a group of companies collaborated to produce a new standard called EISA. EISA is similar to MCA in that it allows devices to communicate more effectively with the computer, but designers can use the EISA standard without having to worry about royalties.

The EISA standard is most often encountered in 80386 and 80486 based systems, and allows a 32 bit interface to be used if required. So far the only boards that seem to use the 32 bit interface are memory boards that allow 386 and 486 systems to access memory in excess of 16MB. Therefore systems using EISA will only have one such 32 bit slot, the remainder being 8-bit and 16-bit connectors.

Any slot may be used for any type of adapter card, assuming the card is configured for the appropriate standard (ISA, MCA or EISA). On early machines, IBM recommended that the second slot be used for the display adapter although there is no clear reason for this. The one thing to bear in mind when allocating slots for option cards is where the cabling will go that is connected to each card. Thus it is generally advisable to have floppy and hard disk controllers over to the right, as they will be nearest the disk units. Display cards often have no internal cabling and can be positioned over to the left. Other cards may have internal and external connections and should be positioned appropriately.

A typical configuration for a 386 based system (as in Figure 3.4) might be as follows:

Slot Interface Card

1   32-bit memory expansion card, containing 8MB of RAM

2   VGA display adapter card, no internal connections, external connection to monitor

3   Mouse card, no internal connections, external connection to mouse

4   Multi-IO card, providing one serial and one parallel interface (in addition to those provided by the motherboard), internal connection to a parallel connector, external connection to serial cable

6   16-bit floppy disk controller, internal connections to two floppy drives, no external connections

8   8-bit IDE hard disk interface card, internal connection to hard disk unit, no external connections

3.5 SUPPORT CIRCUITRY

Most of the chips on the motherboard perform supporting operations, doing routine tasks and thereby allowing the microprocessor to get on with running the software.

Whilst these chips were standardised by IBM, other companies may purchase them from different manufacturers who in turn renumber the devices with their own codes. Therefore the chip numbers quoted below refer to the original PC, XT and AT machines, and may not exactly match the chips used by other compatible systems. However, the chips are required for the computer to function, and will be present in some form or other.

The chips that are of particular interest are:

- the interrupt controller
- the clock generator
- the programmable timer
- the bus controller
- the direct memory access controller.

The technical reference manual for a computer system will identify these chips, and also give their locations on the motherboard. The following sections describe their uses.

3.5.1 THE INTERRUPT CONTROLLER

To the left of the microprocessor there is the 8259 interrupt controller. The IBM PC is described as an interrupt driver machine because all I/O devices are connected with the CPU, and gain it's attention by causing an interrupt signal to occur. The 8259 is the chip which processes the interrupts from the peripherals and generates the signal which is sent to the CPU. On 286 and 386 systems there are likely to be two interrupt controllers to allow for the 15 different interrupt lines, as opposed to the eight available on a PC.

Interrupts are one of the key things that make the computer different from any other man-made machine because they enable the computer to have the ability to respond to an unpredictable variety of work that comes to it. With the interrupt feature the computer can suspend whatever it is doing, and switch to another task, based on something that causes the interruption - such as pressing a key on the keyboard.

Every part of the computer which might need to request the attention of the micropro-cessor is allocated an interrupt number. For example the keyboard has its own interrupt, in order that the microprocessor is aware when a key has been pressed or released; the PC internal clock has its own interrupt which informs the computer's time keeping program each time the clock has ticked - about 18 times a second. Disk drives, printers etc all have their own interrupts. When installing certain option cards into a system, it may be necessary to allocate interrupts. This is discussed in Chapter 8.

3.5.2 CLOCK GENERATOR

At the far right of the second row of chips is the clock generator. In a PC this is identified with the number 8284 and in the AT has the number 88284. The clock generator chip uses a quartz crystal, like those used in quartz watches, as the accurate basis for its timing. The clock generator subdivides the crystal's ultra-fast beat into the fast beat required by the computer, and generates it in a form that other parts of the circuitry can refer to.

3.5.3 PROGRAMMABLE TIMER

This chip is closely related to the clock generator and is identified by the number 8253 on a PC, and 8254 on an AT. It is able to produce other timing signals that occur every so many clock cycles. It is the fact that the rate can be changed that makes this chip programmable. For example, if the computer's main clock runs at six million cycles per second (ie 6MHz), as it does in the AT, and something else is to be performed 6,000 times per second, then the timer chip may be programmed with a count of 1000, which means that for every 1,000 clock cycles the programmable timer will put out a signal representing six million divided by 1,000, or 6,000 times a second. This facility can be used to produce regular timing signals for many purposes, for example, generating sounds on the computer speaker.

3.5.4   BUS CONTROLLER

Information signals pass around the components of the computer through a bus. This is a communication channel, or a set of wires, that act as a common carrier for signals passing from any one part of the computer to any other part. It is referred to as a bus because all the signals ride on it.

The option card sockets at the back of the system board are connected to all the lines of the computer's bus which means that whenever something is plugged into an option slot it can talk to every part of the PC that uses the bus, including the memory and the microprocessor. The bus controller chip, which is identified as the 8288 on a PC and the 82288 on an AT is responsible for controlling and regulating the flow of this information.

3.5.5   DIRECT MEMORY ACCESS

Usually positioned next to the 8253 is the 8237 which is a Direct Memory Access (DMA) controller, used to interface with the disk drives. There are likely to be two 8237 chips in 286 and 286 systems. The DMA facility enables the computer's memory to communicate directly with the disk drives, without data having to pass through the microprocessor. This leaves the microprocessor free to process more instructions, and therefore significantly enhances the performance of disk-related tasks.

The IBM PCJr had no DMA facility, and was therefore very slow when accessing disk data. Thus if examining a PCJr, it will be found that no 8237 DMA controller chip is present.

3.6   RANDOM ACCESS MEMORY (RAM)

The RAM of a computer is where the programs and data are temporarily stored while the program is being executed and the data is being processed. The memory is the computers workplace and is often thought to be analogous to a desk top. It is that part of the computer in which all the main activity takes place.

Early computers had relatively small amounts of memory. Even well into the '60s it was unusual to find computers, including mainframes, with more than 512K. Consequently memory is still measured in terms of K which represents 2^{10} or 1024 bytes or characters. As memory has become cheaper and microprocessors have become more powerful, machines became capable of using millions of characters of memory. Therefore most modern personal computers are sold not with kilobytes, but with megabytes of memory.

The computer's memory is said to be *volatile*, ie it is not permanent. This means that the contents of the memory will be lost when the power is switched off. It is because of the volatile nature of the computer memory that long term storage devices such as disk drives and magnetic tape drives are required.

To cope with this volatility a few computers are supplied with built-in batteries which effectively never allow the power to be switched off, whilst older computer systems coped by using bubble memory which is a non volatile form of magnetic memory.

However, the vast majority of PC systems provide RAM in the form of integrated circuits (ICs or silicon chips). These are small, compact and inexpensive, and are available in many different capacities, the most common of which are 64Kb, 128Kb and 256Kb. Note that Kb here represents Kilobits, as opposed to Kilobytes. Thus it is necessary to have eight individual 64Kb chips to generate 64KB of memory. RAM chips are volatile, and therefore all information in RAM must be stored to disk to ensure its permanency before the system is shut down.

3.6.1 SINGLE INLINE MEMORY MODULE (SIMM)

A storage device being offered by many systems is the SIMM. The term Single In-line Memory Module refers to the format and layout of the edge connector of the board that forms the base for the device. A SIMM appears as a mini option card, approximately four inches long by ¾ inch high, and each sits in a special connecting slot on the motherboard. Each SIMM typically carries up to 4MB of RAM chips, and slots are normally provided for four, or even eight, independent SIMMs. Therefore 16MB or 32MB of memory can be installed on the motherboard, although typically only 1MB or 2MB will be supplied with the system by the vendor. The simple design of the SIMMs means that it is very easy to add more memory by plugging in another SIMM or replacing an existing one with one of a higher capacity. SIMMs are set to become the standard way of implementing memory in any computer configuration due to their small physical size and their ease of use.

3.6.2 DYNAMIC VS STATIC

A further differentiation that is applied to RAM is whether the chips are Dynamic or Static RAM chips.

- Dynamic RAM (DRAM) requires external circuitry to be present on the mother-board that takes care of *refreshing* the data. The refreshing operation ensures that the data does not degenerate while it is being stored.

- Static RAM (SRAM) requires no external circuitry, as all of the logic to perform the refreshing operation is built into the chip. Thus the supporting circuitry is more compact, simpler and less expensive.

Not surprisingly, SRAM costs more than DRAM, and therefore tends only to be used in situations where the simplification of external circuitry is more important than the cost of the RAM chips. Such applications include option cards, memory boards, and memory for compact, notebook-sized portables.

3.6.3 MEMORY SPEED

In addition to its capacity, volatility and type, memory is also categorised by its speed. Speed of memory chips is usually measured in nanoseconds (ns), although it may be quoted sometimes in terms of *wait-states*.

The speed that is referred to is actually the amount of time that the memory chip requires to respond to a request for data. Thus if the chip is rated at 200ns, it will take 200 nanoseconds to return the information stored at a particular location once the microprocessor has requested it.

If the speed is quoted in terms of wait-states, then this value is a measure of how many clock-cycles the CPU has to wait for the data to be produced. Thus if a system is quoted as having three wait-state memory, it means that every time the CPU requests some data, it has to wait three clock cycles before it gets what it asked for.

Up until the advent of the 386 processor, RAM chips typically offered speeds of between 100ns and 200ns. However, modern systems demand faster response times, so chip speeds are gradually increasing. Standard RAM chips currently offer speeds between 60ns and 120ns, although it is possible to find devices that have response times of 30ns or less! These are very expensive chips, and will only be used in situations where speed is of the utmost importance. A typical example is the use of fast RAM chips for memory caching purposes.

3.7   READ ONLY MEMORY (ROM)

There will be one or more socketed chips on the motherboard that are physically quite large, and have a metallic sticker placed in the middle. On an original PC these chips are located on the fourth row of chips below the expansion slots, and this location seems to have become standard for the majority of systems.

These chips are the Read Only Memory (ROM), and contain the basic routines which the computer requires in order to operate. On the PC one ROM chip holds the basic input/output system (BIOS) which is a set of programs controlling information transfer between the CPU and the I/O devices. The BIOS provides control for all devices except the disk drives. Included in the BIOS is a self test program called the POST, or Power On Self Test, which is executed when the system is turned on. It is this chip that identifies a computer, and when the IBM PC was first copied by Far Eastern manufacturers some models had copied the IBM ROM BIOS which contravened the copyright laws. In addition to the BIOS the PC has four more ROM chips which hold cassette BASIC (Beginners All-purpose Symbolic Interpreter Code), a simple programming language provided to allow users to create their own applications software.

Other systems use ROM chips for different applications such as assemblers, other programming languages and applications software. However, there are relatively few software packages available in the form of a ROM chip, despite the fact that they allow much quicker access to the program and reduce the amount of disk space required. On some 80286 machines and most 80386 and 80486 systems, a special program is provided in the form of a ROM chip that allows the user to determine the configuration of the system. This is the SETUP routine, and can usually be invoked by pressing a particular combination of keys (eg Ctrl+Alt+Esc on the Tandon 386 system) whilst the system is booting up. For PS/2 machines this routine totally replaces the DIP switches and jumpers used on other systems to identify memory and peripherals.

Another important use for the ROM chips is in the implementation of data security systems. These typically function at power-on by passing control of the system to the ROM, which typically require a password and identification code to be entered before access to the system is permitted. This is covered in more detail in Chapter 11, *Hardware, Software and Data Security*.

In addition to the ROM chips, there may be a number of empty sockets provided for future expansion. These are traditionally of a fixed size, and as noted above are most often situated in the middle of the motherboard.

3.8 SYSTEM COMPARISON

The table shown in Figure 3.6 summarises the system control chip types and reference numbers that are most often used in the different categories of PC and compatible systems.

DESCRIPTION	CHIP NUMBERS			
	PC compatible	AT compatible	80386 System	80486 System
Microprocessor	8088/8086	80286	80386	80486
Optional math co-processor	8087	80287	80387	N/A
Bus Controller	8288	82288		
Clock Generator	8284	82284		
Direct Memory Access Controller	8237	8237x2		
Interrupt Controller	8259	8259x2		
Programmable Interval Timer	8253	8254		
ROM	1 to 5 chips	1 to 7 chips	1 to 7 chips	1 to 7 chips
RAM	Usually 4 rows of 9 chips	Usually 4 rows of 9 chips	Usually 4 SIMMs	Usually 4 or more SIMMs
Expansion slots	From 3 to 10 8-bit slots	From 3 to 10 with 1 to 5 16-bit slots	From 3 to 10, with 3 to 7 16-bit slots & 1 32-bit slot	From 5 to 12 with 3 to 7 16-bit slots & 1 32-bit slot

Figure 3.6   Chip types used by PC systems

3.9 THE CRYSTAL

A quartz crystal is used to generate a timing signal with which the computer controls all its processes. The crystal is usually located towards the edge of the motherboard on the right upper side.

This device is used in conjunction with the clock generator and programmable timer chips to produce a range of different signals to drive various parts of the motherboard. It is the speed, or frequency of these signals which determines the speed of operation of the computer. The frequency of the chip is quoted in MHz (Mega-Hertz) or GHz (Giga-Hertz), and the value of any particular crystal is normally written on the device. Note that this value may be different to the speed of the microprocessor, due to the fact that the clock generator and programmable timer alter the original frequency to the desired value.

The quartz crystal is almost unique amongst chemical compounds in its ability to vibrate at a constant frequency when supplied with an electric current, hence its use in computer circuitry. As the value at which it vibrates can be very accurately determined, they are ideal for providing extremely accurate timing signals. This value is independent of the physical size of the crystal, rather it is determined by the chemical composition of the quartz. In fact, the physical size of the crystal is normally very small. The metal canister which holds it is usually 90 percent full of special substances to reduce the amount of electrical interference.

3.9.1 UPGRADING SYSTEM SPEED

A commonly held belief is that the speed of a computer system can be uprated simply by changing the crystal. As these crystals cost only a few pounds, it is quite understandable that this form of upgrade is of interest to most users.

Unfortunately, it was possible to use this technique only with the very first IBM PC, XT and AT type machines. If such a system is in use then it is possible to upgrade the speed from the 4.77MHz or 6MHz as standard to around 7MHz and 10MHz respectively, simply by swapping the crystal. If this is attempted, it is possible that there may be a few problems with reliability, but these are very infrequent and can usually be tolerated for the increase in speed that has been gained.

Later systems were altered to prevent this modification; the change consisted of an alteration to the system BIOS, which would enable the computer to check whether or not it was running at the correct speed. If the system detected it was running at a high clock rate then it would not boot up. There is no technical reason for this restriction; it seems to have been put in place with the sole aim of making users upgrade their systems by the conventional (and expensive) path, rather than by the unauthorised method.

3.10 DIP SWITCHES

DIP switches, sometimes referred to as system switches or bit switches, offer additional flexibility to the user when configuring the computer in a variety of different ways. The term stands for Dual In-line Package, and refers to the layout of the two rows of pins that are soldered into the motherboard from the underside of the switch body.

DIP switches are the traditional means used to inform the system about various factors, including how much memory is installed in the machine, what type of monitor is connected, whether a maths co-processor is present and how many floppy disk drives are attached.

DIP switches are troublesome devices, primarily because they are often located in difficult to reach positions on the motherboard. Access is sometimes restricted by option boards which have to be removed before the switch setting may be changed. The switches themselves are tiny and require the use of a small screwdriver or a similar fine-pointed tool.

All the switches can be positioned in one of two positions, referred to as being ON or OFF. There are normally eight switches on each block. If switches are incorrectly set, the system may not be able to recognise certain installed devices, or may try to register devices which are not present. If this is the case error messages will usually be displayed, either at start-up or when a diagnostics routine is run.

The Guide to Operations manual that comes with the computer has a full list of switch setting options. If additional devices are installed there should be information on amending switch settings supplied with the documentation for the device.

The original IBM PC has two sets of dip switches, whereas the IBM PC/XT has only one. Most compatibles have only one set. Some machines do not have DIP switches but have similar devices called jumpers which use small connectors placed over selected pins. The Epson is an example of such a system. Other systems, such as the IBM PS/2 range and many 386/486 based computers, have no DIP switches or jumpers at all, but provide a configuration routine in the form of a ROM chip. All hardware configuration information is determined by the user through this routine, thus removing the problems associated with DIP switches and jumpers.

An area in which DIP switches continue to be used is on adapter cards. These add-on cards and devices are designed to work with a wide range of machines, so it is not possible to use a ROM based routine to determine the configuration. The manuals and other documentation supplied with the device should give sufficient information to allow the DIP switches to be set correctly. They are most often used to specify the interrupt lines and the memory addresses through which the card can communicate with the computer.

3.10.1 SETTING DIP SWITCHES

As stated above, many systems use DIP switches or jumpers to determine the hardware configuration. The following example illustrates how the DIP switches are used on a Tandon 386 system. On such a system there is only one bank of switches, which specify the memory configuration and the presence of a maths co-processor, and these can be set as shown in Figure 3.7. All other configuration information is determined by a ROM based routine.

Switch Settings				Base Memory (Below 1Mb)	Extended Memory (Above 1Mb)
SW 1	SW 2	SW 3	SW 4		
On	On	On	On	512K	None
Off	On	On	On	640K	None
On	Off	On	On	512K	512K
Off	Off	On	On	640K	384K
On	On	Off	On	512K	1M
Off	On	Off	On	640K	1M
On	Off	Off	On	512K	1.5M
Off	Off	Off	On	640K	1.384M
On	On	On	Off	512K	3M

Figure 3.7   Switch settings for Tandon memory configuration

The Tandon 386 supports both the 80287 and 80387 maths co-processors. However, if the 80287 is to be used then an additional option card must be installed. The setting of SW6 determines the type of co-processor that is installed:

- Setting SW6 to OFF tells the system that an 80387 co-processor has been installed.

- Setting SW6 to ON, and installing the additional option board, tells the system that an 80287 has been installed.

If neither device is present in the system then the position of SW6 has no effect upon the configuration.

3.11 SUMMARY

Although it is impossible to supply diagrams for every motherboard available, this chapter has introduced the reader to the components that will appear on such a circuit board. It is important to ascertain the types and locations of the components on a motherboard to facilitate removal or replacement of existing ones, or addition of new ones.

100 percent IBM compatible machines will contain exactly the same devices as the original PC machine, although they may be positioned differently. However, it must be remembered that other machines may use alternative components. One of the easiest ways to identify these components is to obtain the appropriate technical reference manual for the system in question, as this will normally give pictures of the motherboard and identification numbers for the more important chips.

4   Maximising Memory Usage

4.1   THE LIMITATIONS IMPOSED BY DOS

The MS-DOS restriction of 640KB accessible memory continues to frustrate the PC user. It is, however, worth remembering that when the IBM PC was first released in 1980, the onboard RAM capacity was 16K. The fact that this could, through the use of expansion boards, theoretically be expanded to 640KB was considered irrelevant, as the maximum motherboard expansion was 64K. It is appropriate to note that at the time RAM chips were not cheap.

With the 640KB RAM as standard in many PC clones, and configurations increasingly being supplied with 1MB, 2MB or 4MB, the 640KB DOS restriction is a real one. However, the various ways of bypassing or evading this barrier and the related issue of memory speed is not necessarily straightforward.

The 640KB barrier was primarily due to the design of the 8088 processor. This chip has 20 pins on the address bus which means it is capable of addressing 1MB of memory directly. This must include BIOS, any other ROM installed on peripherals such as hard disk controllers etc, and the memory required for the screen mapping. As a result 384KB is allocated to the system. This area is known as the *system memory*, leaving 640KB available for applications and data, which is known as the *real* or *base memory*.

The situation was further complicated in 1984 when the 80286 processor arrived in the form of the IBM-AT. This processor can address up to 16MB of memory, using 24 address lines. However, to ensure compatibility Intel restricted the performance of the chip, causing it to be run in a mode compatible with an 8088. At power on, the 80286 is in *real mode*, with 1MB of addressable memory and all the other limitations of the 8088. It is possible, by changing a signal on a single pin at power up to put the 80286 processor into *protected mode*, giving access to the full 16MB. This is not, however, directly accessible through MS-DOS.

It was at the time of the AT launch that IBM introduced the term *extended memory* which refers to memory between 1MB and 16MB on an 80286 based PC. Extended memory was initially only available when working in protected mode and thus not directly accessible through MS-DOS. Therefore protected mode is accessed through software such as VDISK and RAMdisk as well as various disk caching packages, to give access to the additional memory. Other operating systems such as Unix, Xenix and OS/2 take advantage of extended memory in order to perform multi-tasking and multi-user operations.

The important point about extended memory is that the term refers to memory between 1024KB and 16MB. Therefore an AT compatible computer with 1MB of accessible memory uses the basic 640KB and the addresses between 1024KB and 1408KB. The 384KB between 640KB and 1024KB is the restricted area required by the system for ROM and Video RAM (VRAM), as shown in Figure 4.1.

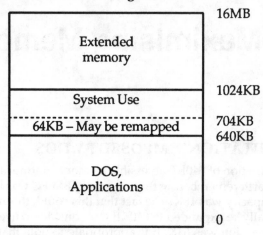

Figure 4.1   Memory usage for an 80286 processor

4.1.1 BREAKING THE BARRIER

There are three primary ways of overcoming the 640KB DOS limitation:

- Remap a portion of the system area
- Use expanded memory
- Use extended memory directly.

4.1.1.1 Remapping the system area

There are a number of products available that will remap the memory usage so that some of the memory in the addresses 640KB-1024KB can be accessed. This is based on the fact that IBM originally reserved 384KB for system use in the PC design, but not all of this space is actually required. Therefore by remapping some physical RAM into the spare space an additional 64KB can be released for programs and data, giving a total of 704KB to the user. This facility is available to both 8088 and 80286 machines, whereas extended memory is only available to 80286 systems.

4.1.1.2 Expanded memory

Due primarily to the growth in spreadsheet usage, it became necessary to overcome the 640KB barrier more effectively. The result of the research and development performed into this area was an *expanded memory specification* (EMS). The first EMS was produced jointly by Lotus and Intel in 1985 and was soon followed by the Lotus-Intel-MicroSoft EMS referred to as LIM EMS 3.2.

This software controlled facility originally allowed MS-DOS programs to access up to 8MB of RAM using a technique called bank switching. The principle behind the technique is to set up a page frame of 64KB in the area between 640KB and 1024KB into which up to four 16KB pages of data from the Expanded RAM area can be mapped.

There were limitations to LIM EMS 3.2 and the latest offering is LIM EMS 4.0 which provides up to 32MB of expanded memory and can be successfully used by multi-tasking products such as Windows and DESQview, as well as many applications programs.

The main disadvantage of using this method is speed, as the relevant area of extra memory has to be transferred to the 64KB page frame before the data can be accessed. This may seem to be a small overhead, but when the operation has to be repeated hundreds or thousands of times it can be very noticeable. A second disadvantage is that a special software driver is required, which uses a small amount of the base memory of the computer, thus reducing the amount available for the applications software.

4.1.1.3 Extended memory

Some modern software products can directly access extended memory, giving access to the full 16MB, or 32MB in the case of 386 systems, on-board capacity. This technique means that data can be stored and retrieved at the same speed as if real or base memory were being used, without the need for the special software driver.

Examples of these products are Windows 3, Lotus 1-2-3 Release 3, AutoCAD and DataEase, all of which require high-specification systems before they can be used to best advantage. As this technique offers the fastest and simplest methods of data storage, it is likely that more and more products will be developed to take advantage of this feature.

4.1.1.4 Practical systems

The division of PC memory into real, extended and expanded memory has caused much confusion, particularly with regard to where one finishes and the other begins. A typical configuration that is advertised in the computer press is an AT compatible with 640KB of real memory, 384KB of Extended memory which is used for disk caching or RAMdisk, and 2MB or more of LIM EMS RAM which is used for applications that have been written to support it directly such as Lotus 1-2-3, SuperCalc, Symphony etc.

Other EMS products such as QEMM from Quarterdeck are available which handle the memory mapping, and with this software it is possible, using MS-DOS, to move RAM-resident software and software drivers into the area between 640KB and 1024KB and to then emulate LIM EMS 4.0 memory in Extended memory which negates the need for physical RAM mixtures.

The 80386 processor has removed many of the memory management problems as, for example, an 80386 system with 4MB of RAM and a copy of a suitable EMM driver can give any combination of real, extended or expanded RAM that users require. It does however bring new problems, not least of which are associated with speed as the 80386 processor can run at speeds of 16 to 33MHz, and most popular memory chips are too slow to cope with the faster processor clock speeds. Windows 3.0 is especially useful when working with a 386 system as it will decide whether a package requires expanded or extended memory, and installs it appropriately.

4.2 MODERN OPERATING ENVIRONMENTS

Whilst many users are happy to work directly through DOS, issuing all commands at the DOS prompt, many more are now turning to the modern operating environments such as Gem and Windows. One of the key reasons for this is the way in which these *front-end* systems simplify the operation of the computer, allowing users to run programs and manage files through a graphical interface, primarily by using the mouse, rather than having to know and understand the somewhat complex DOS commands.

However, there is a second benefit to some of these systems, particularly Windows; they make much more efficient use of the facilities offered by the PC than is possible through DOS. Thus the facilities provided by Windows allow a number of programs to be executed one after another (or even simultaneously!) even if they have totally different memory configuration requirements.

4.2.1 OPTIMISING MEMORY USE WITH WINDOWS

The current version of MicroSoft's Windows operating environment, 3.0, provides three different modes of operation. Not all of these are available on all computer systems though, and hence functionality can be somewhat limited on certain systems:

- Real mode is the simplest of all. Any PC can run Windows in Real mode as long as it has at least 640KB of RAM, although for best performance it is recommended that additional expanded memory is installed. Real mode offers the most limited flexibility, as it does not directly access any extended memory. Real mode provides maximum compatibility with previous versions of Windows applications.

- Standard mode is only available on computer systems with 80286 or greater processors, and is the default mode of operation. Standard mode provides access to extended memory, and allows the user to switch between non-Windows applications. Standard mode requires that the computer system have at least 1MB of memory.

- 386-enhanced mode allows Windows access to the virtual memory capabilities of the 80386 and 80486 processors. This feature allows Windows to use more memory than is actually available by using the disk as temporary storage. It also allows non-Windows applications to be multi-tasked. To use 386 enhanced mode the computer system must be based around an 80386 or 80486 processor, and must have at least 2MB of memory.

Thus programs running under Windows, on an appropriately configured system, may use any combination of conventional, expanded, extended and virtual memory. Furthermore there is no need to reboot the machine or make changes to the configuration data when changing between applications that have different requirements, as Windows handles all of the memory management itself.

4.2.2 MAKING THE MOST OF DOS VERSION 5.0

In mid-1991 Microsoft announced the long awaited release of DOS Version 5.0. Users the world over had been hoping that DOS 5 would finally solve the memory and disk management problems that they were experiencing, and although the new release doesn't provide solutions to every difficulty it is at least a step in the right direction.

One of the most fundamental changes to the way DOS manages the computer's memory is that it now has the ability to load the majority of the DOS kernel into high memory, thus freeing up to 620KB or so of conventional memory for use by applications. Furthermore, when working with the 80386 and 80486 processors, more of the new features become available, allowing the user to load device drivers, buffer space and TSR programs above the 1MB barrier. Thus DOS effectively uses extended/expanded memory for storing this data.

However, DOS 5 goes no further than this, and to obtain the full flexibility desired by many users it is still necessary to use third-party products, or choose the Windows operating environment. Much of the design and development work behind DOS 5 was done in consultation with *power users* as they have become known, namely those PC users involved in programming, systems design, and technical journalism. Much of this consultation was through the CompuServe and BIX networks, and the responses that MicroSoft received were said to indicate that users wanted even more in the way of power and flexibility. Whilst many of the requests were not met by DOS 5, the interaction did serve to inform MicroSoft about exactly what PC users wanted. It seems likely that the next DOS release will go even further towards the goals that have no been firmly set in place.

4.3 SUMMARY

The issues of memory management tend to baffle many users when they are first confronted. However, it has been shown that the memory in a PC can be divided into three groups:

- Real memory - ie the 640KB directly accessed by DOS.

- Extended memory - used by some special software, and more recently by popular systems such as Windows, Lotus 1-2-3, AutoCAD etc. Other operating systems make better use of extended memory to provide multi-user and multi-tasking abilities. These include OS/2 and Xenix.

- Expanded memory - used in conjunction with a special software device driver to allow many software packages to access memory beyond the standard DOS barrier.

In the past these categorisations have lead to considerable confusion amongst users. These problems are being resolved in new releases of some software packages which are able to directly access extended memory, thus allowing large amounts of data to be handled. Additionally new operating systems and operating environments are becoming available which are gradually removing the need to differentiate explicitly between the different memory types, thus simplifying matters considerably. However, it should always be remembered that in order to obtain this flexibility it is necessary to use the most up-to-date hardware and software, which means it is rapidly becoming impractical to use older systems in the modern business environment.

5 Troubleshooting Component Faults

5.1 INTRODUCTION

Preceding chapters in this book have concentrated on the components that make up the personal computer and how they work. Only once this knowledge has been attained is it possible to start diagnosing and, where possible, repairing component faults. Of course, many faults exhibit themselves by producing corrupt data or by losing data altogether. This chapter does not discuss how to recover lost or corrupt data, but concentrates on how to find and isolate the part of the system that is the cause of the problem.

Warning

Always establish what the warranty situation is before attempting to dismantle a system. Suppliers may not undertake repairs if the equipment has been tampered with.

5.2 A STRUCTURED APPROACH

Most important is to approach any troubleshooting situation in a structured, orderly manner. Figure 5.1 shows a basic flowchart that illustrates the steps for approaching most faults and involves both the user and the troubleshooter. When the steps in Figure 5.1 have been covered and the fault has still not been remedied the system should be handed to the control of the troubleshooter. A second flowchart is supplied for the basic procedures required from this point and this master flowchart references five further charts which deal with problems specific to disk drives, the system board, the power supply, the monitor and the keyboard. If from the reported fault the troubleshooter is of the opinion that the fault most likely lies with a particular component such as the disk drives or the power supply, having checked for obvious problems, it might be appropriate to move directly to the specialist flowcharts rather than to pursue all the preliminary checks listed below.

5.2.1 SPARE PARTS

At various points in the following pages it is suggested that components are substituted with compatible parts that are known to function for test purposes. If these components solve the problem a permanent replacement can be made. It will obviously depend on the size of the troubleshooting department as to the amount of spare parts that can be held. A popular approach in larger organisations is to have one or two 'phantom' machines. These are fully configured systems that are on the company's asset register,

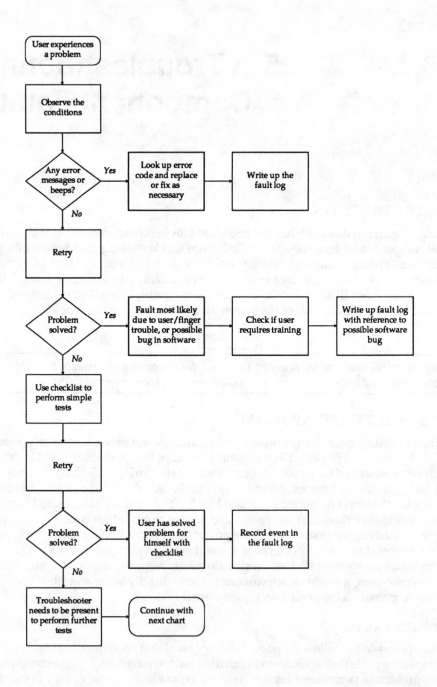

Figure 5.1   Basic troubleshooting flowchart

but which are not designated to an individual or department. The phantom machines may in some cases be specially purchased, but they might also be systems that have been released due to user upgrades. These systems can be used either as substitute systems so that the user can continue working whilst the troubleshooter endeavours to solve the problem, or in some cases they can be used as 'part swappers' in order to test potential failed components on other machines.

In addition to phantom machines, if possible retain redundant parts when upgrading components such as disk drives, memory chips etc, as the old parts may be useful in an emergency situation to restore a system to use, even if only to enable data to be transferred. It may, of course, not always be cost effective to do this as many suppliers will give special prices on new equipment if the old is traded in.

The following list is a guideline as to the general spares any troubleshooter should hold. It is important to note that it may be necessary to hold several of each part if there are a range of different PCs in the organisation and the troubleshooter should be aware, for example, of what type of cable the disk drives in each type of computer requires.

- Cables of all types
- Power supplies
- Memory chips
- Floppy disk drives and controllers
- Keyboards.

If the system is critical to the firm and must be running continuously then the following must also be available:

- Hard disk drives
- Hard disk drive controllers
- Graphics cards
- Parallel interface cards
- Serial interface cards.

The following sections support the flowcharts and give guidelines that will help in the identification of most types of fault.

5.2.2 DON'T PANIC!

When a user reports a fault it is quite likely that the system has failed in the midst of some critical work - it is also quite likely that the data involved is not fully backed-up and thus the user is likely to be panicking. It is too easy to say 'calm the user down', but at least keep calm yourself and prepare to ask the correct questions in order to most speedily ascertain the source of the problem.

5.2.3 OBSERVE THE CONDITIONS

Information that is usually easy to ascertain from the user is exactly what was happening when the fault occurred. This involves asking questions such as "Did the fault exhibit as the system was switched on?" "Was a program running?" "Were you entering information at the keyboard?" "Were you attempting to save or retrieve a file?"

Eyes, ears and nose are all useful detectives when trying to ascertain the source of a problem. Users must be encouraged to understand what the lights on their computer represent in order that questions such as "Were the disk drives lights on?" "Is there a power light showing?" "Did the system beep, flash or display any kind of error message on the screen?" can be asked. If a disk drive is failing due to a fault with the motor or other moving parts, it may make unusual sounds when trying to access data on the disk. Finally, in some circumstances, usually those connected with power faults, there may be a smell of burning material.

$$\boxed{\text{Warning}}$$

If a user reports any kind of evidence suggesting power problems, ensure immediately that all mains power has been disconnected from the computer, but do not allow the user to touch the computer further.

If the user is able to report some useful observations, such as seeing an error code displayed on the screen or hearing a series of beeps, it may be possible for the fault to at least be diagnosed, if not repaired without needing to proceed further along this flow-chart. A full list of all the error codes and beep messages for the IBM personal computer range, including the PS/2 is supplied in Appendix 4. The description supplied with the error code will enable the troubleshooter to isolate the problem at least to a major component such as the disks, monitor, keyboard etc. The appropriate flowchart for that area should then be consulted in order to further diagnose the problem. In fact, in some cases the error message is so specific as to report the chip that has failed.

One example of this perhaps more common than most others is the error message given when a memory chip has failed. In many PCs the message will be displayed in the form of a four digit number followed by 201. For example 1004 201. The 201 indicates that it is a RAM failure and the 1004 identifies which chip has failed.

Figure 5.2 represents a typical bank of memory chips that may be found in a PC. There are four banks labelled bank 0 through to bank 3. The first chip in each bank is called parity and is responsible for controlling the remaining chips in the bank. The numbers identified as error code represent the second half of the four digit number. Therefore with an error message of 1004 the failed chip is on bank 10 and is the third chip after parity in that bank.

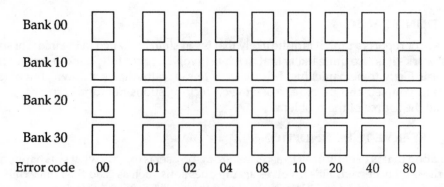

Figure 5.2   PC memory chip positioning

If the four digit number begins with 40, the failed chip is located on an expansion board. Furthermore there maybe an additional message displayed indicating whether the failed chip is on the motherboard or expansion card. This takes the form of Parity Check 1 for the motherboard and Parity Check 2 for an expansion card. Figure 5.3 is a table indicating how memory error messages are constructed.

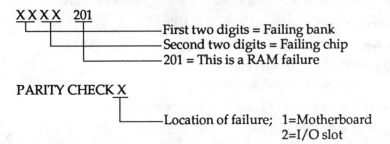

X X X X 201

First two digits = Failing bank
Second two digits = Failing chip
201 = This is a RAM failure

PARITY CHECK X

Location of failure; 1=Motherboard
                      2=I/O slot

Figure 5.3   Memory error message syntax

In some systems a more complex form of numbering is used. For example in an IBM AT a 10 digit error message precedes the 201, as shown in Figure 5.4. In this case the byte address is supplied in hexadecimal notation followed by the failed chip reference.

Byte address	Bank	Chip number								
040000 to 07FFFF	Bank 1	8	9	10	11	12	13	14	15	P
		0	1	2	3	4	5	6	7	P
000000 to 03FFFF	Bank 0	8	9	10	11	12	13	14	15	P
		0	1	2	3	4	5	6	7	P

The four digit number corresponds to the chip number:

0001=0	0010=4	0100=8	1000=12
0002=1	0020=5	0200=9	2000=13
0004=2	0040=6	0400=10	4000=14
0008=3	0080=7	0800=11	8000=15

A value of 0000 indicates the parity chips (P) have failed, and both should be replaced

Figure 5.4   AT memory chip positioning

From Figure 5.4 it can be seen that if the fourth chip on bank 1 had failed the following error message would be displayed:

05CE32 0010 201

With any error message, if further diagnosis is not possible, always report displayed error messages or beeps to an engineer as it will help them in their diagnosis.

5.2.4   WRITE DOWN WHAT HAPPENED

Users must be encouraged to record problems on paper. This should include a list of all the conditions observed at the time of the system failure. Users should have a checklist that they can answer at the time a fault occurs. Figure 5.5 is an example of such a checklist.

Checklist to be Completed in Case of System Failure

- What were you trying to do at the time of failure?
- Is there any error message being displayed?
- What is your PC doing that it shouldn't be?
- What is your PC not doing that it should?
- What parts of your system appear to still be functioning?
- Which power lights are still on?
- Is any unit smelling?
- Are any peripherals unduly hot?
- Can you run a software program other than the one running at the time of the failure?
- Is the software installation correct?
- Have you changed your SETUP, CONFIG.SYS or AUTOEXEC.BAT files?
- Have you installed a new version of DOS recently?
- Have you recently installed new software?
- Have you installed any new peripherals?
- Has anyone different had access to your system recently?

Figure 5.5   User checklist

In some cases the act of completing the checklist can lead to a problem diagnosis and maybe even repair. This will largely depend on the experience of the user. For example, if a user had changed CONFIG.SYS it is likely that he or she has enough knowledge to be able to change this file again and in some cases to thereby rectify the fault. Of course, a little knowledge can be a dangerous thing, and the user may not be able to get the system back into a working order. It does, however indicate to the troubleshooter where the source of the problem lies.

5.3   ROUTINE CHECKS

In addition the checklist of questions in Figure 5.5, users should be supplied with a few basic routines that they can perform before reporting a fault, as shown in Figure 5.6.

If any of the points in the checklist show a potential problem, it is of course important to retry after correction. Furthermore, as many faults are due to finger trouble or user error, it is often advisable to coach the user through a retry exercise. This will depend to some extent on the nature of the problem. For example, if it is suspected that the system has been attacked by a virus, the user should leave the system alone and the troubleshooter should tackle the problem with the aid of virus detecting software.

Main system

- Are all external cables properly connected to the correct devices?

Printer

- Is the printer power on?
- Are the cables to the printer correctly connected?
- Is the online light showing prior to attempting to print?

Monitor

- If there is a separate power source is it connected and powered on?
- Are the contrast, brightness and colour buttons correctly set?

Keyboard

- In the case of switchable XT/AT keyboards, is it correctly set?

Disks

- If working with floppy disks, are disks inserted correctly and is the drive door properly closed?
- If experiencing write problems with floppy disks, are there write protect tabs in place?
- Retry

Figure 5.6   User guidelines for routine checks

Even if a retry procedure does not solve the problem, it might cause it to re-exhibit, which in turn can help the troubleshooter diagnose the cause. If the problem is related to a floppy disk, it is always worth trying another disk and even another disk drive before attempting more in depth diagnostics.

5.4 PROBLEM REPORTS AND FAULT LOGS

It is important to maintain a detailed log of all faults encountered, relating to both hardware and software, including a description of the action taken to remedy the fault. This should be a two tier operation with a fault log and a problem report.

The fault log is a brief description of the problem as it was reported and there should be a fault log for every computer installed in the firm. Figure 5.7 is an example of such a log. Notice the reference to the computer by name and by serial number. The fault log may either be kept in the troubleshooting department, or it may be left with the computer.

A separate problem report should also be kept that outlines more details of the problem and the steps that were necessary to solve it. Figure 5.8 shows a typical problem report for the last fault listed on the fault log.

FAULT LOG

MACHINE MODEL: TANDON 386/20   **SERIAL #:** 1-0899 - 54723

Date fault Occurred	Details of Fault	Date Fault Reported	Name	Date Fault Fixed	Name	Problem Report Ref.
11-1-91	WOULD NOT BOOT FROM C: DRIVE AT ALL	11-1-91	J. ANDERSON	11-1-91	P. THOMAS	110191/0134
27-1-91	BAD DATA WRITTEN TO FLOPPY BY A: DRIVE	28-1-91	J. ANDERSON	28-1-91	P. SNELLINGS	280191/0279
15-3-91	PRINTER WILL NOT WORK AT ALL.	15-3-91	H. BARNTON	15-3-91	P. THOMAS	150391/044
23-5-91	WOULD NOT BOOT FROM C: DRIVE AT ALL	23-5-91	J. ANDERSON	23-5-91	P. THOMAS	230591/0529
24-5-91	LOST FILES & CORRUPT DATA ON C: DRIVE. WP5 CANNOT READ IT'S OWN DATA FILES	24-5-91	J. ANDERSON	30-5-91	P. THOMAS	300591/0624

Figure 5.7   Computer system fault log

PROBLEM REPORT

Reference: 300591/0624

Date and Time Fault Occurred: 24-5-91, 10:30 AM

Details of Problem: WORDPERFECT 5 CANNOT ACCESS ITS DATA FILES. SOME ARE CORRUPTED, SOME ARE LOST COMPLETELY.

Location of System: FLOOR 3, MARKETING OFFICE, JOAN ANDERSON'S DESK

Networked (Yes/No): NO

Hardware Configuration: TANDON 386/20, 80MB HARD DRIVE, TWIN FLOPPIES, HPLJ PRINTER, VGA DISPLAY.

Software Configuration: MS-DOS 3.2, WORD PERFECT 5.1, VENTURA PUBLISHER, 1-2-3, COMMS SOFTWARE. APPROX 25MB OF DATA FILES.

Operation Attempted: TRIED TO LOAD WORD PERFECT DATA FILES.

Details of Remedial Procedure: RECENT HISTORY OF HARD DISK PROBLEMS. AGREED TO CHANGE HARD DISK UNIT
- REMOVED SEAGATE 80MB MFM UNIT
- INSTALLED SEAGATE 110MB MFM UNIT.
RE-INSTALLED SOFTWARE + DATA FILES ONTO NEW DISK.

TESTED WITH MULTIPLE READ/WRITE OPS.

RETURNED 30-05-91

Figure 5.8   A typical problem report

It is surprising how often problems recur and in time keeping problem reports make solving future problems much quicker and easier. If for any reason it is impractical to use a manual system such as that shown in Figures 5.7 and 5.8, there are a number of software packages available now that allow this data to be stored on a computer, thus making cross referencing and fault finding even easier. In larger organisations a database interrogation system could be developed (as suggested in Chapter 1) that cross-references with the asset register.

All the flowcharts in this chapter end a successful diagnosis and repair with the instruction to write up the fault log and problem report.

5.5 HAND CONTROL TO THE TROUBLESHOOTER

At this point in the troubleshooting flowchart it is likely that it is no longer possible for the user to solve the problem his/herself, either alone or with the troubleshooters help. Instead the troubleshooter will have to look more closely at the system in an attempt to isolate the failed component or peripheral. The best approach for this is one of exclusion. Figure 5.9 is the flowchart that the troubleshooter should pursue from this point.

Where possible, begin by carefully checking that the system SETUP, CONFIG.SYS and AUTOEXEC.BAT files appear to be in order and that the software in use has been correctly installed. This should already have been incorporated in the checklist above, but it is wise not to entirely trust the judgement of the user and as the basic setup of a system is a common source of problems, it is always worth double-checking.

Before opening up the computer box, it may be worth running the diagnostics disk that should have been supplied with the computer to see if any errors can be detected this way. The proprietary utilities might also be useful at this stage to check things such as the disk drive spindle speed or the presence of bad sectors on the disk.

When all external checks have produced nothing helpful, the next step is to open up the system box and investigate inside.

5.6 HEAT AND MOISTURE

It is surprisingly common to find interface cards and chips not properly seated into their sockets on the motherboard. Chips in particular are prone to a disease called "chip creep", the main cause of which is vibration. Moisture is a problem area as well, causing corrosion of the chip pins, which in turn leads to bad connections. Therefore if cards and chips can be pushed more firmly into their sockets, and this appears to solve the problem under investigation, it is important to check the environment that the computer is located in. Stacked systems with printers on top of the computer is generally not recommended as this can produce both excess heat and undue vibration. Computers in hot rooms without air conditioning can be prone to humidity and dampness. If it is not possible to improve the air conditioning, the purchase of a portable dehumidifier can help the situation. Early warning systems are useful in changeable environments. For example, in a typical British summer, humidity levels can vary from non-existent to quite high.

Heat can cause problems in other ways. In particular it can be responsible for a range of intermittent faults. For example if the vents on the system box are blocked, then there is not the correct circulation of air inside the system. This can lead to the disk drive motor overheating – which in turn causes the casing of the drive to overheat and ultimately in

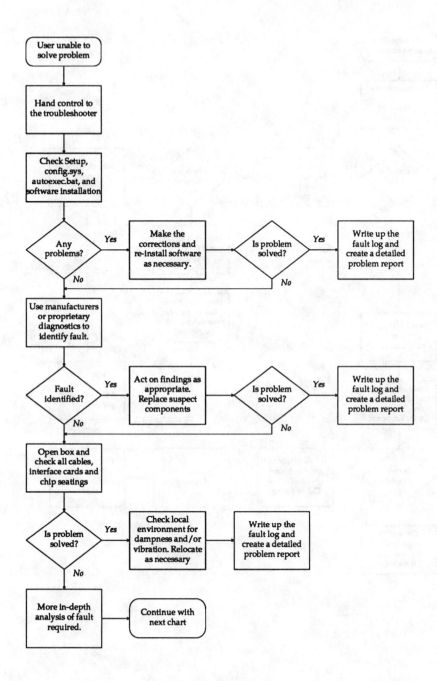

Figure 5.9   Advanced troubleshooting flowchart (a)

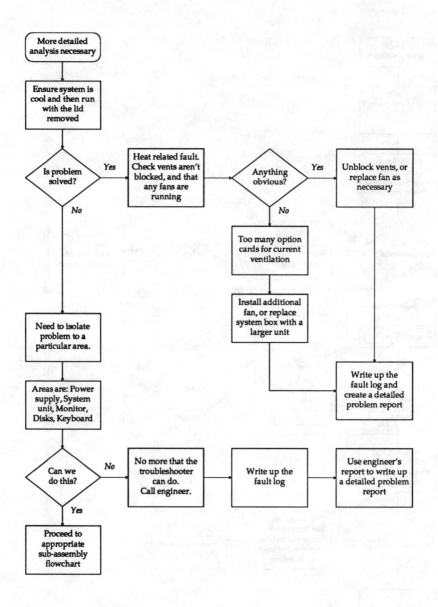

Figure 5.9   Advanced troubleshooting flowchart (b)

an extreme case the disk surface itself. The power supply unit can also overheat if the vents are blocked, or if the internal fan fails, which can lead to intermittent power problems, or in an extreme case to complete power supply failure. The heating of components such as the power supply and the disk drive can also affect chips on the motherboard which can then fail.

To test for heat related problems the system should be cool and then run for a period of time with the lid off, and perhaps with an additional fan to ensure components cannot overheat. If this seems to solve the problem, but the vents and fans in the system are all clear and operating well, the problem is then likely to be associated with the number of option cards installed in the system. The more option cards in the box, the less room there is for the air to circulate and thus the ventilation supplied with the original specification cannot cope with the load. The problem can sometimes be solved by installing an additional fan into the existing system. However, in a very overcrowded system it is usually preferable to transfer everything into a larger system box with better ventilation.

5.7 DIAGNOSE A PARTICULAR PERIPHERAL OR UNIT

At this stage most of the prospective problems that can affect the system in general have been assessed. If the fault still has not been isolated it is necessary to isolate the problem to a particular area of the system.

The five areas of the system that have been categorised here are:

- the power supply
- the disk drives
- the system unit
- the monitor
- the keyboard.

5.8 THE POWER SUPPLY

Figure 5.10 is a flowchart illustrating the troubleshooting steps that can be followed to ascertain whether the power supply unit (PSU) in the system is at fault.

Computer systems require different power supplies depending on their configuration. For example an XT with few option cards installed does not require as much power as a 386 system with several option cards. The table in Figure 5.11 gives an indication as to the power supply requirements for different configurations. When troubleshooting the power supply, the rating of the power supply is one of the first things to check and if the system is underpowered a replacement power supply should be installed.

If the ratings appear to be within limits the next area to check is the stability of the power supply in terms of output. This is achieved by connecting a volt meter to each of the connectors coming from the power supply.

If this test shows a single wire in one connector to be faulty, it might be possible to swap this connector for another unused one and thus avoid the necessity of purchasing a new power supply. If however, several wires are showing faults, it is likely the power supply unit itself is faulty and it should be replaced.

Some power problems, and especially intermittent ones, can be caused by an unstable mains power supply. If this is suspected it is usually possible for the Electricity Company

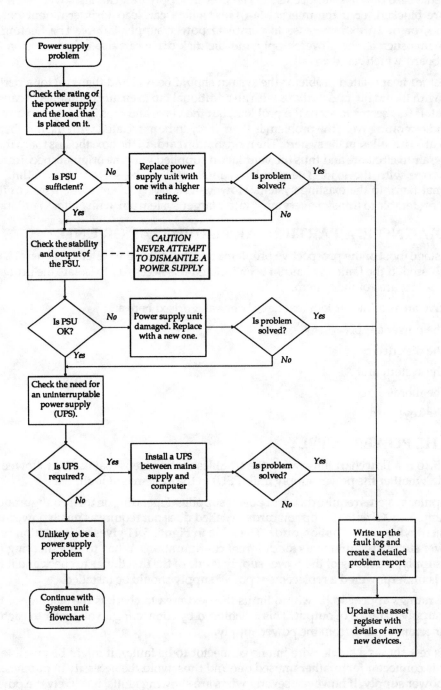

Figure 5.10   Flowchart for diagnosing power problems

to test the supply. In any case, it is advisable to install an uninterruptable power supply (UPS) which will both ensure a stable and constant power supply and provide backup power in the case of total power failure.

5.9 DISK DRIVES

The stability and output of the power supply can also exhibit by causing the disk drives to fail intermittently and thus the section above on checking this should be followed when troubleshooting disk drive problems.

If power is not deemed to be the source of the fault it is necessary to establish which drive or drives have failed. Figure 5.11 shows the procedure that should be followed when diagnosing disk drive based problems.

The sections below discuss the likely problems when either the hard or floppy drives are at fault. However, if all drives have failed the fault must be caused by something common to all drives.

In some systems the disk drive controller card handles all the drives installed in the system and this should be swapped for a working one. If the problem is solved the controller card should be permanently replaced, but if not then it is likely to be something on the motherboard and it is probably time to hand the system over to an engineer.

5.9.1 FLOPPY DISKS

Always begin by checking the condition of the disk media in another working system. If it fails in the other system, format a new disk and try using this in the original system. If it works, is either the media that is faulty, or the disk drive is corrupting the media. If the disk still does not work, then the problem is more likely to be connected with the drive unit. Figure 5.12 shows the procedure that should be followed to identify the problem.

Around 80 percent of floppy disk drive failures are due to dirty heads on the drive. In much the same way as it is recommended to clean audio tape drives and video tape drives, it is also important to regularly clean the heads of floppy disk drives. There are two ways to do this. Either a proprietary drive cleaning kit may be used which involves placing a few drops of cleaning solution onto a special disk and then inserting the disk in the drive and making the drive turn. Alternatively the heads can be manually cleaned with a cotton bud and cleaning solution. This would normally only be necessary if a drive had been badly neglected and the disk cleaning kit was not able to clean the heads.

The problem is to decide how regularly the cleaning operation should be performed. Factors that influence this decision include the environment the computer is located in and the amount of usage the disk drive has. If the computer is located in a factory or in some other dusty environment, the heads will gather dust more quickly than on a computer in a clean office environment. Similarly, if the computer operator smokes (which should be strongly discouraged in any case), this will cause the heads to clog up with ash and tar and cleaning must be performed more regularly. With regards disk drive usage, much of the dirt that accumulates on the drive heads comes from the floppy disks and thus the more disks that are inserted in the machine, the more likely particles will gather on the drive heads.

Some drive cleaning kits suggest cleaning every day. This is definitely too often and will be detrimental to the life of the disk. Once a week should be the most frequent period

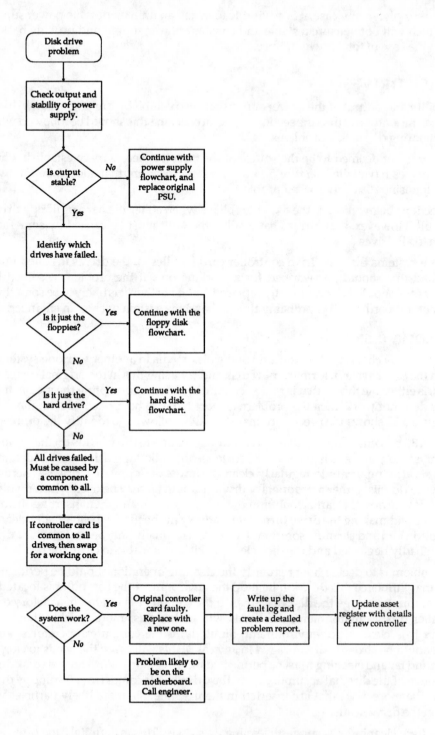

Figure 5.11   Flowchart for diagnosing disk problems

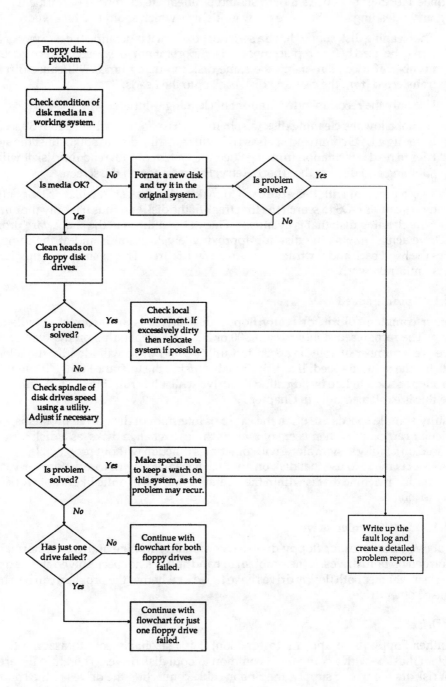

Figure 5.12   Diagnosis of floppy disk problems

and once a fortnight or once a month should be adequate for most environments. When using drive cleaning kits there are a few guidelines which should be followed:

1   The cleaning disk should have a series of boxes on it indicating the number of times it may be used before replacement. It is important not to exceed the recommended number of uses as re-using the same disk too many times will cause dirt to be transferred from the cleaning disk back onto the heads.

2   Use only the recommended amount of cleaning solution.

3   Do not allow the cleaning disk to spin in the drive for more than about 30 seconds. Entering a DOS command such as DIR will cause the disk to spin whilst the system tries to read information from it. When the system cannot read the disk it will stop spinning and display the Abort, Retry, Fail message on the screen.

There is a problem with this approach to making the disk spin which is that entering DIR always causes DOS to search the first track of the disk and thus it is only the outmost part of the cleaning disk that is ever used. One of the utilities in the shareware program TestDrive actually spins the disk for approximately 30 seconds and at the same time moves the head back and forth across the read/write area. This ensures that the cleaning disk is uniformly worn.

5.9.1.1   Spindle speed

Another common culprit for faulty floppy disk drives is an incorrect spindle speed setting. The recognised standards are 300 or 360RPM, depending on the type of drive. There are a number of spindle speed test utilities and these will identify the tolerance limits for the spindle speed. If a disk drive is outside the tolerance range it can usually be brought back into line by adjusting the drive whilst it is running the test utility. How to do this is explained fully in Chapter 7.

Faulty spindle speeds are often the cause of intermittent disk drive problems, and in particular can exhibit when users of two machines exchange disks, as a disk formatted and used on a faulty system alone will sometimes function without problem. If, however, an attempt is made to use that disk on another system it may not work. Similarly, a disk from another machine that is within the tolerance range will quite likely not work in the faulty machine.

5.9.1.2   Identify which drive

The above techniques for floppy disk drives are fairly routine and would normally be performed on both drives. If the problem in hand still has not been solved it is necessary to be clear whether both floppy drives have failed or whether the problem can be isolated to one or other drive.

Both Drives

If neither floppy drive appears to function, it is reasonably safe to assume that the problem must be with a component common to both disk drives. Therefore the areas at most risk are the power supply, the ribbon cable connecting the drives to the controller card, the controller card itself or possibly, but least likely, a problem on the system board. Figure 5.13 shows the procedure that should be followed. It is assumed at this stage that all power supply related faults have already been examined; if this is not the case, refer back to the power supply section.

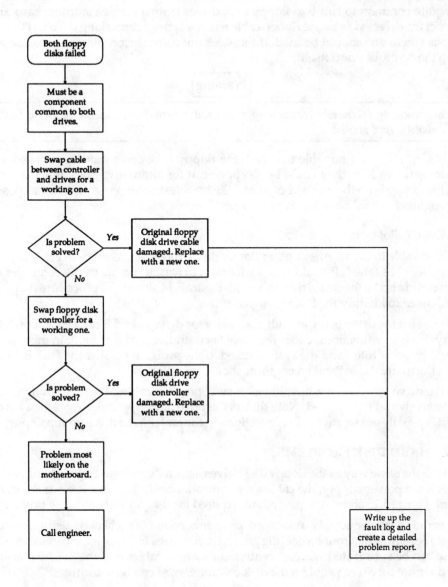

Figure 5.13   Floppy disk problems – both drives

The simplest area to check first is the cable connecting the drives to the controller card. It is quite common to run two floppy disk drives from a single controller card and to connect the drives via a single ribbon cable with two connectors along it. To test this cable a replacement one should be tried. If this does not solve the problem the next step is to swap the controller card itself.

| Warning |

Care must be taken when swapping a controller card from another machine that a compatible card is used.

Although it is just possible that both the floppy disk drive units have failed and if circumstances allow, they could be swapped out for alternative ones, it is more likely that the failure is on the motherboard and the troubleshooter has gone as far as possible. The engineer should be called at this stage.

One Drive Failed

If it is possible to isolate one or other floppy disk drive it is necessary to establish which component has failed. It could be, as with both drives, the cable or the controller card, but it could also be the disk drive unit itself. Figure 5.14 shows the procedure that should be followed to identify the faulty component.

To test for the drive being at fault, the cables for drive A and B can be swapped. If the faulty drive now functions, either the cable or controller card is at fault. In this case each should be substituted and the system tested. If the problem persists the fault is likely to be on the motherboard and an engineer should be called.

If the drive still does not function after swapping the cables, the drive unit itself is at fault and should be replaced. Note that as the price of floppy disk drives today is quite low it is usually not worth further investigating the fault on the drive for repair purposes.

5.9.2 HARD DISK PROBLEMS

In much the same way as the floppy disk drives, failures connected with a hard drive can be with the power supply, the cables, the controller card, the drive itself or the motherboard. Figure 5.15 shows the procedure required for diagnosing hard disk problems.

Assuming power supply associated problems have been checked using the power supply section of the troubleshooting guide, the next area to check is the connector cables. These can be substituted with alternative compatible cables and the machine tested. If this does not solve the problem the disk controller card can be substituted.

| Warning |

If it is thought likely that the drive itself has failed, on no account should an attempt be made to open up the drive as not only would this invalidate any warranty that might be on the equipment, but it will almost certainly render the drive useless.

If it is possible to substitute another drive, this should be tried and if the system works a replacement drive can be permanently installed. If the problem persists it is likely to be a motherboard failure and an engineer should be called.

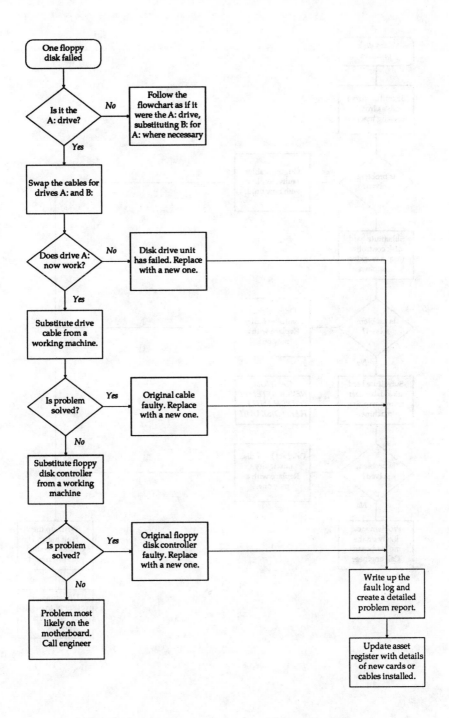

Figure 5.14   Floppy disk problems – one drive

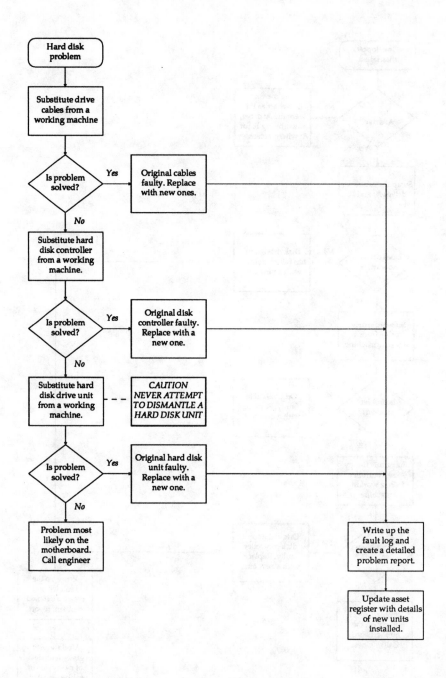

Figure 5.15   Diagnosis of hard disk problems

5.9.2.1 Integrated drive electronics

A new form of disk drive technology is becoming increasingly popular on modern PCs. Integrated Drive Electronics (IDE) refers to systems that have the majority of the controller logic for a disk drive on the drive itself and on the motherboard, thus negating the need for a complex drive controller card. If this type of drive gives problems, there are less components that can be substituted and it may be necessary to exchange the drive unit in order to see whether the drive or the motherboard is at fault.

5.10 SYSTEM BOARD

Figure 5.16 shows the flowchart that should be followed when suspecting a fault is connected with the motherboard itself.

Although it should already have been done in the early stages of the troubleshooting procedure, the chip seatings, interface card and cable connections should all be double-checked and the system retried.

It is likely that by the time the troubleshooter reaches this stage a number of other checks will already have been performed in an attempt to isolate the source of the problem. Therefore, it has proved difficult to isolate the problem with the computer configuration as it is currently set.

The next step is therefore to strip the system to the simplest possible configuration. This means removing any expanded memory cards, communication or network adapters and any other interface cards not essential to the operation of the system. Before attempting to test the machine, make sure that any dip switches or jumpers have been adjusted as necessary and that the SETUP, CONFIG.SYS and AUTOEXEC.BAT have been revised accordingly. If the system now works, the problem is likely to either be incorrectly set switches, SETUP or CONFIG files or to be due to a faulty peripheral card.

To further isolate the problem, each peripheral card should be re-installed and the system tested after each installation until the problem recurs. This will indicate the board at fault. The board can then be checked for switch setting and chip seatings, but if it still fails it should be replaced.

BEWARE
Always write down any changes to system board or option card switches. They may have to be reset at a later stage and serious problems can be caused if they are incorrectly set.

If the basic configuration still fails their is little else the troubleshooter can do. It is worth checking to see whether any new chips have recently been installed - additional memory or a co-processor for example. Chips have a right and wrong way round in the socket and if they have been incorrectly installed this can cause a system to fail. If this is the case, do not use the existing chip or chips but replace them with working ones and see if the system functions. Unfortunately, incorrectly installed chips can sometimes cause more serious problems on the circuitry of the motherboard and thus even after replacement the system will not function and an engineer is required. The correct installation of new chips is discussed in Chapter 8.

If all the chips appear to be correctly installed, the troubleshooter has gone as far as practical and the engineer must be called.

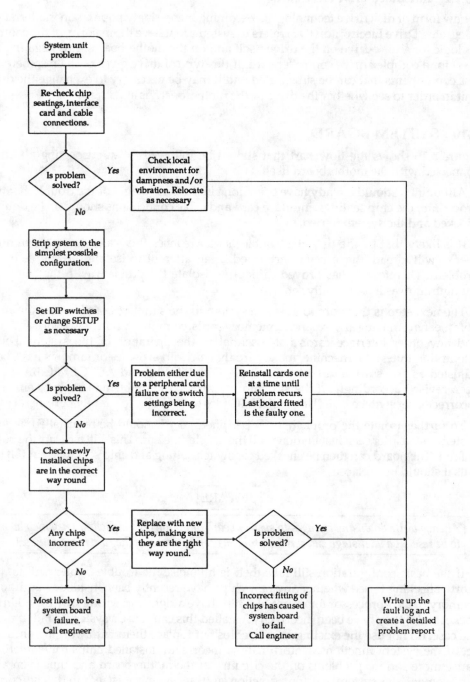

Figure 5.16   Flowchart for diagnosis of system unit

5.11   DISPLAY UNIT

There are some routine checks that can be performed on external peripherals such as the monitor and keyboard. Figure 5.17 shows the flowchart for the monitor.

Display unit problems can be caused by incorrectly installed software. This may only exhibit when the software is working in a particular mode. For example a spreadsheet can be perfectly well displayed, but a graph drawn using the same package may not be viewed at all if the installation procedure was not completed correctly. If new software has recently been installed, or if the monitor problem only occurs when working with a particular package these compatibility issues should be carefully checked. Some software packages do not entirely clear their settings from memory when they are exited and thus occasionally a monitor might fail to function correctly when moving from one software package to another. If this is the case, a utility should be used to clear the memory completely before the second package is loaded.

Assuming the software is correctly installed the next step is to re-check the interface cards are correctly seated and the connections to the motherboard and the monitor are in order. Some interface cards have dip switches or jumpers that may need adjusting. If the interface card is suspected as being faulty it should be substituted for a compatible card that is known to work with the type of monitor in use. If the system now functions a permanent replacement can be made. If the problem appears to be with the monitor itself it should be substituted or sent to an engineer for repair.

WARNING

Never attempt to dismantle a monitor. It contains lethal voltages and should only be handled by a trained technician.

5.12   KEYBOARD

The flowchart in Figure 5.18 shows the routines that can be followed in the case of a suspect keyboard. The first area to check is that the correct drivers have been installed, either through the SETUP screen or in the CONFIG.SYS file.

Some keyboards are multi-functional in that they can be set to work with an XT or an AT type machine. This is usually controlled through a switch on the back of the keyboard. If this switch is incorrectly set the keyboard will invariably cease to function completely.

If the keyboard problem is associated with sticky keys or odd keys that do not always function, it may be that the key contacts need cleaning. The cleaning of keyboards should actually be performed on a routine basis and details of how to go about it are given in Chapter 7. If this solves the problem it is worth considering the practicalities of using a keyboard cover – particularly if they system is in a dusty or dirty environment. In any event a dust cover for the entire computer is advisable when it is not in use to minimise general dust settling on the system.

If these basic routines do not solve the problem the keyboard should be substituted for another known working one. This will prove whether it is the keyboard or the device circuitry on the motherboard that is at fault. If it is the keyboard that is faulty, it is usually more cost effective to purchase a new one than to attempt further repairs on the faulty one. If the problem lies with the motherboard circuitry, it must be handed to an engineer for further tests.

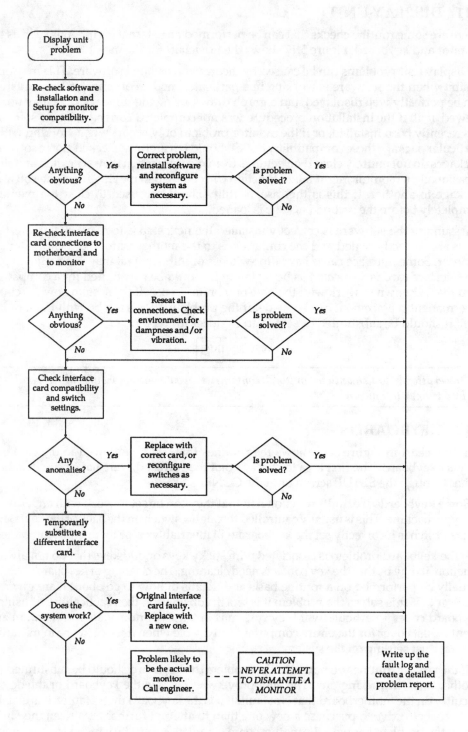

Figure 5.17   Flowchart for diagnosis of display unit

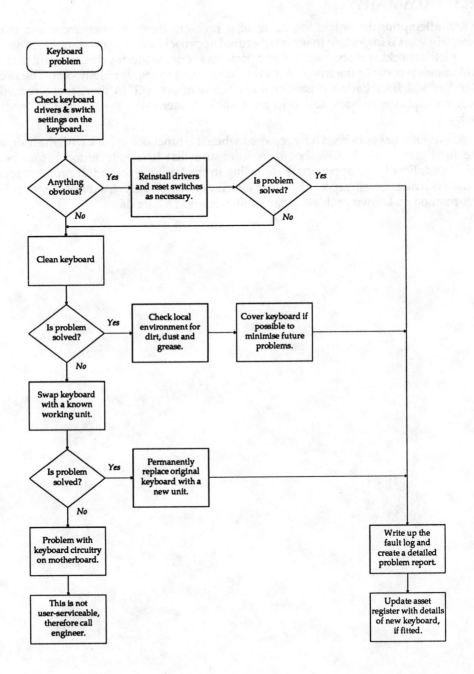

Figure 5.18   Flowchart for diagnosis of keyboard

5.13 SUMMARY

When attempting to isolate the cause of a problem from an often extensive list of possibilities, it is important to use a structured approach. Ensuring that users are able to complete a checklist of observations and perform a series of routine checks for themselves will alleviate some of the trivial tasks that are passed to the troubleshooter. The use of standardised flowcharts for each main component set will, in time, make recurring problems quicker to trace and help the troubleshooter test a system in a methodical fashion.

A computer has only been fully repaired when it is functioning back with the user, and the final task of the troubleshooter is to ensure that it is fully tested before being reinstated. Finally, an appropriate recording in the fault log and a full problem report must be made for all reported faults, which again will help troubleshooters collect information on known problem areas if faults recur at a later date.

6 Software Diagnostics

6.1 WHAT IS THE ROLE OF SOFTWARE DIAGNOSTICS?

Software diagnostics involves the use of manufacturers programs, proprietary software, and third party utilities to assist in diagnosing faults that may have occurred in a computer system. Before discussing the role of software and the troubleshooter in more detail, it is worth clarifying the term *software* along with *hardware* and *firmware*.

With computers today it has become increasingly difficult to make a sharp distinction between hardware and software. In the first place hardware both runs and is run by software. Outside of the computer, software has no particularly meaningful existence, although software can be listed, read and understood, it has no function until it is loaded in a machine. On the other hand, without software, hardware also has no function and has sometimes been referred to as nothing more than high tech paperweights. Despite these difficulties, it is possible to define the terms:

– Hardware has traditionally been defined as the physical components of the system. Thus clearly the monitor, printer, disk drives, keyboard and system box are all hardware components. However, each of these items are nothing more than boxes until they are joined together in a system through the use of software. This software is referred to as systems software and consists of the instructions which are supplied on chips within the systems box, as well as the operating system which is loaded by the computer when it is first switched on.

– Software is normally defined as a series of electronic instructions which are required by the machine in order for it to perform any useful function. The instructions required by the different peripherals of the machine in order to make it work are referred to as the operating system, whereas the instructions required to make the machine perform useful tasks such as debtors, payroll or ledgers, is referred to as applications software.

– Firmware is a term used to describe electronic instructions which are supplied on chips or integrated circuits. All computer systems will have some firmware which may be restricted to the ROM BIOS. Other computers make extensive use of firmware and may have the configuration settings, operating system and even some application systems supplied on integrated circuits.

Software can often help in the diagnosis of computer faults. This software might be as basic as the Power On Self Test (POST) supplied as firmware on the ROM BIOS, which is always automatically executed at the time of start-up, or it might be the manufacturers special diagnostics program supplied on a disk. In addition, there are available on the market nowadays a wide range of special utility software aimed at helping the user track down problems with his/her system, as well as programs for tackling some of these problems.

6.2   HOW A COMPUTER SYSTEM BEGINS TO WORK

Clearly the secret to the success of the computer is the ability for all the components to work in harmony so that the system functions in the desired way. At no time is this more important than when the computer is first switched on.

6.2.1   THE COLD BOOT AND THE WARM BOOT

A Cold Boot refers to the procedures which occur within the computer when the system is first switched on or energised. A Warm Boot refers to the procedures which occur when the computer is electronically reset. Whilst these procedures are similar in many respects, there are some important differences:

6.2.1.1   The cold boot

When the system is first switched on or booted up the switching power supply sends a POWER GOOD signal to the clock generator which then generates a +5 volt RESET pulse that is sent to the appropriate pin of the CPU (different CPUs use different pins for different tasks). This signal starts the boot-up procedure. This is referred to as a COLD BOOT because the system was not energised before the boot began. The word boot is used to describe this feature because the whole system is being reset and initialised with all the start up conditions necessary to operate (boot is short for BOOTSTRAP and this word goes back to the days of mainframe computers which were said to pull themselves up by their own bootstraps). The software required for the booting procedure is in the ROM BIOS. This is the program which makes the system come to life. The system then commences a series of tests referred to as the Power On Self Test, or POST. The exact procedures that are executed during the POST are listed in Figure 6.1.

6.2.1.2   The warm boot

During the bootstrap procedure the BIOS monitor checks to see whether the system has been previously energised when the reset pulse occurred. If a positive result is obtained then all the RAM tests described in the cold boot procedure are by-passed. The pressing of the CTRL, ALT and DEL keys simultaneously generates a non-maskable interrupt (NMI) which causes a system reset to be initiated. In some systems, the same effect is produced by pressing a Reset button. The Power-On Self Test (POST) is then performed, but the RAM tests are by-passed.

Some compatibles have particularly good POSTs which report on the monitor the results of each step in the self test. Others systems show the amount of memory being tested while others including the original IBM PC only show a flashing cursor or dash during the POST.

The list of operations shown in Figure 6.1 indicates the process followed by the BIOS of the original IBM PC when it was started with a cold boot. This POST includes a number of hardware diagnostic routines that check the fundamental components of the system. Other systems will obviously differ slightly when they execute their POST, although the general operations will be the same.

Switch on power

Power supply sends power good signal

Clock starts

+5V reset pulse to pin 21 of CPU

DS ES SS and IP registers set to zero

CS register is set to address 0FFF0H

CPU executes first instruction

Jump to power-on selftest

Interrupts are disabled

CPU flags are set

Read-write test of CPU registers

Checksum test of BIOS ROM

Initialise programmable DMA chip

Test for ROM start

(If yes, skip memory test)

Test first 16k of RAM

Initialise 8259 programmable interrupt controller

Test 8253 timer for count speed

Initialise and start 6845 CRT controller

Display cursor

Test installation of expansion box

Test additional RAM

Test keyboard

Test cassette interface

Test optional ROM

Test ROM containing BASIC

Test installed disk drives

Test printer and RS232 port

Enable NMI interrupts

Beep speaker

Perform disk drive interrupt

Await operator keyboard action

Figure 6.1   The POST process for an IBM PC

6.3 DIAGNOSTICS SOFTWARE

In order to gain further information about a reported error during the POST, or to seek out errors that did not display themselves at start-up, most IBM compatible computers have a diagnostics disk. IBM in fact have two levels of diagnostics referred to as Diagnostics and Advanced Diagnostics. The Advanced Diagnostics performs a range of more detailed tests than the standard diagnostics program.

| BEWARE |

> *Do not attempt to use a diagnostics program that does not claim to be compatible with the computer you are using. For example, using the IBM diagnostics on some non-IBM machines will cause error messages to be displayed when there are not really errors.*

Diagnostics software is usually invoked by placing the program disk into drive A and either switching on or rebooting the computer. The main menu of options will then be displayed on the screen. Figure 6.2 is an example of a typical diagnostics menu.

SELECT AN OPTION

0 SYSTEM CHECKOUT

1 FORMAT DISKETTE

2 COPY DISKETTE

3 PREPARE SYSTEM FOR MOVING

4 SETUP

9 END DIAGNOSTICS

Figure 6.2   A typical diagnostic menu

It is quite common for diagnostics software to include options for formatting and copying disks, but these activities may equally well be performed from within DOS.

The option to PREPARE SYSTEM FOR MOVING is particularly important when moving hard disk computers as this program stabilises the disk in such a way that the disk head cannot be damaged. This program is also usually executable from within DOS and often has the filename PARK.

The SETUP option is a program that many computers require to have run when they are first installed. This establishes things such as the speed the processor will operate at as well as identifying high density disk drives and setting the real time date and time.

The main systems checks will be performed by selecting the SYSTEM CHECKOUT option. Once system checking commences the first step is usually for the program to identify the configuration of the computer and a report such as the one shown in Figure 6.3 will be produced. If the list is incorrect or incomplete answering N to the prompt will allow the user to state what the configuration is.

THE INSTALLED DEVICES ARE

1   SYSTEM BOARD

2   1024KB MEMORY

3   KEYBOARD

4   MONOCHROME AND PRINTER ADAPTER

6   2 DISKETTE DRIVE(S) AND ADAPTER

9   SERIAL/PARALLEL ADAPTER - PARALLEL PORT

11   SERIAL/PARALLEL ADAPTER - SERIAL PORT

17   1 FIXED DISK DRIVE(S) AND ADAPTER

IS THE LIST CORRECT (Y/N) ?

Figure 6.3   Configuration list for a typical system

Once the list has been accepted an option to test selected items or to test everything will be given. In addition tests may usually be performed once or a number of times. In most situations it is sufficient to test each component once, although if intermittent faults are being experienced then it is worthwhile performing the tests multiple times, in order to try and isolate the problem.

Some of the items for testing will probably have their own menu of options. Figure 6.4 shows the options available for the display and printer adapter. The options are set by the fact that a monochrome display was established as part of the configuration list. If a colour monitor had been attached then the menu for display tests would be different.

IBM MONOCHROME DISPLAY AND
PRINTER ADAPTER TEST

0   DISPLAY ADAPTER TEST

1   DISPLAY ATTRIBUTES

2   CHARACTER SET

3   80X25 DISPLAY

4   PRINTER ADAPTER TEST

10   RUN ALL ABOVE TESTS

11   VIDEO TEST

12   SYNC TEST

ENTER NUMBER OF DESIRED ACTION

Figure 6.4   Diagnostic options for display & printer

The menu for diskette drive test will also vary according to the number and type of disk drives that were specified on the configuration list. Figure 6.5 shows the menu for two floppy diskette drives and adapter.

```
                2 DISKETTE DRIVE(S) AND ADAPTER
                   DISKETTE DIAGNOSTIC MENU


                    OPTION                    DRIVE
        1    SEQUENTIAL ACCESS           ONE DRIVE
        2    RANDOM SEEK                 ONE DRIVE
        3    VERIFY DISKETTE             ONE DRIVE
        4    SPEED TEST                  ONE DRIVE
        5    DSKT CHANGE TEST            ONE DRIVE
        9    RETURN TO CONTROL PROGRAM


        FOR OPTION 9 TYPE "9" AND PRESS "ENTER"
        FOR OTHER OPTIONS (1 THRU 5) TYPE THE
        OPTION NUMBER, DRIVE ID (1,A), AND PRESS
        "ENTER"
```

Figure 6.5   Diagnostic options for floppy disk tests

BEWARE

All these options require a blank formatted disk to be placed in the selected drive - any data that may be on the disk will be destroyed and a warning message to this effect is usually displayed on the screen.

The testing of the fixed disk will not normally erase any data and Figure 6.6 shows the type of tests that will be performed.

When the diagnostic program comes to test the serial/parallel adapter parallel and serial ports a prompt may be displayed on the screen to insert a *wrap plug*. This is a special plug that fits into the parallel and serial ports of the computer to simulate an actual cable in position. Not all diagnostics programs go to this degree of testing and if they do then the wrap plug may be supplied with the software.

Once all the tests relating to the specified configuration list have been performed the main diagnostic menu will be returned to the screen. On exiting from this menu the system is usually reset in the same way as performing a warm boot.

If errors are discovered during a test they will be reported on the screen, usually together with a reference number which can be looked up in the technical manual. A full explanation of the error and what is required to rectify it will be found there. Some diagnostics programs give an option to create an error log. This is an ASCII file containing a list of any errors with their reference numbers which can subsequently be printed out.

```
                    FIXED DISK DIAGNOSTIC MENU


        1    WRITE, READ, COMPARE (ON TEST CYLINDER)
        2    SEEK TEST
        3    HEAD SELECT
        4    ERROR DETECTION AND CORRECTION
        5    RUN ALL TESTS
        6    READ VERIFY
        7    FORMAT MENU
        9    RETURN TO CONTROL PROGRAM


        FOR OPTION 9 TYPE "9" AND PRESS "ENTER"
        FOR OTHER OPTIONS (1 THRU 7) TYPE THE
        OPTION NUMBER, DRIVE ID (1,C), AND PRESS
        "ENTER"
```

Figure 6.6   Diagnostic options for hard disk tests

6.4 DIAGNOSTIC SOFTWARE FOR OTHER SYSTEMS

Diagnostics software is available for many different systems. Although the software performs the same task, it will normally use different screen displays to those shown below. It may also use a different interface, for example allowing the use of the mouse to make selections.

An example of alternative diagnostics is shown in Figures 6.7 to 6.9 below. These displays are produced by the diagnostics software supplied with the IBM PS/2 system, which uses overlaid windows to show results of different tests.

6.5 OTHER SOFTWARE FOR THE TROUBLESHOOTER

There are many other software products on the market which are useful to the trouble-shooter. These range from general utility packages such Norton Utilities and PCTools which provide general disk management and data recovery programs, to more in depth products such as Disk Optimizer and TestDrive.

6.5.1 GENERAL UTILITIES

General utility packages such as Norton Utilities and PCTools have been available for many years. These two products are the most popular, but it should be remembered that they are by no means the only ones available. Other systems such as Mace Utilities and Baker's Dozen offer similar features, but may concentrate more closely on different aspects of the system.

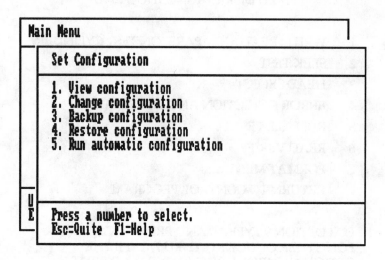

Figure 6.7   The PS/2 diagnostics menu options

```
┌─────────────────────────────────────────────────────────┐
│ View Configuration                                        │
├─────────────────────────────────────────────────────────┤
│                                                           │
│   Total System Memory                                     │
│      Installed Memory ..................... 6144KB (6.0MB) │
│      Useable Memory ....................... 6144KB (6.0MB) │
│                                                           │
│   Built In Features                                       │
│      Installed Memory ..................... 2048KB (2.0MB) │
│      Diskette Drive A Type ................ 1.44MB 3.5"   │
│      Diskette Drive B Type ................ 1.44MB 3.5"   │
│      Math Coprocessor ..................... Not Installed │
│      Serial Port .......................... SERIAL_1      │
│      Parallel Port ........................ PARALLEL_1    │
│                                                           │
│   Slot1 - Empty                                           │
│                                                           │
│   Slot2 - Empty                                           │
│                                                           │
│   Slot3 - Empty                                           │
│                                                           │
├─────────────────────────────────────────────────────────┤
│ Esc=Quit                                                  │
│ F1=Help                          ↓    End    PageDown     │
└─────────────────────────────────────────────────────────┘
```

Figure 6.8   First page of the configuration report

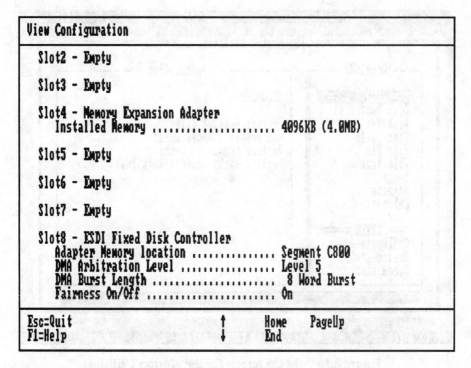

```
View Configuration

   Slot2 - Empty

   Slot3 - Empty

   Slot4 - Memory Expansion Adapter
      Installed Memory ...................... 4096KB (4.0MB)

   Slot5 - Empty

   Slot6 - Empty

   Slot7 - Empty

   Slot8 - ESDI Fixed Disk Controller
      Adapter Memory location .............. Segment C800
      DMA Arbitration Level ................. Level 5
      DMA Burst Length ...................... 8 Word Burst
      Fairness On/Off ....................... On

 Esc=Quit                      ↑       Home    PageUp
 F1=Help                       ↓       End
```

Figure 6.9   Second page of the configuration report

6.5.1.1   The Norton Utilities

The Norton Utilities concentrates its efforts into the recovery of data after it has been lost or corrupted in some way. Indeed the *undelete* feature offered by Norton Utilities is what made the package famous in the first place, as it effectively allows the user to reverse the DOS DELETE and ERASE commands. However, in addition to this feature, which is still one of the most comprehensive, a number of other facilities are provided. These are accessed from a graphical interface, in which the mouse or the keyboard can be used to select the desired commands. Figure 6.10 shows the main display produced by the Norton Utilities.

It can be seen that the programs are grouped under headings of Recovery and Speed, with further options (not shown on this screen) for Security and Tools.

– Recovery utilities provide routines and procedures to safeguard data before problems occur, to automatically recover data after problems occur, and to allow the user to make changes to the disk at a very low level.

– Speed utilities can help improve the performance of the system by testing various components to ensure that they are working at maximum efficiency.

– Security utilities allow the computer to be protected against virus attacks, and also to prevent unauthorised access to data.

– Tools utilities help the user to make more efficient use of the computer by simplifying common tasks.

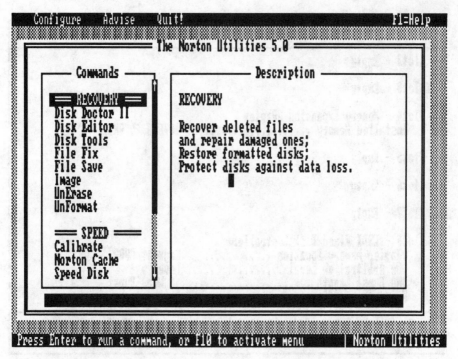

Figure 6.10   Main screen for the Norton Utilities

The right hand side of the screen gives more information relating to the currently highlighted utility. This allows the user to determine which command they actually require, and how they should use it.

One of the most useful utilities provided is called SysInfo, and is located under the tools category. SysInfo provides details about the configuration of the computer system, allowing the troubleshooter to see whether there are any obvious problems. Of course, SysInfo is not as accurate as the manufacturers diagnostics, but it is more wide ranging and looks at a broader variety of components. In fact Norton produces more than a dozen displays which provide important information, including the following:

- – System configuration
- – Disk configuration
- – Disk usage
- – Memory configuration
- – Memory usage
- – Computing performance
- – Disk performance
- – Overall performance index
- – Summary of CONFIG.SYS and AUTOEXEC.BAT files.

Figure 6.11 below shows the SysInfo display relating to the basic system configuration.

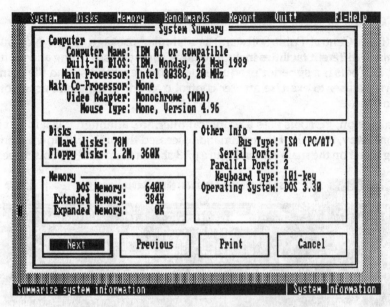

Figure 6.11   Summary of system configuration

One final point to note about the Norton Utilities is that it provides an Advice feature. This is a special help system that aims to answer any queries that may arise when error messages are produced on the screen. Thus for example, if the system fails to boot up and produces a message saying *"Insert system disk and press any key"*, this can be looked up in the advice system to determine the appropriate course of action. Figure 6.12 below shows some of the DOS error messages that are covered by this feature.

Figure 6.12   The Norton Utilities Advise feature

6.5.1.2 PCTools

PCTools (from Central Point Software) is a similar package to The Norton Utilities, offering many different facilities including file recovery, disk editing and security tools. However, PCTools is a superior product in terms of general disk and file management, as it allows the user to exercise greater control over the placing and usage of files and subdirectories

As with Norton, PCTools uses a graphical interface, although it is laid out in a more conventional way, with all of the commands accessed through pull-down menus, rather than being listed on the main screen Figure 6.13 shows the main PCTools screen display.

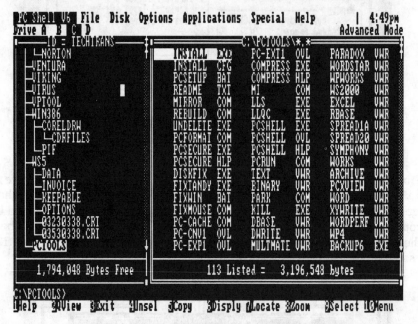

Figure 6.13   The PCTools main display

It can be seen that there are two main windows, the first showing the directory structure graphically, and the second listing the files in the current directory. Files can be selected with the mouse by using a point and click technique, and can then be moved, copied, deleted etc as necessary. Thus all file manipulations are performed much more efficiently than is possible through DOS.

One area in which PCTools is of particular use is as a front-end for applications programs. By selecting the *Applications* menu option, a list of application programs is produced, allowing the user to select which one they want to use. The software automatically changes to the relevant directory, and issues the command to execute the program, together with any parameters that may be necessary. This means that any software package can be started simply by pointing to its name in the list. New software packages can easily be added to the list when they become available, although if required PCTools will scan the entire disk when it is first installed to determine what applications are in use. Figure 6.13 shows the PCTools Applications menu options for a fully installed system.

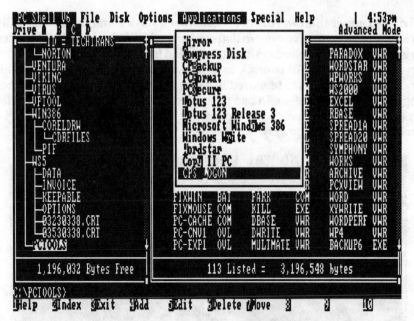

Figure 6.14   The PCTools applications menu

PCTools comes complete with several applications programs of its own. These are effectively utilities that could otherwise have been integrated into the main program, including a disk backup utility, a program to safeguard the hard disk against damage or accidental reformatting and a disk optimiser. These are obviously very similar to the features offered by other utilities. In addition to these general purpose utilities, there are a number of more specialised applications.

– The first of these is a cut-down version of LapLink, a program that allows files to be transferred between two computers that are linked with a suitable serial cable. Laplink is an excellent product for transferring files between systems with incompatible disk drive types, and for transferring files that are simply too large to be accommodated on a single floppy disk. Furthermore, some computers (especially Notebook computers) are supplied with no floppy drive at all, but have a version of LapLink installed on a ROM. Thus there is no other way of transferring data from such a machine to a desktop system.

– The second application is an entire desktop manager. This is a special program that runs as a TSR, and hence remains in the background memory of the computer even when other applications are executing. The desktop manager provides a wide range of general time and resource management features such as:

• an appointments scheduler
• a calendar
• a flexible diary
• a calculator.

Users familiar with SideKick, a similar system, will have no difficulty in getting to grips with PCTools' desktop manager, as it works along similar lines.

– The third application worthy of special mention is a communications utility. This is a very comprehensive system that can be used with the majority of modems that are available. The application has an auto-dial feature (although it only works with an auto-dial modem of course), and allows frequently used telephone numbers and log-on sequences to be stored in a special format, thus simplifying the task of logging-on to any system. In fact the system comes ready-programmed to dial in to the Central Point technical help line, so users experiencing difficulties can get technical support as quickly as possible.

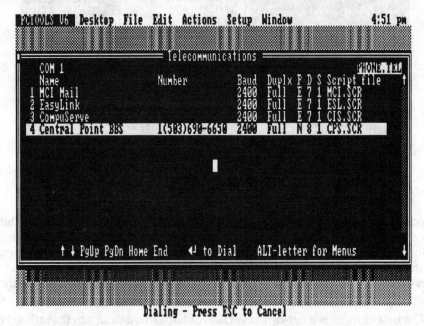

Figure 6.15   The PCTools communications utility

6.5.1.3   Disk optimisers

The more a disk drive is used the slower it will become. This is because the operating system functions by saving data in the next location on the disk where it can find an empty space without being concerned to keep all the data together. A file stored in this way is said to be a single logical unit, although it could be scattered into many different physical units. This will inevitably lead to progressively slower access times.

Because of the random nature with which MS-DOS treats the location of data, files become scattered all over the physical disk. As files are stored in clusters of 2K, 4K, or 8K, a relatively small file of 40K could be spread over 20 different locations, and thus be significantly de-optimised. The reason for this is that in order to read or write data from or to such a file the system could have to reposition the disk head as many as 10 times at 10 different locations on the surface of the disk. As head positioning is the most time consuming element in retrieving data this re-positioning activity is the overhead work-load which causes a deterioration in access time. The more a file is changed the worse the problem often becomes. Furthermore, the problem is not restricted to data files as program files may also be scattered over the disk.

This problem of scattered data and programs may be solved by software such as Disk Optimizer which consolidates the various clusters and thus makes the physical data layouts correspond with the logical data file. The effect of this process is that the new data or programs will be rewritten into a contiguous area. This process can significantly increase the speed of access of the disk.

Figure 6.16 shows how a disk could appear before and after optimising.

Before Optimisation

SYS	SYS	SYS	SYS	AA	AA	BB	CC	DD	DD
CC	CC	CC	EE	EE	EE	FF	EE	FF	GG
GG	GG		HH	HH	II	HH	HH	JJ	II
II	KK			KK	KK		KK		LL

After Optimisation

SYS	SYS	SYS	SYS	AA	AA	BB	CC	CC	CC
CC	DD	DD	EE	EE	EE	EE	FF	FF	GG
GG	GG	HH	HH	HH	HH	II	II	II	JJ
KK	KK	KK	KK	LL					

Figure 6.16   Disk usage before and after optimisation

The optimising procedure can take between five and 90 minutes to run, depending on the state and capacity of the disk. The increased speed of the system after optimising will be between five and 50 percent, also depending on the original condition of the system. Disk intensive applications such as databases and accounting suites benefit most from disk optimisation and such systems should be optimised about twice per month.

When using disk optimisation systems, it is very important to take a backup of the disk prior to beginning the operation. The reason for this is that the software works with the disk at a very low level, and if there was to be a power cut, or if the system fails in the middle of the process, it is quite likely that data could be lost or corrupt.

6.5.1.4   TestDrive

In addition to the programs mentioned above, there are numerous shareware utilities available which focus on more specific areas. These can be acquired for a very small fee, although they are seldom free of charge as many users think. Some of these products may be of assistance to the troubleshooter in ascertaining what might be wrong with the system, and helping to put it right.

One of the best examples of such a product is TestDrive. This is a special program that provides a full diagnostic checkout for floppy disk drives. It is able to diagnose almost any problem that has occurred with the disk drive without requiring the user to have in-depth technical knowledge of any kind. Figures 6.17 and 6.18 show sample displays produced by TestDrive while it is running.

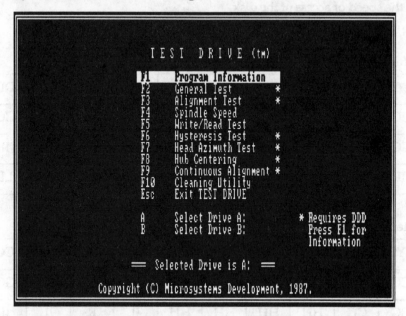

Figure 6.17   The TestDrive main menu options

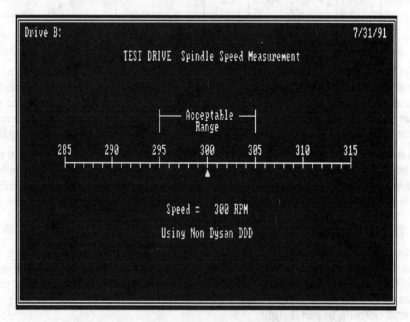

Figure 6.18   The TestDrive spindle speed test

6.6 SUMMARY

The software available to help the troubleshooter ranges from the simple POST supplied in the form of an IC on the motherboard, to sophisticated diagnostics and utility programs. The use of a combination of these will enable the troubleshooter to diagnose many common problems that occur with a personal computer, including memory failure, disk problems, interface card faults etc.

Utility software can also be used to improve the performance of the system, or to organise work in a more logical manner. The Norton utilities, PC Tools and The Disk Optimizer are all software packages that fall into this category, allowing the user to control information on hard and floppy disks in the most efficient way.

7   Preventative Maintenance

7.1   WHAT DOES PREVENTATIVE MAINTENANCE INVOLVE?

On mainframe and large mini computers preventative maintenance is performed on a regular basis. Preventative maintenance means that the computer is checked at regular intervals in an attempt to forestall component failures which will cause the machine's operation to be interrupted. In this sense, preventative maintenance is not generally performed on personal computers. Preventative maintenance in the personal computer context means taking a series of precautions which will help reduce the occurrence of the common faults discussed in Chapter 5.

7.2   FACTORS AFFECTING COMPUTER RELIABILITY

The precise reasons why computers fail are numerous, but beside intrinsic component weakness and simple wear and tear, failure can usually be pinned to one of the following six factors:

- The user
- Heat
- Dust/ash
- Power
- Corrosion
- Magnetism/static.

This chapter explains how to minimise the above factors affecting the on-going performance of the system.

7.3   THE USER

Perhaps the most common cause of computer problems is the user. User-related problems are often trivial matters, such as incorrectly adjusted monitor controls or disconnected cabling. If users are trained correctly to begin with, the number of problems of this type will decrease.

This training should include not only the fundamental issues of how to use the software correctly, but also the underlying factors such as suitable naming for files, correct use of directories and organising the work area to minimise problems. In general, tuition is not expressly given for these issues, and the user is left to find out for themselves how they should be organising their work.

Installation training should routinely be given to all new users when their system is installed. This may only be as little as half an hour, but should include topics such as how to handle diskettes, how to switch the computer and peripherals on and off, and in what order this should be performed.

It is also useful to ensure that each system has a checklist along the lines of the one shown in Chapter 5, which can be consulted when a problem initially occurs. This will reduce some of the work that the troubleshooter has to do, as it will enable the user to diagnose and correct simple problems, such as disconnected cables, maladjusted monitor controls etc.

Most importantly, ensure that users know how to get help when they need it – ie leave them the troubleshooting department's telephone number!

7.4 HEAT/COLD

The disk drives, chips and other parts of the circuitry in a computer are sensitive to *excessive* heat or cold. A good general rule of thumb is that if the environment is comfortable for the user, then it is comfortable for the computer as well. However, whilst this may well be the case when the system is in use, it may be found that the temperature varies considerably when the computer is not in use, for example when it is being transported or if it is left in an unheated office overnight. The solution to this situation is to allow the computer to reach room temperature before switching on, especially if it is moved.

7.4.1 EXCESSIVE HEATING

When a computer is functioning normally a certain amount of heat will be generated by the electronic and mechanical components. This has been recognised in the design of the system and all computers have open slots forming air vents which help dissipate heat to the outside of the case. The power supply will also draw in air from within the system which will be expelled through the fan.

If the parts of a computer are not excessively hot to touch then it is unlikely that the system is experiencing excessive heat and that should not be the cause of any potential problem.

Whilst a suitably rated power supply will be capable of providing power for the basic components of the computer as well as a number of additional adapters that may be attached to the motherboard, there can be a heat problem when additional adapter cards are in place. The design of the CPU is such that the motherboard is flat and the natural heat emitted by the chips rises to the top of the unit box and eventually out of the vents. When a number of adapter cards are inserted there is restricted space for the heat to rise, and little room for the air to circulate. This restriction, together with the additional heat being generated by the chips on the adapter card itself can occasionally cause overheating problems.

When components are subjected to repeated excessive heating the result is premature aging and failure. The heat generated may not be uniform across a particular device, for example in the case of many chips there is more heat at the input/output connectors where the leads meet the chip itself. The heating, and subsequent cooling (when the system is switched off) of these components causes the contacts in the chip or device to break down, eventually leading to open-circuit failure. When hot the device can produce intermittent "soft errors" whereby data is lost or corrupted. The effect is known as "Thermal Wipeout" and can be a chronic problem in overloaded systems which are not properly cooled.

7.4.1.1 Solving heat-related problems

The preventative measure for this kind of problem is to do everything possible to ensure that the system is properly cooled. With a basic system not using multiple adapter cards it should be sufficient to ensure that the ventilation slots are kept clear – ensure that the computer is not pushed up against a wall, and check that the ventilations slots are not covered with paper or messages. Also, check that the fan in the power supply is functioning; visual examination is sufficient. If a number of adapter cards are in use then it may be worthwhile installing an additional fan which can be positioned just behind the system box face plate. Electronic technology is constantly advancing, and whilst the majority of systems have ordinary, continuous operation fans, there are a few systems that are equipped with fans with a thermal sensor interface. These monitor the internal temperature of the system and speed up when temperatures rise. The result is that the fan is more efficient, it lasts longer, and it is quieter in normal operation as it runs only at a slow speed.

After an extended period of time the normal heating and cooling of the chips in a computer can cause them to work loose from their sockets, a process sometimes referred to as "chip creep". This often results in intermittent system failures. To prevent this occurring it is a good idea to regularly check that the chips are firmly in their sockets.

Heat is a common contributor to disk failure. Hard disks will start to screech, and will fail in a shorter time period, whilst floppy disks can physically melt, warp or crack. The basic rule to follow with regards the care of disks is the same as that for computer systems: if the environment is comfortable for the user, then it is comfortable for the disks as well. This applies equally well to excessive sunlight, as the effect of leaving a disk in direct sunlight has exactly the same effect as leaving a gramophone record in the sun – it warps. The disk drive head will have great difficulty in reading a warped disk and the data will probably be lost.

7.4.2 EXCESSIVE COOLING

Whilst on the subject of heat, it is worth giving a mention to cold. The electronic components of a computer system do not mind the cold, in fact in some cases it can enhance their performance. However the mechanical parts such as the disk drives and the printers are not so happy. The recorded acceptable temperatures for floppy disk drives is between 40 to 115 degrees Fahrenheit, with hard disk drives being slightly more tolerant of the ambient temperature. However at the low end of the scale there can be mechanical sluggishness leading to erratic data storage and retrieval. The floppy disk itself can become brittle if left for too long in a cold environment.

7.4.2.1 Solving cold-related problems

The way to prevent errors occurring due to cold is simply to allow the system to stand until it has reached room temperature before switching on. This is usually only necessary when systems have been transported and thus exposed to excessive cold, or perhaps if the system is used in a workshop/factory floor which has no direct heating.

7.5   DUST/ASH

Large computer systems are generally kept in specially air conditioned 'clean' rooms where dust is kept to the minimum. However with personal computers the exposure to household and office dust is inevitable. There are however a number of preventative measures that can be taken to ensure that dust does not become the originator of system failures.

Dust will settle on any piece of equipment left on a desk or on the floor. However, it is especially attracted by the static emitted from the computer system and also by heat. Because of this the most obvious part of the system to be affected by dust and static is the display unit, in exactly the same way as a television screen. The screen should be regularly cleaned with a household cleaner, or with a damp cloth and detergent. It is advisable to use an anti-static spray to help prevent dust collecting due to the static.

The natural heating of components within a system attracts dust and the collecting dust in turn insulates the circuit devices and prevents the heat being dissipated. Whilst it is possible to vacuum the inside of a computer from time to time, the best preventative maintenance that can be performed is to try and keep down the amount of dust being generated in the computer environment.

- Keep dust covers on the computer when not in use and especially when the environment is being cleaned – there is an enormous amount of dust generated by a vacuum cleaner when carpets are swept.

- Floppy disks are very sensitive to dust as there is always a section of the delicate mylar material exposed. There is a lining to the vinyl disk jacket which is designed to pick up dust particles, but there is a limit to the amount and size of dust particles this can cope with. To help prevent dust collecting on disks always keep them in the protective sleeves when not actually using them and then keep them in closed disk boxes.

- If the computer is being used close to a dusty or dirty area, then try to ensure that any interconnecting doors are kept closed as much as possible.

Cigarette smoke is a menace to computers. Not only do the particles of ash settle on the screen and in the keyboard, but ash on the surface of a floppy disk will both corrupt the data on the disk as well as damage the hardware of the disk drive. This can be especially difficult to remove as eventually a layer of sticky tar builds up, coating the sensitive parts of the drive head. The preventive measures to be taken here are simple. Do not allow smoking whilst working with, or in the vicinity of, the computer.

7.5.1   WORKSHOPS AND FACTORY FLOORS

Another common source of problems occurs when computers are used in workshop environments. These can be dirty and dusty, and in many cases greasy. This leads to grease or oil finding its way into the keyboard mechanism, and insulating the contacts beneath the keys. The simplest remedy is to cover the keyboard with a thin flexible plastic sheet. These are often seen on the keypads of supermarket cash tills, and are the most effective way of ensuring that no dust, dirt or grease interferes with the operation of the keyboard. Another area susceptible to grease is the disk drives and disks. There is no simple remedy to this problem, other than ensuring that disks are handled correctly, replaced in their protective sleeves when not in use, and stored in a closed disk box.

Workshop environments are among the most hostile for computers, and thus it is essential that care is taken to minimise the risks when installing and operating personal computers.

| HINT |

When not in use all the peripherals should be protected by anti-static dust covers. These are inexpensive and will go a long way towards keeping the machines free of dust and ash.

7.6 POWER

It is very important to maintain a 'clean' power supply to the computer. When the local power supply is subjected to an excess of use the amount of power being sent down the lines can fluctuate. This may be exhibited by lights dimming in a room. Even quite small fluctuations in the power line to a computer can cause the system to fail, possibly with disastrous results. Power-line problems can be divided into three categories:

– Brownouts
– Blackouts
– Transients

7.6.1 BROWNOUTS

Brownouts are planned (or sometimes unplanned) voltage sags when less voltage is available to drive the computer system. These voltage sags are quite common, especially when a system is being used near some large electrical equipment such as air conditioners, factory machinery etc. Another cause of brownouts is the electricity distribution body themselves; in order to ensure that their network is not overloaded at peak periods, they may institute a temporary brownout. These typically last between a few seconds and 10 minutes, although it has been known for a brownout to continue for significantly longer.

The system should be designed to cope with voltage drops of up to 20 percent, but if the drop is too low, insufficient power is sent to the motherboard and the data being processed may become garbled. During brownouts the system may operate intermittently, overheat, or simply shut down and lock out.

On occasions there may be a surge in the voltage and within limits the system should be able to cope with this. However the effect of the power supply having to cope with a higher voltage will cause components to heat up more quickly.

7.6.2 BLACKOUTS

A blackout is a complete loss of voltage in the power-line and which can be caused by storms and lightning. It can also be caused by power lines being damaged or by an incorrect switching action within the power station.

When power is lost all data being held in RAM will be lost. If data was being written to disk at the time of failure it is likely that only a partial save will have been effected, which in some situations can have the effect of corrupting the disk.

It is important to always unplug and switch off all computer components when a power failure is encountered because when power returns there is usually a surge of electricity which can damage the system.

7.6.3   TRANSIENTS

Transients refer to spikes of voltage which can be sent down the power line without notice. These unexpected surges can be very substantial, sometimes up to as much as 2000 volts. If a large spike comes down the line whilst the computer is switched on it is possible that it may destroy the sensitive circuit devices.

7.6.4   PREVENTING POWER RELATED PROBLEMS

In order to prevent power-line problems one of two courses of action can be taken. Either the power being supplied can be conditioned to ensure that the last leg of its journey is an evenly distributed flow of power, or alternatively an auxiliary or backup power source can be provided. Two devices are available to counteract the problems:

- The spike catcher
- The uninterruptable power supply.

7.6.4.1   The spike catcher

The spike catcher is the simplest of the two devices, and serves only to prevent transients and spikes from reaching the equipment. They vary in price from under £20 to over £250.

The cheapest devices protect only against spikes of high voltage, and are often based on a device called a varistor, which is placed between the live and earth wires of the supply. Whilst the difference between live and earth is under about 400V, the varistor does nothing, but once the voltage increases, the varistor effectively short circuits the two wires, diverting the excess energy to ground rather than allowing it to go to the equipment. The more advanced spike catchers have varistors between all three power lines, so that surges on any of them are prevented.

More expensive units include filters to combat electrical noise. This is a form of interference that may in certain cases produce errors in a computer system. The electrical noise on the power lines is transferred through the power supply onto the circuit boards. It can then cause signals to be garbled, as the components do not know the difference between the true signal and the noise. Thus, the addition of filters into the power supply ensures that errors due to noise are minimised.

The most expensive spike catchers include protection against very large power surges. Varistors may be unable to cope with very large surges, and in most cases they will be destroyed by them. Thus to guarantee protection from large surges it is necessary to buy the more expensive devices. These work on a variety of different principles, one of the most common being the gas-discharge tube. This is a glass tube containing a special gas which is electrically connected into the supply. As the voltage rises beyond safe limits, the gas begins to ionise, and creates a path for the excess current. This form of device can be effective against the highest surges, such as those produced during lightning strikes.

7.6.4.2   The uninterruptable power supply

An uninterruptable power supply (UPS) is effectively a large battery which is automatically switched into the power circuit if the main supply fails. The battery is trickle charged whilst the main supply is operating correctly, thus it should not need any special maintenance, replacing or manual recharging. A UPS normally includes some form of spike catcher and filtering circuitry to minimise noise.

UPSs are available in a range of different specifications. They are rated in terms of Watts (W) or Volt-Amps (VA) to indicate how much power can be supplied. A 400W system is designed to power an IBM-XT class machine, including its disk drives, monitor and printer. For an IBM-AT type machine, an 800W system is recommended. Obviously, if a large number of option cards are installed, or there are more peripherals than normal, then a more highly rated UPS will be required. The above figures are based on the UPS powering the system for 15 minutes or so after power failure. However, in many cases, all that is required is for power to be maintained for five minutes or so, until the user has had time to save files and shutdown the system properly. There are several utilities available which perform this process automatically when a power failure occurs.

There are two distinct types of UPS:

- *The inline UPS*

   The inline UPS is constantly connected to the power supply of the computer, and in turn is constantly being charged from the mains supply. If the mains power supply fails, the UPS is no longer being charged but it continues to supply power to the computer system as before, until it's charge runs out.

- *The offline UPS.*

   The offline UPS is slightly different. In normal use the computer system is powered directly by the mains supply. When a power failure occurs, a special switch is automatically thrown to connect the UPS battery to the computer rather than the mains.

Whilst the time required to switch the offline UPS into the system is minimal, it has been found to cause occasional problems, especially when used to power high performance computer systems. Thus it is recommended that such systems use an inline UPS, as these have proved to be the more reliable.

A UPS costs considerably more than a simple spike-catcher. However, it does offer a much greater degree of protection for applications where it is essential that no information is lost. The lowest rated, offline, UPS costs from £200 upwards. Inline UPSs cost slightly more for a similarly rated device. There is almost no upper limit on the price, as UPSs are available which can power complete buildings! When choosing a suitable device, it is essential to select one with a sufficient rating; if there is any doubt about an appropriate UPS then advice should be sought from a reputable dealer.

7.6.5 USING A UPS OR SPIKE CATCHER

Both UPSs and spike catchers are easy to use. In many cases it is simply necessary to plug the system into the device, and then plug the device into the mains. In the case of the UPS it may be necessary to make a hardware connection to the power supply of the PC, or actually bypass it altogether by re-routing the power connections directly to the UPS circuitry.

The only other factor that needs to be considered when using a UPS is whether or not it is working. The only way the answer to this question can be determined is by checking and testing the system on a regular basis. It will do no harm to the system at all to test the UPS with the following procedure:

- Power up the system normally, but boot from a DOS disk that installs no special caching software etc. Similarly, ensure that no RAM drives are in use.

- Exit from any menu system of applications that are automatically executed.
- With the DOS prompt on the screen, switch off the mains power supply to the UPS.
- Most systems will then give an audible warning, alerting the user to the fact that there is a problem.
- Check the computer still works, and then switch everything off.
- Allow to settle for 30 seconds or so, restore power to the UPS, and restart the system in the usual way.

7.7   CORROSION OR RUSTING

The metal connector pins on interface cards, chip pins and cables can become corroded. This is a chemical change in which the metal of the pins and sockets is gradually eaten away. Corrosion can be very damaging.

There are three types of corrosion which affect personal computers:

- Oxidation
- Atmospheric corrosion
- Galvanic corrosion.

7.7.1   OXIDATION

A film of oxide forms on the metal surface, reducing the contact between two pieces of metal. The oxidation process accelerates at high temperatures and the metal is actually worn away as the electrical contact surface is converted to an oxide, which gradually crumbles into dust.

7.7.2   ATMOSPHERIC CORROSION

Chemicals in the air can attack metals in the computer system circuitry, causing pitting and a build up of rust. In the early stages sulphur compounds in the atmosphere are converted to sulphuric acid which lies in small droplets on the surface of the metal connectors. The acid eats at the metal, causing pits to form.

If caught early the contacts can be wiped clean of the corrosion, restoring the metal brightness, but after a while the sulphuric acid becomes a hard layer and cannot be wiped away. The effect is to reduce electrical contact.

7.7.3   GALVANIC CORROSION

With galvanic corrosion tiny cracks in the metal plating on a pin or connector let moisture borne electrolytes, such as salt, penetrate the metal plating. The plating surface becomes scaly and rough as the plating is eroded and oxides form. The effect is the same as other forms of corrosion.

Corrosion may be minimised by regular cleaning of the pins on chips and connectors.

- Chips work themselves out of their sockets after extended use. By turning off the power and carefully pushing them back into their sockets they will be cleaned and the electrical contact improved. Always make sure the power is switched off before undertaking these steps.

–   Contacts may also be cleaned, but should always be rubbed lengthwise. Note that it is very important not to touch the contacts with fingers as the perspiration and natural oil on fingers contains enough sodium chloride to initiate rusting on the contacts. Solvents and spray cleaners are sold which may be used to clean the pins.

7.7.4   THE EFFECT OF WATER ON A COMPUTER SYSTEM

Water, whether it is in the form of coffee, tea, orange squash or pure H_2O, can have a drastic effect on a computer system under certain circumstances, but may do little or no damage if treated correctly.

If a drink is spilt into the system unit, monitor, printer or disk drives of a computer system that is connected to the mains, it is likely that severe damage may be caused. In such circumstances power should immediately be removed from the system by switching off at the wall socket; don't touch the unit at all as it may be hazardous. Advice and assistance should then be sought from an engineer, who should be able to identify the damage and remedy any problems.

If something is spilt into a computer system that is not connected to the mains then it is quite likely that there is no damage at all. The first step in the remedial process is to drain all loose liquid from the device. This may mean supporting the unit over a sink for several minutes. Once all excess liquid has been removed, a cleaning solvent can be used to remove any other traces from the circuit boards or other devices; this is especially important if the liquid contained sugar, as this will form a syrup when it dries if left untreated. Once all traces of the substance have been removed dry the unit thoroughly before switching on again; in fact it is advisable to leave it for a day or two in a warm, dry atmosphere in order to be certain it is safe to use.

Keyboards are very resilient to having liquids spilt on them, and in most cases will not be damaged by such an accident even if the computer system is operating at the time. To remedy the situation, the first step is to unplug the keyboard and drain any excess liquid. Once this has been done, it can be cleaned with a solvent and then dried. There have recently been a number of documented instances where no solvents or cleaners were available, and so the users resorted to cleaning the keyboard under a running tap. Fortunately they took time to dry the keyboard completely, and on reassembly the devices were found to work with no problems whatsoever. In two cases the drying process was speeded up through the use of an ordinary hairdryer, which has the added advantage of blowing away any particles of dust or dirt that may have accumulated.

7.8 MAGNETISM

Data is stored on disks by the use of magnetic technology, and just as magnetic fields may be used to write the data, they may also inadvertently be used to destroy it. Such magnetic fields are most often created by high voltages or currents, such as those found in audio speakers and video monitors. Thus if a disk is brought too close to such a device it may become corrupt.

Magnetic fields are also generated by electric motors and care should be taken that disks are not placed near such pieces of equipment. Common culprits include photocopiers and printing devices, although the most commonly encountered source of magnetic fields in every office is the telephone. Disks placed next to telephones, especially the older styles ones, can quite quickly become unreadable.

Magnetism can also effect transfer of data through cables and therefore care should be taken as to where interconnecting cables are laid. This is especially important in the local area network environment, where such disruptions can result in total network failure.

7.9   DISK DRIVE MAINTENANCE

7.9.1   HARD DISK MAINTENANCE

As hard disks are sealed in dust tight cabinets, the only preventative maintenance which can be done is to ensure that the disk is placed in a location which will minimise electrical noise interference problems, and to check that all external connections to the device are sound. Static can also be a major problem and the environment in which the disk is placed should have anti-static mats placed at appropriate points. Any faults encountered with this type of disk drive must be handled by a qualified engineer. If an attempt is made to open the sealed unit by non-qualified technicians the drive warranty is immediately deemed invalid, and the data on the disk will be unreadable.

When these disks give problems they often have to be replaced. Therefore make sure that a full back-up copy of all data is maintained at all times.

7.9.2   FLOPPY DISK DRIVE MAINTENANCE.

Floppy disk drives require maintenance in several ways, the most common of which are the following:

- Head cleaning
- Disk speed adjustment
- Disk drive alignment.

7.9.3   HEAD CLEANING

Heads need cleaning to remove the oxide which builds up on the surface of the head. It is a procedure which should be undertaken regularly, about once every 40 operating hours depending on the environment in which the system is used.

Head cleaning diskettes of various kinds are available, normally consisting of a special diskette which works with a cleaning solvent. There is also an abrasive head cleaning product available, which must not be overused, or irreparable damage will be caused.

Most cleaning systems contain a cleaning disk with or without the solvent. This cleaning disk should not be left in the disk drive for more than 30 seconds. Proprietary disk cleaning kits have a limited life and it is important not to use the kit more than the manufacturers specified number of times. Typically a kit can be used 15 to 20 times and there is usually a label which can be marked each time the cleaning disk is used.

Disk heads can also be cleaned manually with a cotton swab and alcohol. However, great care must be taken not to damage the heads or the delicate mechanical components of the disk drive.

In place of cleaning solvents, surgical alcohol or methanol may be used. However, whatever solvent is used it must not leave a residue when it evaporates. At all times ensure that there is sufficient ventilation so that all the solvent can evaporate before the system is used.

The exact period between cleaning depends of the degree of usage of the system. On average a diskette can be expected to provide three million read/write passes before enough ferrous oxide wears off to require the drive head to be cleaned. Some poor quality disks will degenerate the head much more quickly. However, the environment in which the computer is used will also determine the frequency of cleaning, as dirt and dust in the air will contaminate the drive heads. This is especially relevant for systems used in workshops or on the factory floor, as these may experience severe problems.

Keeping the disk drive door closed when the system is not in use contributes to keeping dust and dirt out and therefore extends the period of use between cleans.

Procedure for cleaning the disk drive head for drive A.

- Turn the computer power on

- Dampen the cleaning disk with the solvent

- Insert the dampened cleaning disk in the drive

- Close the drive door

- Reset the system with Ctrl-Alt, Del and the disk will spin in the drive whilst it searches for information on the disk. The effect of the spinning causes the head to be cleaned

- After 20 or 30 seconds open the drive door and remove the cleaning disk.

> BEWARE

> *Never allow the cleaning disk to spin in the drive for more than 30 seconds.*

- With some systems the disk drive will automatically stop after five seconds. In this case repeat the reset procedure three or four times.

- Turn off the computer

- Let the drive read/write head dry thoroughly before operating the system and in particular before inserting a data diskette into the drive.

When cleaning the drive head for disk drive B the system should be booted up into DOS and then the DIR command issued for drive B with the cleaning disk inserted. The effect of this command is for the drive to search for information on the disk and the spinning of the disk causes it to be cleaned.

Remember to wait for a few minutes before inserting a diskette into the drive, especially if the system has to be booted from floppy. Failure to observe this precaution may cause the disk to be damaged, and the head to be contaminated again. This is because certain solvents used for cleaning will melt the mylar forming the disk

7.9.3.1   To clean the drive head manually

The tools required for this procedure are:

- Flat-head screwdriver

- Phillips screwdriver

- Adequate lighting

- Tray to hold loose screws.

The head cleaning procedure for one of the original IBM PC disk drives is as follows:

- Turn off the power.
- Disassemble and remove the disk drive from the chassis.
- Remove the head cable from the connector at the front right corner of the drive.
- Remove the two Phillips screws holding the analogue card on the drive – these are located on both sides in the front.
- Slide the analogue card towards the back of the drive until the card is free of the grooves in the drive mechanism – it may be necessary to wiggle the card to get it to slide.
- Lift up the analogue card from the front.
- Lift the black head-load arm and look for discolouration on the surface of the pad, or on the read/write head below.
- Using a special foam or wrapped cotton swab dampened with cleaning solvent, gently rub the head and the pad.
- Be sure to let the surfaces dry completely before re-assembly.
- When the head and pressure pad are dry, carefully slide the analogue card back into the grooves in the drive mechanism.
- Reinstall the two Phillips screws.
- Reconnect the head cables.
- Reinstall the disk drive using a reverse procedure to that outlined above.

Some disk drives have different layouts to the original PC, and so the above procedure may differ slightly. However, the underlying technique of gaining access to the read/write head is the same.

7.9.4   DISK SPEED TESTS AND ADJUSTMENTS

Variation in the disk drive speed can be caused by normal mechanical drive wear or by excessive moving and reconnecting of the drives. Adjusting the disk drive speed is similar to the retuning of a motor car engine and is a worthwhile procedure to exercise as part of routine PC maintenance.

The standard 360K IBM PC disk drive rotates at 300 rpm and works with soft sectored disks. This means that the computer software identifies the beginning and the end of each sector on each track of the disk. No timing holes are used as they are with some hard disks and for this reason the speed of rotation is critical to the accurate synchronisation of the software with the signals stored on the disk. If the speed deviates as little as 10 rpm from the norm then the drive may not be able to correctly read the disk.

Incorrect speed means that the data is written to an incorrect location on the disk. The next time the heads access this area on the track the computer will hang up and will give a disk error. Speeds between 291 rpm and 309 rpm are normally acceptable. Speeds outside this range cause either intermittent or permanent error. Speeds outside the limits of 270 and 309 will erase the synchronisation timing marks on the disk making the disk itself useless. To recover from this the disk will have to be reformatted.

7.9.4.1   Adjustment of disk speed

The tools required for this procedure are:-

- Flat-head screwdriver
- Phillips screwdriver
- Jewellers flat-head screwdriver
- Tray to hold loose screws

The procedure for adjusting the disk drive speed is relatively simple, and should be carried out with the aid of a disk drive diagnostic program such as TestDrive:

- Turn off the power.
- Disassemble and remove the disk drive from the chassis.
- Set the drive mechanism on its side crossways on the top of the power supply.
- Reconnect the drive cable and the power supply cable to the drive.
- Find the speed adjustment control potentiometer at the back centre of the drive (it has a groove on the top into which a small flat-headed screwdriver may be placed).
- Reconnect the power cord to the computer.
- Turn the computer on – be careful not to touch any of the exposed electronic components whilst the power is on.
- Insert the disk containing a disk speed test program into the drive to be adjusted.
- Close the disk drive door.
- Follow the test procedures as displayed on the screen.
- Use a jewellers screwdriver or a tweaker to adjust the disk speed by gradually turning the speed adjustment potentiometer until the disk speed is reported as being within the range 299–301 rpm.
- Remove the disk.
- Turn off the power.
- Disconnect the disk drive cable and power supply cable from the drive.
- Reassemble the disk drive using a reverse procedure to the one outlined above.

$$\boxed{\text{NOTE}}$$

The speed of rotation is different for 1.2MB 5¼ inch floppy disks. These devices are specified to rotate at 360rpm in order to make the most of the high-density disk media. Thus when testing such a disk drive it is important to ensure that the test program supports the high-density format, and that it is set to the appropriate mode of operation.

7.9.4.2   Disk drive alignment

This procedure is best left to the service centre as to properly realign the disk drive requires the use of special equipment including a dual-trace oscilloscope, special alignment disks and various disk alignment tools which are generally only available to qualified technicians.

However, disk drive diagnostic systems such as TestDrive do include a check to determine whether or not the alignment is acceptable. Thus it is perfectly possible for the troubleshooter to diagnose the problem using such a system, and then contact an engineer to perform the necessary adjustment.

The most delicate alignment adjustment necessary is that of adjusting the read/write head alignment, or tracking. The symptoms for this being a requirement are that a disk is formatted and used in one disk drive without any problems, but cannot be used in a different disk drive at all. If it is necessary to replace the electronics analogue card that is built onto the drive, the tracking should be checked because every card is tuned for the drive and a new card could affect the tracking.

| HINT |

It often costs as much to have a floppy disk drive repaired as it does to buy a new one. Therefore it may be appropriate to keep a spare floppy disk drive on hand.

7.10   FLOPPY DISK CARE

It is important to pay due care and attention to floppy disks in order to prolong their working life and to minimise the failure rate. Fortunately the 3½ inch disks are becoming more popular, especially with the spread of laptop and notebook computers. One of the advantages of the 3½ inch disks is that they are much more robust and reliable than their 5¼ inch counterparts.

The following guidelines illustrate some of the main areas in which care is required when handling floppy disks:

- Handle the diskettes carefully
- Do not leave disks lying around
- Always keep disks in their protective sleeves
- NEVER touch the exposed disk surface
- Keep disks away from direct sunlight.

The guidelines for disk care are sometimes printed on the back of the disk sleeve as shown in Figure 7.2.

Some general guidelines for prolonging the life of a disk are:

- ALWAYS buy good quality brand name disks
- NEVER touch the disk surface
- ALWAYS ensure that the disk is properly in the drive before closing the drive door
- ALWAYS store disks in their protective sleeves
- AVOID writing on labels that are already on the disk, but if this is necessary always use a felt tip pen and never a biro or pencil
- NEVER rub out information on a disk label using an eraser
- ALWAYS store disks in a cool, dry place
- ALWAYS back-up all data regularly

- **ALWAYS** store working disks and back-up disks in different places
- **NEVER** allow smoking in the vicinity of disks or computers
- **NEVER** leave disks by monitors or televisions where static may affect them
- **NEVER** leave disks in the vicinity of electrical machines such as telephones or vacuum cleaners. Audio speakers must also be avoided
- **NEVER** bend disks.

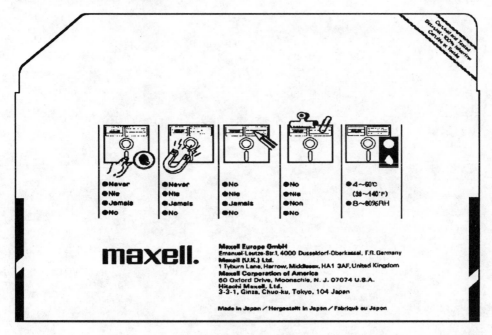

Figure 7.1 Floppy disk sleeve showing guidelines

Whilst it is safe to put disks through X-ray machines, it is essential to ensure that they are not put through a metal detector or body scanner such as those encountered at airport security checkpoints. These devices work by emitting a magnetic field which is reflected from metal objects. These magnetic fields will destroy data on a computer disk. X-ray machines do not emit magnetism, and thus are safe.

When sending disks through the post or travelling with disks always wrap them in silver foil, and place them in a sturdy box or carton, or a purpose made disk envelope. These precautions will help to ensure that the valuable data that was stored on the disk at the start of the journey is still there when it reaches its destination.

7.11 SUMMARY

Preventative maintenance involves two processes:

- The regular checking of the computer system in an attempt to forestall component failures.
- The taking of precautions which will reduce the occurrence of common faults.

There are many reasons why computer systems fail, although the cause can often be traced to one of five factors, namely heat, dust, power problems, corrosion, and magnetism or static electricity. If measures are taken to reduce the incidence of these in the region of a PC then there will be fewer faults.

Suitable training will help ensure that users are aware of the possible risks, and they should be actively encouraged to avoid smoking, drinking or eating while working with a computer system.

8 Installing Optional Devices

8.1 INTRODUCTION

There are many optional extras available for personal computers, a factor which has significantly enhanced the PC's popularity. Some of the products change the way in which the PC works, adding extra features that are not provided on the standard model. This means that the PC can be used for a wide range of applications, from office work such as accounts processing, word processing, desktop publishing and graphical design to more specialised applications such as electronic design, controlling machinery, monitoring security systems etc. Other products do not add extra functionality to the system, but enhance the power, capacity and overall performance of the existing components. Still more make it simpler for the operator to complete the task in hand, thus improving the efficiency of the system as a whole.

Irrespective of precise details, devices can be categorised into three distinct groups:

- Products supplied in the form of plug-in option cards, such as video cards, fax boards, disk drive controllers etc.

- Products supplied in the form of other hardware, such as disk units, external modems, scanners, graphics tablets etc.

- Products supplied in the form of integrated circuits, such as RAM chips, SIMMs and maths co-processors.

All devices in each category are installed in a similar way, and the same guidelines apply to the procedures that are required irrespective of the exact nature of the product.

WARNING

Before opening the system unit, ensure that the power is switched off and the cable is removed from the wall socket. Failure to observe this simple precaution could expose the troubleshooter to a serious risk of electric shock.

8.2 OPTION CARDS

Option cards are the most popular way of enhancing PC systems. Cards are available to perform a wide array of different tasks, including:

- Extra memory (expanded or extended)
- Video adapters
- Mouse interfaces

- Additional serial and parallel interface ports
- Modems
- Hard disk drives (known as Hard Cards)
- Specialist analogue and digital I/O ports
- Scanners
- Game control adapters (Joysticks)
- Specialist printer control cards
- Musical and sound effect boards.

Option cards can be fitted with a minimum of effort, and in most cases can be installed and operational within a few minutes. All option cards should come with installation instructions that tell the user how to fit the new card. As these will be specific to the device, they should be followed as closely as possible. However, the following sections outline the key points which must also be borne in mind when fitting such devices.

8.2.1 CHECK COMPATIBILITY

The option card must be compatible with the system in use. In the majority of cases the card will be specified as being suitable for *IBM PCs and 100 percent compatible machines*. However, there are some manufacturers who specify that their boards are only for true IBM systems, and if they are installed in a compatible they may not work correctly.

The second factor relating to compatibility is whether or not the card matches the architecture of the system. Personal computers are generally based on one of the following design concepts:

- 8-bit ISA
- 16-bit ISA
- 32-bit EISA
- 16-bit MCA
- 32-bit MCA.

Similarly, option cards are specified as being suitable for one or more of the above architectures and it is essential to purchase a board that is compatible with the particular architecture of the system in use. Having said this, there is a small amount of variation:

- 8-bit ISA systems (generally 8088/8086 PCs and compatibles) must only use 8-bit ISA boards
- 16-bit ISA systems (generally 80286, 80386 and 80486 based AT and PC compatibles) can use either 8-bit or 16-bit ISA boards
- EISA systems (80386 and 80486 AT and PC compatibles) can use 8-bit ISA, 16-bit ISA or EISA boards
- 16-bit MCA systems (low-end PS/2 models) must use only 16-bit MCA boards
- 32-bit MCA systems (high-end PS/2 models) can use 16-bit or 32-bit MCA boards.

Thus the more advanced the architecture, the more flexible the system in terms of what devices can be installed.

The option board must also be compatible with any other cards that are installed in the system. This applies to several different categories of option card, as the design of the PC limits the system to using only one of each at any time. The following list outlines some of the problem areas:

– *Video cards*

Systems can usually only have a single video card installed, and conflicts will arise if this restriction is not heeded. There are a few exceptions to this rule however, the most notable being the large screen monitors, such as the Taxan Viking range, which are used for CAD and DTP applications. These devices can sometimes be used in conjunction with a second display unit such as a CGA or Hercules monitor and adapter card.

– *Memory cards*

Owing to the fixed addresses employed by the majority of memory cards, it is not usually possible to install more than one into any system. To add more memory to a system, beyond that provided by an existing memory card, it will be necessary to replace the card with a larger capacity one.

– *Serial and parallel interface cards*

There is a limit to the number of interface ports supported by PC systems, as the original BIOS designs supported only two serial ports and one parallel port. However, option cards are available which exceed this, and provide four serial ports and two parallel ports, controlling them with special software device drivers. This is the absolute limit that can be installed in any system if they are to be controlled through DOS, as it is not possible to access devices other than COM1, COM2, COM3, COM4, LPT1 and LPT2.

There are other incompatibilities that may be encountered, although the above examples are among the most common. Documentation supplied with the board should give sufficient information to determine if any incompatibilities are likely.

8.2.2   INTERFACE CONNECTION

Assuming that the board is compatible with the system, it will be necessary to find a free slot in which it can be fitted. Only two factors need to be borne in mind here:

– Slot size
– Card size.

8.2.2.1   Slot size

The slot needs to be able to accommodate the card's edge connector;

– A 32-bit card requires a 32-bit slot
– A 16-bit card requires a 16-bit slot or a 32-bit slot
– An 8-bit card requires an 8-bit slot, a 16-bit slot, or a 32-bit slot.

The positioning of a card in the system is only limited by the type of card in terms of its 8-bit, 16-bit or 32-bit connector. An 8-bit card can be installed in any slot, a 16-bit card can be installed into a 16-bit slot or a 32-bit slot, but a 32-bit card must be installed into a 32-bit slot. This aside, it doesn't matter whether the card is fitted in the leftmost or rightmost slot. However, in order to accommodate the new card it may be necessary to reposition the existing ones.

Care should be taken to ensure that all internal cabling is not stretched, and that cables are appropriately routed so that they are not snagged when the system unit lid is removed. This is most easily achieved by positioning the card as near to any devices it is connected to as possible.

8.2.2.2   Card size

Cards are quoted as being either full-length or half-length. This is a measurement of the physical size of the card, and bears no relationship to the interface connection; full-length cards are approximately 30cm long, and half-length cards are between 12 and 20cm long. It is important to ensure that there is sufficient room around the slot chosen to accommodate the card, and to help in this most systems have their option card slots specified as being either half-length or full-length.

This physical restriction is less common on desktop systems, but may be encountered when working with laptops and portables. Generally speaking, such systems do not provide any full-length card positions, and perhaps only one or two half-length ones. If multiple interface cards are required, a special interface box must be used to house them. This will either fit directly onto the back of the computer, or it may be connected by a short cable to a special socket on the PC.

8.2.3   INTERRUPTS AND MEMORY ADDRESSES

As well as the physical positioning and interfacing of the card, it is also important to bear in mind the logical requirements of the device, ie exactly how it will communicate with the rest of the computer system. The PC provides two ways in which option cards can communicate with the CPU, disks and other components:

–   Interrupts

–   Memory addresses.

8.2.3.1   Interrupts

An interrupt, or IRQ, is a special signal that is generated or recognised by the option card, and the occurrence of an interrupt causes the device to start operating in some way. There are only a limited number of interrupts available on personal computer systems:

–   PCs and compatibles have eight standard interrupts, numbered IRQ 0 to IRQ 7, although only six are available at the expansion slots. Figure 8.1 shows typical usage of the interrupts on a PC.

    The NMI (Non-Maskable Interrupt) is a special instance of an interrupt, and is reserved for use by the system. Similarly, as IRQ 0 and IRQ 1 are not available at the expansion slots, they are also reserved for the system. The interrupts numbers shown in Figure 8.1 have been grouped to show which are available at the expansion slots and which are not.

–   ATs and compatibles have 16 standard interrupts, numbered IRQ 0 to IRQ 15. Only interrupts 2, 3, 4, 5, 6 and 7 are available on 8-bit slots, whilst interrupts 10, 11, 12, 14 and 15 are additionally provided on 16-bit slots. Any board specified as using IRQ 2 will automatically be redirected to using IRQ 9, as IRQ 2 has a special use in the AT. The NMI and interrupts 0, 1, 2, 8 and 13 are reserved for use by the system. Figure 8.2 shows the typical usage of the interrupts on an AT system.

	IRQ	Use
Reserved	NMI	Parity check & 8087
	0	Time of day clock
	1	Keyboard
Available at slots	2	Network adapter (if fitted)
	3	Secondary asynchronous communications, COM2: (if fitted)
	4	Primary asynchronous communications, COM1: or AUX:
	5	Fixed disk controller (if fitted)
	6	Floppy disk controller
	7	Parallel printer port, PRN: or LPT1:

Figure 8.1   Typical usage of PC interrupt lines

	IRQ	Use
Reserved	NMI	Parity check
	0	Timer
	1	Keyboard
Available at 8-bit slots	2	Cascaded interrupt from second interrupt controller
	3	Serial port COM2: (if fitted)
	4	Serial port COM1:
	5	Parallel port LPT2: (if fitted)
	6	Diskette controller
	7	Parallel port LPT1:
Available at 16-bit slots	8	Real time clock
	9	Redirected from IRQ 2
	10	Reserved (ie can be used by option cards)
	11	Reserved (ie can be used by option cards)
	12	Reserved (ie can be used by option cards)
	13	80287 Co-processor (if fitted)
	14	Fixed disk controller
	15	Reserved (ie can be used by option cards)

Figure 8.2   Typical usage of AT interrupt lines

Usually it is not possible for two cards to share an interrupt, so each must be allocated its own. These are most often specified by setting DIP switches or jumpers on the card (see below), although some cards are very inflexible in this respect and force the user to allocate a particular interrupt.

Invariably the user has no idea what interrupts are in use in a system, and on attempting to install a new device is faced with a major problem. To avoid this situation, it is recommended that an up-to-date record is kept for each system, detailing which interrupts are used by each card. This should be updated whenever a change is made to the configuration. Figure 8.3 shows such a listing.

The PS/2 is significantly simpler to work with than PCs and ATs, as the design of the

IRQ	Use
2	Available
3	Available
4	COM1: serial port located on multifunction card in slot 3
5	Available
6	System – Floppy controller in slot 8
7	Parallel port LPT1: located on multifunction card in slot 3
10	Mitsubishi scanner controller in slot 4
11	Available
12	Available
14	System – Western Digital Hard disk controller in slot 7
15	Vega Video7 SVGA card in slot 1

Figure 8.3   Interrupt line allocations for an AT

system was reconfigured to allow more than one option card to use each interrupt. Thus choosing interrupts for PS/2 machines is much simpler, negating the need to keep a detailed log of the interrupt configuration.

8.2.3.2   Memory addresses

Whilst the interrupts can trigger the device into action, they cannot be used to transfer data. To allow for information to be passed between the device and the rest of the system, it is necessary to allocate certain memory addresses. These locations can then be accessed by both the hardware and the software, thus allowing intercommunication.

The design of the PC, and all its successors, allows for 1024 such locations, or I/O ports as they are also known. Each I/O port must be allocated to a particular device, and ro two devices should share a location. Generally speaking, with 1024 ports there should be more than enough to cater for all the different cards that may be installed. However, as with the interrupts, some cards are relatively inflexible, limiting the user to choosing from a small range. Figure 8.4 shows the usage of the I/O ports for a PC or XT.

Hex Range	Device	Hex Range	Device
000–0FF	System Use	348–357	Reserved
200–20F	Game control	360–367	PC network
20C–20D	Reserved	368–36F	PC network
210–217	Expansion unit	378–37F	Parallel printer port 1
21F	Reserved	380–38F	Reserved
278–27F	Parallel printer port 2	390–393	Reserved
2B0–2DF	Alternate EGA	3A0–3AF	Reserved
2E1	Reserved	3B0–3BF	Monochrome display
2E2–2E3	Data acquisition	3C0–3CF	EGA
2F8–2FF	Serial port 2	3D0–3DF	CGA
300–31F	Prototype card	3F0–3F7	Disk controller
320–32F	Fixed disk	3F8–3FF	Serial port 1

Figure 8.4   I/O port usage for a PC

I/O ports 000-0FF are reserved for use by the system, whilst ports 100-3FF can be accessed from the expansion slots. Any I/O port addresses NOT listed in Figure 8.4 are available for use by expansion boards. This includes addresses 100-1FF.

There are very few differences in the use of the I/O ports between the PC and the AT. The system still uses ports 000-0FF (although they can be accessed by software), and ports 100-3FF are still accessible from the expansion slots. However, the precise usage of each port differs slightly, as shown in Figure 8.5. As with Figure 8.4, I/O ports not listed in this table can be used for expansion boards, including ports 100-1FF.

Hex Range	Device	Hex Range	Device
000-0FF	System Use	360-363	PC network
1F0-1F8	Fixed disk	364-367	Reserved
20C-20D	Reserved	368-36B	PC network
210-217	Expansion unit	36C-36F	Reserved
21F	Voice communications	378-37F	Parallel printer port 1
278-27F	Parallel printer port 2	3A0-3AF	Reserved
2B0-2DF	Alternate EGA	3B0-3BF	Monochrome display
2E1	Reserved	3C0-3CF	EGA
2E2-2E3	Data acquisition	3D0-3DF	CGA
2F8-2FF	Serial port 2	3F0-3F7	Disk controller
300-31F	Prototype card	3F8-3FF	Serial port 1

Figure 8.5   I/O port usage for an AT

To minimise the problems encountered in allocating I/O ports to option cards, it is advisable to keep an up-to-date record of the locations used by each card. Figure 8.6 is an example of such a record.

Hex Range	Device
160-16F	Mitsubishi scanner controller card in slot 4
1F0-1F8	Fixed disk controller in slot 7
20C-20D	Reserved
210-217	Expansion unit
2E1	Reserved
364-367	Reserved
36C-36F	Reserved
378-37F	Parallel printer port 1 on multifunction card in slot 3
3A0-3AF	Reserved
3B0-3EF	Vega Video7 SVGA card in slot 1
3F0-3F7	Floppy disk controller in slot 8
3F8-3FF	Serial port 1 on multifunction card in slot 3

Figure 8.6   Listing of I/O port usage

8.2.4   DIP SWITCHES

DIP switches are most often used on option cards to specify various aspects of the configuration. They may also be used on the motherboard of the system to indicate what additional devices are installed. Each set of switches must be correctly set in order for the new device to work correctly.

The DIP switches on the card will almost certainly need to be examined, and possibly altered, in order to specify the IRQ and I/O ports that have been allocated. Additionally, there may be switches that determine what features are exhibited by the card, what speed it works at etc. Other switches may be present that allow the speed of the computer to be specified, as well as what other devices are already installed. It is very important to set these switches before the card is physically installed as it is almost impossible to reach them with the card in the slot.

The DIP switches on the motherboard are less likely to need changing. These switches control basic configuration settings, and will only need changing if an extra memory card is installed, or perhaps if the display adapter is changed. These switches are often located in very inaccessible positions, and it may be necessary to remove the option cards to gain access. Thus it is again important that they are set correctly before the card is physically installed.

8.2.5 INSTALL THE CARD

Once the interface settings have been specified, and any other DIP switches have been set if required, the card can be physically installed into the system.

When performing the installation, it is important to handle the card with great care. If possible, an anti-static wristband should be worn to prevent any possibility of damaging the card with static electricity. If an anti-static wristband is not available then it is essential to touch the top of the power supply unit before handling the computer or the option card. This serves to discharge any static that may be on the user's clothes or body. When handling the card, hold it only by the edges, and avoid touching the circuits. The exposed edge connectors should never be touched, as this will speed up the corrosion process.

Before fitting the card into the computer, connect any internal cabling that is required. Once the board is installed, it becomes quite difficult to gain access to any of the connectors on the card. These cables are most likely to be connected to other devices (such as the disk drives), to other cards (such as the video adapter), or possibly to the power supply of the system. At this point the cables should only be connected to the card, the other ends should still be free.

With all necessary cables attached, the board can be inserted into the system unit. It should be located in the guides that run at the front and back of the system box, and then gently pushed down into place. It may be necessary to rock the card from end to end if it is a tight fit, but be very careful not to rock it from side to side, as this can seriously damaged the printed circuits. More force may be required to push the edge connector into the socket as this is often a tight fit.

Once the board is slotted into the socket, it can be fixed in place with the small retaining screw at the upper rear edge. This should not be overtightened as it may be necessary to remove it again at a later date.

When the card is securely fixed, the loose ends of the internal cabling can be connected to the relevant components. The cables should be routed with the following points in mind:

– The cables should not be stretched, as they will be more likely to fail if this happens.

- The cables should not be routed near the top of the system unit, especially if it has a sliding lid. Failure to observe this precaution will almost certainly lead to the cable being snagged, and possibly damaged, when the lid is removed in the future.

- The cables should not be positioned to any device which will get hot, as they may melt. Devices subject to excessive heating will be fitted with a *heatsink*. These small metal components fit over the top of ICs and radiate excess heat away. They are normally black, and will have a number of fins fitted to them to aid cooling.

Once the cables have been connected, the system unit lid can be replaced. If there is any doubt regarding the likelihood of the system working correctly, it may be necessary to leave the system unit open while the computer is tested, although this is not generally recommended.

8.2.6   CONNECT EXTERNAL DEVICES

If the card has any external cabling, then it should be connected. The cable should be secured using the two fixing screws on the connector, as this will minimise the possibility of problems occurring due to poor connections.

In order to test the system it will be necessary to connect the card to an appropriate device. Thus video adapters should be connected to monitors, serial interface cards should be connected to modems or serial printers etc.

Any other devices that were disconnected whilst the card was installed should be reconnected at this point, ready for the system to be thoroughly tested.

8.2.7   SWITCH ON

With the system fully reassembled, it is time to test it. The computer should be switched on, as should any external peripherals such as monitors, printers and modems. The initial system responses, such as the results of the POST and any error messages that may be displayed, should be noted. If necessary, insert a floppy disk to boot the computer into DOS.

If any problems are obvious then the symptoms should be noted and the machine switched off again. It is unlikely that any damage will occur as a result of poor installation, but it is possible. If the system fails before booting into DOS then it will be necessary to recheck the installation of the board. In particular, the following points should be noted:

- Is the board compatible with the system in use?

- Has the board been configured to use appropriate interrupts and I/O ports?

- Has all internal and external cabling been correctly fitted?

- Does the board require an external power supply, for example from a monitor? If so, try switching the monitor on before the computer.

- Is the board fitted correctly, and is the edge connector fully inserted into the socket?

8.2.8   MODIFY CONFIGURATION

If the system boots up correctly then it can be assumed that there are no fundamental problems with the installation. At this point it is necessary to modify the software configuration of the system to make it recognise the new device. This modification can take four forms:

- Changes to the SETUP data (where appropriate)
- Changes to CONFIG.SYS
- Changes to AUTOEXEC.BAT
- Installation of special software.

SETUP will almost certainly need to be modified when memory cards are installed, or if new parallel and serial interfaces are fitted. The SETUP screen should be accessed in the normal way, and the relevant device options selected as necessary. On exiting SETUP, the system will most likely reboot.

CONFIG.SYS will need modification if a non-standard device is installed. These include external floppy disk controller cards, expanded and extended memory cards, extra serial and parallel interfaces etc. The modification will normally consist of adding a line such as DEVICE=XXX.SYS, where XXX.SYS is the name of a file supplied with the card. Full instructions for this command will accompany the card.

AUTOEXEC.BAT may also need modification if a non-standard device is installed. The changes that may be required in AUTOEXEC vary greatly between different devices, although it will normally involve the insertion of one or more commands to run special programs.

Special software may need to be installed for certain devices, such as scanners, sound boards and modems. DOS provides no direct way of controlling such peripherals, and it is therefore up to the manufacturer of the new device to supply appropriate software.

8.2.9 TEST

Once the software has been installed or modified as necessary, the device should be tested as thoroughly as possible. This may take some time, and should involve using all of the features of the new product. It is also important to test the original peripherals and components, as these may fail to work if there is a conflict in the usage of IRQ lines or I/O ports.

If problems are experienced in getting the new device to work, there are a number of areas that should be checked:

- Check for conflicts between IRQ lines and I/O ports
- Check that the software has been correctly installed
- Check that the correct commands are being issued, and the any software is being used in the correct manner
- If a new video board is installed, check that existing software is reconfigured to use the new display standard
- If the problem persists, and cannot be diagnosed using the techniques discussed in Chapter 5 then it will be necessary to call an engineer, or contact the supplier of the device for further assistance.

If everything has been fully tested and found to work correctly, the records of IRQ and I/O port usage should be updated with the new information, as should the asset register entry for the machine in question. These record keeping systems will ensure that any future problems involving this computer can be solved as quickly and efficiently as possible.

8.3 HARDWARE DEVICES

Devices installed in the form of add-on hardware are generally simpler to install than option cards. These devices typically add extra features to the system, including the following:

- Extra hard disk drives
- Extra floppy disk drives
- Mice
- Scanners
- Graphics tablets
- External modems
- Printers.

As with option cards, full documentation should be supplied with the device, including instructions on installation procedures. The following sections provide additional information that should be considered during the installation process.

8.3.1 CHECK COMPATIBILITY

The component or peripheral should of course be compatible with the system, and with any other devices that are already installed. Compatibility is easier to achieve with this form of device as they generally work through controller cards or interfaces that are already present in the system. However, for this reason it is important to check for compatibility between the controller and the actual device, especially in the case of hard and floppy disks.

It is also important to check the specifications of devices that make use of the serial or parallel ports. The IBM PC uses the RS232 standard for serial interfacing, and whilst this is by far the most common, it is not the only standard. Some devices may use the RS423 standard which is slightly different. Similarly, the IBM PC uses a uni-directional parallel interface, with data passing from the computer to the peripheral. However, some devices expect the parallel port to be bi-directional, as found on the PS/2 and certain PC compatibles.

8.3.2 SET DIP SWITCHES

It is unlikely that any DIP switches on the motherboard will have to be altered, as the add-on hardware devices are not interfaced at this level. It is more likely that DIP switches on the adapter card will have to be changed, to specify exactly what type of device is being connected. This applies mainly to specialised adapters such as hard and floppy disk drive controllers, specialist printer adapter cards and dedicated mouse cards.

Hard disk controllers and hard disk units must have the drive specification DIP switches set to corresponding values. These switches are provided so that a single controller can be used for two or more disk drive units. Failure to set the DIP switches appropriately will mean that the controller is unable to communicate with the drive.

The actual peripheral may have DIP switches on it as well. For example, the Apple LaserWriter Postscript printer has a set of DIP switches that specify which interface is being used, as well as the protocol employed for communication. Some hard disks have switches that must be set depending on the exact controller card that is being used, as well as those described above for specifying the drive specification.

Some disk drives also have *terminating resistors*. These are small electronic devices that prevent electronic interference from affecting the transmission of data along the cable between the drive and controller. The terminating resistors should only be fitted to the last drive in a chain, although it is quite common to find disk drives supplied with them already installed. If they are omitted, or if they are erroneously installed in a drive in the middle of the cable, they are unlikely to cause obvious problems, although the operation of the drive may be intermittent under certain circumstances. This most often shows itself as an unusually high number of *device not ready* errors being reported.

8.3.3   INSTALL THE DEVICE

Installation of the device can take many forms. If it is an internal device, such as a hard or floppy disk, then it will be necessary to open the system unit and physically fix the new unit into the disk drive chassis. Anti-static precautions should be taken to minimise the likelihood of damaging the system.

If it is an external device, then installation simply involves siting the unit in an appropriate position. It should be positioned such that any controls are accessible, and any status lights or displays are easily visible. Consideration should also be given to where the cabling between the peripheral and the computer can be positioned.

8.3.4   CONNECT CABLING

The cables between the unit and the adapter should be connected. Internal connections will be in the form of ribbon cable, and this should be routed in the same way as for option cards. Note that most hard disks require two cables; one for data transfer, and one for commands. Floppy disks are usually connected with a single cable that is "daisy-chained" between the drives. In addition to the ribbon cables, disk drive units will also require a power connection.

External cables can take different forms. Parallel connections tend to use ribbon cable, whilst serial connections are most often made with multi-cored flex. As with internal connections, the cables should not be stretched, they should not be bent at sharp angles, and they should be placed in a position in which they are unlikely to be caught or damaged by anyone walking past.

The actual connections within the cable will depend entirely on the peripheral it is connecting. Parallel cables have a straight 1:1 correspondence at either end. Serial cables are available in three types:

- One-to-one RS232 cables, as used for connecting the computer to a modem, or to another PC configured as a modem (eg when using LapLink)

- Null-Modem cables, as used for connecting the computer to a printer, a terminal, or a PC configured as a terminal

- Some devices need custom-made cables that are not available off-the-shelf, and therefore have to be specially constructed to individual requirements

It is important to use the appropriate cable for the type of device or connection that is being made. Failure to do so will mean that the peripheral appears not to work, or only appears to work intermittently.

8.3.5   SWITCH ON

Once the cables have been connected the computer can be switched on, together with any peripherals. It is unlikely that the system will fail to boot correctly as the POST does not check the external devices. One exception to this is if the hard disk unit has been changed, when it will be necessary to boot from a floppy.

If problems do occur then check all cabling, and also the DIP switch settings on the adapter card. If these are incorrect, the system may think it is connected to an incorrect device, and could therefore crash before the POST finishes.

8.3.6   MODIFY CONFIGURATION

Depending on exactly what was installed, it may be necessary to modify the software configuration of the system in some way. This can take four different forms:

- SETUP will need to be modified if the hard disk unit is changed. This is specified through a simple numeric code that determines the geometry of the drive (number of heads, sectors and tracks). The numeric code for a particular drive should be supplied in the documentation that accompanies the unit; if it is not, contact the vendor immediately as it may prove impossible to continue using the system until this information is correct.

- CONFIG.SYS will need to be changed if a non-standard device is connected to the serial or parallel port. Examples of such devices include mice, external disk drives, and data acquisition systems. The change will normally involve the insertion of a command such as DEVICE=XXX.SYS. Detailed instructions should be supplied in the documentation accompanying the product.

- AUTOEXEC.BAT may need to be changed if the serial port is being used, or if any special device-specific software needs to be loaded. For example, the MODE command will almost certainly need to be issued if a modem or serial printer is being used. Similarly, most mice are connected to the serial port, and therefore require their MOUSE.COM program to be executed (some systems have a MOUSE.SYS which must be referenced from CONFIG.SYS).

- Specific software may need to be installed in order to use the device, and it is not uncommon for the manufacturers of the peripheral to include some simple software that allows the new device to be fully tested.

  Similarly, special software will be required to perform the formatting and preparation of any new hard disk units that are installed. This should be supplied with the new disk, as in many cases it is specific to the particular model purchased. The vendor should be contacted if no appropriate software is supplied.

8.3.7   TEST

The system should be fully tested, and all the features of the new device should be tested as thoroughly as possible. This can involve using a variety of software applications and test programs, and can be quite time consuming.

If problems are encountered, the following areas should be examined:

- Is the adapter installed and configured correctly?
- Is all cabling of the correct type and fitted securely?

- Does the new device have power?
- Is the software installed correctly?
- Was the system rebooted after changes to AUTOEXEC.BAT and CONFIG.SYS?
- If existing software is being used with the new device, has it been reinstalled or reconfigured as necessary?

If the problems persist, then it will be necessary to contact the supplier or a qualified engineer for further assistance.

If everything has been fully tested and found to work correctly, the asset register entry for the machine in question should be updated with full details of the new device.

8.4   INTEGRATED CIRCUITS

Integrated circuits can be installed to improve the performance of the computer system, and may be oriented towards enhancing speed or enhancing capacity. A further possibility is that ROM chips can be installed to add extra software features to the system, such as security systems or programming languages. Thus the devices that may be installed are most likely one of the following:

- Maths co-processor
- DRAM chips for extra memory
- SIMMs for extra memory
- SIPPs for extra memory
- Other ROMs to add extra features.

The installation procedure that needs to be followed is very similar, irrespective of the exact nature of the chip being fitted. It is not unusual when purchasing extra chips to be supplied with only the ICs themselves, and no instructions or guidelines of any kind. This occurs most often when purchasing DRAM chips, as it is more usual for vendors to supply at least some documentation with the more expensive co-processors, SIMMs, SIPPs and ROMs.

The following guidelines illustrate some of the more important issues that must be kept in mind when selecting and installing ICs.

8.4.1   CHECK COMPATIBILITY

Because the new devices will be operating directly with the circuitry on the motherboard, it is of the utmost importance that they are 100 percent compatible with the existing components. This is not quite so difficult to achieve as it may at first seem, as there is a great deal of standardisation in terms of the components used in PC systems. In general, the following guidelines apply to compatibility issues:

- DRAM chips are available that work at different speeds; the slowest operate at around 200ns, whilst the fastest may work at 60ns or less. The chips used to provide extra memory should be of the same speed rating or faster than the existing chips. The speed of the original chips can be found from the technical reference manual for the system. If, for some reason, it is not possible to determine the speed rating, Figure 8.7 gives some speed ratings for typical chips used in PC systems:

System type	Clock speed (MHz)	Wait States	Memory Access time (ns)
PC	4.77	1	200
XT	4.77	1	200
AT	6	1	150
AT	8	1	150
AT	8	0	150
80386sx system	16	1	120
80386sx system	16	0	100
80386sx system	20	1	100
80386sx system	20	0	80
80386 system	20	1	100
80386 system	20	0	80
80386 system	25	0	80
80386 system	33	0	70
80486 system	25	0	80

Figure 8.7   Memory speeds for typical systems

In Figure 8.7 the term *wait state* refers to a design aspect of the system. The wait state specification of a system determines how long the microprocessor waits to receive data from RAM. A 2 wait state system will sit idle for two clock cycles after requesting data from memory; a 1 wait state system sits idle for one clock cycle. A 0 wait state system required the memory to supply the requested data immediately. Thus 0 wait state systems are the fastest, but they also demand higher specification, and hence more expensive, memory devices.

As a rule of thumb when choosing chips, always err on the fast side; the chips may cost slightly more, but they will not cause overall system performance to degrade.

– SIMMs and SIPPs are also quantified in terms of speed. Unlike DRAM chips, it is rare to find SIMMs and SIPPs that operate at 150ns or more, as most devices are much faster, typically being rated at 120ns or less. The values in Figure 8.7 apply equally to SIMMs and SIPPs when determining speed of operation.

– Maths co-processors are available in several different types and speeds. Intel produce the 8087, 80287, 80387 and 80487, but other manufacturers, such as Weitek, produce similar devices. However, in order to use one of the non-Intel devices, it is necessary for the motherboard to have a suitable socket, as they are not pin-for-pin compatible with the more popular Intel versions.

One point worthy of a special mention is that the 80287 has a number of inherent disadvantages, resulting in the fact that overall the performance of the 80287 is quite poor. There is no way around this limitation, as it is inherent in the design of the chip.

It is also important to select an appropriate maths co-processor for the CPU in use. Thus an 8086/8088 based system requires an 8087; an 80286 system requires an 80287; an 80386 system can normally use an 80287 or an 80387. The 80487 is only required by those systems based on the 80486sx microprocessor.

A final point to note with maths co-processors is that they must be of the same speed rating as the microprocessor. Thus if a 33MHz 80386 is in use, it will be necessary to buy a 33MHz 80387 co-processor.

−   ROMs will be specified as being suitable for PCs and compatibles. They are not speed rated in any way, and as long as they are quoted as being compatible with PCs (as opposed to Apple Macintoshes etc), then they should work in any system. However it is recommended that ROMs are purchased from well-known sources as some ROM manufacturers have proved to be less than 100 percent IBM compatible despite their claims to the contrary.

8.4.2   REMOVE OLD RAM IF NECESSARY

Depending on the memory configuration of the original system, and the way in which the memory is being upgraded, it may be necessary to remove the old devices prior to installing the new ones. This is especially the case with systems using SIMMs and SIPPs, as it is very rare for such systems to allow a mixture of different capacity devices to be installed. Older systems using DRAMs tend to be slightly more tolerant, and as long as the chips in each bank are of the same capacity then there should be no problems.

One step that must be taken before any memory is removed is to make a written note of the orientation of the memory chips on the motherboard (this applies only to DRAM chips, as SIPPs and SIMMs are polarised and can only be fitted one way round). All chips are marked in some way, to ensure that they are correctly installed. Figure 8.8 shows typical markings that may be found on chips to denote orientation.

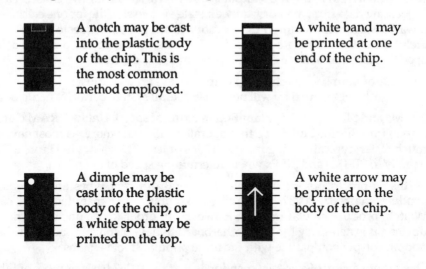

A notch may be cast into the plastic body of the chip. This is the most common method employed.

A white band may be printed at one end of the chip.

A dimple may be cast into the plastic body of the chip, or a white spot may be printed on the top.

A white arrow may be printed on the body of the chip.

Figure 8.8   Orientation markings found on ICs

The four chips illustrated in Figure 8.8 are shown in the same orientation, and so the markings are equivalent in these examples. If chips are supplied with none of the above markings then the supplier should be contacted for further assistance. However, all of the major IC manufacturers use one or more of the above techniques, and so the absence of any markings may indicate lesser quality devices from an unknown source. This may be the case if the chips are obtained at bargain prices.

WARNING

Before handling the memory devices, ensure that anti-static precautions are taken.

Ideally, an anti-static wristband should be worn, and it is highly recommended that one of these inexpensive safety devices be purchased if any chips, SIMMs or SIPPs are to be handled. If this is not available, then it is absolutely essential for the troubleshooter to touch the top of the power supply to earth themselves. This should be done before handling each device.

Care must be taken when removing the devices, and the technique required for chips differ to that required for SIMMs/SIPPs:

– DRAM chips must be removed using a chip extractor. This is a very simple tool that is similar to a pair of tweezers, except that it has a small hook at the end of each prong. The hooks are located under each end of the plastic body of the chip, and it can then be lifted up. Chips are often quite tight fits in their sockets, and it may be necessary to gently rock it from side to side. However great care must be taken to ensure that the pins are not bent excessively.

– SIMMs and SIPPs are preformed modules, based on a printed circuit board, which means that the entire module simply plugs into a socket on the motherboard. As the devices are physically larger and only have a single row of connectors, they are not as difficult as DRAM chips to remove. A firm hold should be taken of the edges of the module, and it can then be pulled straight out from the socket.

Once the device have been removed, they should be put somewhere safe. The reason for this is twofold:

– If one of the new devices being installed into this machine fails, then the original memory can be temporarily reinstalled to get the system back into working order whilst the faulty device is replaced.

– If a different machine needs upgrading, it may be possible to use some of the chips from the current machine rather than purchasing brand new ones.

Unfortunately there is no commercial value for used memory devices, so they cannot be "part-exchanged" for the new ones. The main reason for this is that the original devices are often quite low-spec, and so there is no demand for them at all.

8.4.3   INSTALL CHIPS

Installing the new devices is very simple, although with DRAM chips this can be time consuming and tedious. The first thing to do is to take adequate anti-static precautions, preferably by wearing and anti-static wristband. Some SIMMs and SIPPs, and all maths co-processors, can be easily damaged by static electricity, and with some devices costing in excess of £400, it makes sense to protect the investment.

All devices should be handled carefully, bearing in mind the following points:

– Try to avoid touching the pins of chips and connectors of SIMMs. This is especially important if no anti-static wristband is being worn. If possible, chips should be grasped at either end of the plastic body, whilst SIMMs and SIPPs should be held by the edges of the circuit board. Some maths co-processors are supplied with a special cardboard holder that should first be constructed. The IC is then slid into the holder to simplify fitting, thus preventing the user from accidentally touching any of the sensitive parts of the chip.

- If any pins or connectors on DRAMs or ROMs become bent, they should be straightened by pressing the device against a flat metal surface. Try to avoid straightening the pins by hand. If the pins on a co-processor are bent then consult the vendor for assistance, as these devices are very fragile.

- Don't rush the process, and only handle one chip at a time. Failure to observe this precaution will almost certainly lead to pins or connectors being bent or damaged.

Each chip, SIMM or SIPP should be inserted into its socket bearing in mind the correct orientation. If devices were installed previously then their orientation will have been noted when they were removed. If no devices were present, the orientation can be noted from the circuit board or the socket, as shown in Figure 8.9.

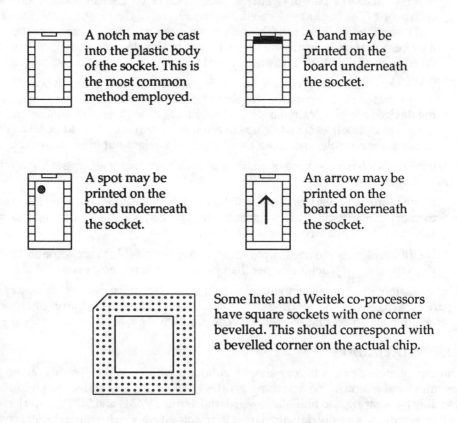

A notch may be cast into the plastic body of the socket. This is the most common method employed.

A band may be printed on the board underneath the socket.

A spot may be printed on the board underneath the socket.

An arrow may be printed on the board underneath the socket.

Some Intel and Weitek co-processors have square sockets with one corner bevelled. This should correspond with a bevelled corner on the actual chip.

Figure 8.9   Orientation markings on the motherboard

The marking shown on the board should correspond to the orientation marking on the chip. These markings may be different, but as discussed in section 8.4.2 they are directly equivalent with each other.

If the correct orientation of memory devices is still unclear, they should be inserted so that they are facing the same way as all other DRAMs, SIMMs or SIPPs in adjacent banks.

> ## WARNING
>
> *If ICs are inserted into their sockets the wrong way round then they are likely to be damaged if the machine is switched on. It is also possible that they may damage other circuitry on the motherboard.*

If the legs of a chip are bent during insertion, it should be removed and the legs straightened as described above. If this goes unnoticed, the system will not complete its POST and will generate error messages, but the chip will NOT be electronically damaged.

Once the devices are located in their sockets they should be firmly pressed into place, to ensure that a good contact is made between the pins and the socket connectors. This action will also minimise the possibility of the chips working loose.

8.4.4 SET SWITCHES ON MOTHERBOARD

A large number of systems still use DIP switches or jumpers on the motherboard to specify the amount of memory that has been installed in the system, and whether or not a co-processor is installed. If this is the case with the system being upgraded, then it is essential that the switches are set to appropriate values. These settings can be found from the technical reference manual for the system.

If the switches are not correctly set, then the system may do one of two things:

– It may simply not recognise some of the memory that has been installed. Note however that most versions of DOS will only recognise the first 640K of memory, and it will be necessary to use a diagnostic or utility program (such as Norton's SYSINFO) to display the true amount of memory installed. In the case of the co-processor, it will not be recognised at all.

– The system may hang before the POST is completed, generating one or more error messages. In this case it will not boot into DOS, and it will not be possible to run any software at all.

8.4.5 SWITCH ON

At this point the system can be reassembled and tested. On switching the computer on, the initial results of the POST should be noted, especially any error messages that may be generated. Chapter 5 illustrated how these error messages can be decoded to give precise information on which chip has failed.

Assuming that the system boots up correctly it will be possible to perform further tests:

– If the memory upgrade was in the sub-640K area then these tests can be directly performed, as DOS will recognise the extra memory immediately. The easiest way to do this is to run CHKDSK, which in addition to describing disk usage provides a report of the amount of memory installed.

– If new ROMs were added then they should be immediately accessible, according to the instructions supplied with them.

– If a maths co-processor was installed then there will appear to be no change at all. However, SYSINFO should report that there is now a co-processor present, and any software that can work with such a device should also recognise it. However, some applications may need to be specifically installed to work with the chip.

- If the memory was installed above the 1MB boundary, it will be necessary to change certain aspects of the software configuration before it can be accessed. Until these changes are made, DOS will not be able to access the extra memory.

8.4.6   MODIFY CONFIGURATION

Memory installed above 1MB can usually be configured as expanded or extended memory. This is achieved in several different ways:

- The SETUP routine supplied on most 80386 and 80486 systems allows the memory to be configured as required. In some cases this is all that is required, and appropriate software can then use the extra storage space. However, it is more common, especially where expanded memory is required, for changes to be made to the CONFIG.SYS and AUTOEXEC.BAT files as well.

  SETUP may also be used to indicate the presence of a maths co-processor.

- CONFIG.SYS may need to be modified to include an appropriate device driver for the new memory. This may be an expanded memory driver, such as EMM.SYS or EMM386.SYS etc, or it may be a driver designed to work with extended memory, such as HIMEM.SYS. Full instructions on the use of these drivers should be supplied with the device.

- AUTOEXEC.BAT may need to be modified to include software drivers that are supplied in the form of executable files. It may also be necessary to install TSR software from AUTOEXEC.BAT that makes use of the new extended/expanded memory, such as RAM disks and disk caching software.

8.4.7   INSTALL SOFTWARE

Some software needs to be specifically installed to use extended or expanded memory, whilst other applications automatically recognise the presence of such memory. Thus it is important to consult the documentation to determine what needs to be changed. Similarly, some software needs to be explicitly told that a maths co-processor is present, while other applications recognise its presence automatically.

For example, Lotus 1-2-3 is able to use as much extended or expanded memory as it can find (depending on the version of the product in use). It does this automatically, with no specific user intervention. However, Ventura Publisher needs to be explicitly told to use expanded memory, as it is incapable of detecting it automatically.

8.4.8   TEST

Once the software has been configured as necessary the system should be tested as thoroughly as possible:

- With memory upgrades this is relatively simple, as it should now be possible to process more data with appropriately configured applications than before. Note that there are some restrictions, especially with expanded memory, that may result in strange situations occurring. For example, certain versions of Lotus 1-2-3 purport to allow the user access to 16MB of expanded memory. However, it has been found that *out of memory* errors occur even when the system information reports that there is more memory free. Chapter 4 supplies further details on expanded and extended memory.

- Co-processors can be tested through repeated computations; for example, most users have an approximate idea of how long their applications take to complete a certain task, such as processing 600K of statistical data, or redrawing the screen. This subjective evaluation can then be measured against the increased performance of the system with the maths co-processor installed, and in cases such as these the difference should be obvious. However, other tasks may not benefit as much and so a quantitative approach may be required:

  The easiest way to measure the performance is to perform a number of tests with the co-processor disabled and time them individually. The co-processor is than re-enabled and the tests repeated. The differences in the speed of execution will provide a measure of the performance improvement.

- ROMs can be tested by attempting to use each of the facilities that the product provides. In the case of a security system, the ROM should intervene as soon as the system is switched on, prompting the user for a password etc. In the case of an application, the software should be immediately accessible from DOS, as should a programming language etc.

8.4.9 INSTALLATION PROBLEMS

If problems are encountered when installing ICs then the following areas should be examined:

- Is the software capable of working with the new devices? For example, there will be no performance gain at all when installing a maths co-processor into a system running word processing software.

- Has the software been configured correctly to work with the new devices? This means checking CONFIG.SYS, AUTOEXEC.BAT and SETUP, as well as the installation of various applications.

- Are the DIP switches and jumpers on the motherboard set correctly?

- Examine each of the chips that were installed to see if any legs or pins are bent. Also check the orientation of the chips; it is surprisingly easy to fit a RAM chip the wrong way round!

- Press down firmly on all of the new devices to ensure that they are well seated in their sockets.

- Try removing the new devices. If the system works with them removed, then it is possible that there is a compatibility problem, or one or more of them may be faulty.

If the problem cannot be diagnosed, advice should be sought from an engineer or the vendor supplying the devices.

8.5 SUMMARY

There is a wide range of optional extras available for personal computers, from extra memory and disk drives, to faster processors, communications cards and graphics cards. Every additional device purchased should be supplied with comprehensive installation instructions which will explain exactly what to do.

Memory chips and boards tend to be the easiest to install and require minimal changes to the configuration of the system (ie CONFIG.SYS and AUTOEXEC.BAT). Additional devices and option cards generally require more time to be spent in ensuring that the system is working correctly once they have been installed, but are still straightforward.

It is particularly important to observe the safety procedures detailed earlier when adding devices and chips. Remember to earth yourself before handling any devices, and to hold chips and boards only by the edges, away from the conducting surfaces. Most important of all is to ensure that the system is disconnected from the mains supply before removing the cover. Failure to do this may result in electric shocks.

Finally, once a new device is installed and tested, update the system documentation to reflect the new equipment. This will help future troubleshooting activities as an accurate configuration list may indicate a more likely source of a problem.

9 Using DOS For System Control

9.1 WHY IS SOFTWARE A TROUBLESHOOTING ISSUE?

There are several reasons why software is of critical importance to troubleshooters:

- Most software products have to be installed in order to function with a particular configuration. If the software is not properly installed the system will fail and it need not necessarily be obvious that it is a software, as opposed to a hardware, fault that has been encountered. An example of this are the device drivers which have to be present when a Hercules graphics card is to be used. Without the device drivers the card will simply not function.

- Software may have been installed in such a way that another application will not function. This can occur in two different ways:

  - Software products can conflict with each other. This is especially true of memory resident programs such as Sidekick and Superkey.

  - Some software products require multiple files to be open as well as a large number of buffers to be set. This uses a substantial amount of memory and can prevent subsequent software from functioning.

To be able to cope with these types of problems, it is essential that the troubleshooter has a good working knowledge of software and especially of the operating system in use.

This chapter has not been written as a thorough introduction to DOS, but rather as an aid to PC users when installing, configuring and performing housekeeping routines. It is assumed that readers will have a basic understanding as to what an operating system is, and the type of tasks that are performed. The chapter will go through a series of routines starting with a new computer and explaining how to partition and format the hard disk and install the software through to writing batch files for menu control.

9.2 PREPARING THE HARD DISK

Before a hard disk can be of any use, there are three necessary preparation procedures that must be followed. These are:

- Physical formatting of the disk
- Partitioning of the disk
- Relative or Logical formatting.

9.2.1 PHYSICAL OR ABSOLUTE FORMATTING

This is sometimes referred to as low level formatting and is usually performed before the disk drive is shipped. The low level format divides the tracks on the disk into individual sectors which eventually hold data. During the format process each sector is tested by writing a specific pattern of data in a repeating sequence which continues until the entire disk has been recorded with data. The pattern usually commences with the outside track and progresses towards the innermost tracks. As each pattern is written it is read back by the system to assure that the portion of the disk has correctly stored the data. If the data is incorrect the area is marked as bad and will be skipped when the next step is performed. This means that when the system is being used, data will not be lost by attempting to write it to damaged areas of the disk.

Because physical formatting programs vary widely from disk drive to disk drive, this chapter does not cover the process. If a low level format has not been performed, then instructions should accompany the disk. The only time an end-user should need to contemplate a low level format is if some severe read/write problems have developed with the hard disk.

9.2.2 PARTITIONING OF THE DISK

MS and PC-DOS up to an including version 3.3 will generally only accept a hard disk of up to 32MB. However, through the use of the DOS program FDISK it is possible to divide a physical disk of almost any size into a number of separate logical drives, none of which exceed 32MB. It should be noted that some manufacturers of IBM compatible machines have provided versions of DOS that overcome the 32MB barrier and allow the hard disk to be logically formatted as one unit. MS-DOS itself allows for this in version 4.0 and above. Even if there is no restriction, it can be good housekeeping to divide large disk drives by choice and the facility to so do will usually be available.

To use the FDISK program it is necessary to boot up the computer with the DOS disk in drive A. With the A> prompt on the screen type

FDISK (E)

Figure 9.1 is an example of an FDISK menu running under DOS version 4.01.

```
FDISK Options

Current Fixed Disk Drive: 1

Choose one of the following
     1. Create DOS Partition
     2. Change Active Partition
     3. Delete DOS Partition
     4. Display Partition Information



Enter Choice: [1]
```

Figure 9.1   The FDISK menu screen

To create a DOS partition, Option 1 should be selected. This brings up a second level menu with the options shown in Figure 9.2.

```
Create DOS Partition

Current Fixed Disk Drive: 1


    1. Create Primary DOS partition
    2. Create Extended DOS partition
    3. Create logical drive(s) in the EXTENDED
       DOS partition



Enter choice: [1]
```

Figure 9.2   The Create DOS Partition menu options

The first menu choice allows a standard DOS partition to be created, and this is the option that most users require. The second and third options are provided for disk that are to be partitioned into two or more logical drives; to use this technique, the first logical drive is defined through the *Create Primary DOS Partition* option, and then the remainder of the disk is allocated as an extended partition using the second option. Finally, this extended partition is further subdivided into as many logical drives as necessary with the third menu option.

On a previously unused disk, the *Create Primary DOS Partition* option should be chosen, and will produce a display as shown in Figure 9.3.

```
Create DOS Partition

Current Fixed Disk Drive: 1

Partition Status    Type    Start    End    Size

No partitions are installed



Total disk space is  732 cylinders.
Maximum space available for partition is  732 cylinders


Enter partition size ...........[ 732]


Press ESC to return to FDISK options
```

Figure 9.3   Creating a partition on an empty disk

The system prompts the user to specify the size of the primary DOS partition. As this display was taken from a DOS 4.01 version of FDISK, the system is suggesting that the entire disk be used as it is capable of working with drives in excess of 32MB. Other versions of DOS differ slightly in this respect.

If the entire drive is to be used as the partition then the Enter key can be pressed to accept the default size. If however the drive is to be divided into a number of smaller partitions, the appropriate size for the primary partition should be specified at this point. Note that the size is specified in terms of disk cylinders, not MB.

Once the partition size has been defined, the user is prompted to specify whether or not the partition should be active. There should only be 1 active partition on a disk, and this is the partition from which the system will boot. This simply means that the system will boot. By responding Y to the prompt, the system will ensure that the primary partition is made active, although it will still be necessary to install the system files (see below). Once the partition has been created (which only takes a short time) the system will reboot from the floppy disk.

If a primary DOS partition already exists on the drive and the *Create Primary DOS Partition* option is chosen, the screen will appear as shown in Figure 9.4

```
Create DOS Partition
Current Fixed Disk Drive: 1
Partition Status    Type    Start    End    Size
  C: 1           A    PRI DOS      0    732    732




Total disk space is  732 cylinders.


Primary DOS Partition already exists


Press ESC to return to FDISK options
```

Figure 9.4   Message screen for an existing partition

In either case it will now be possible to proceed to formatting the disk.

9.2.3 LOGICAL FORMATTING

After partitioning the hard disk the final preparation step is to logically format it. This procedure is sometimes referred to as a *high-level format*. The process establishes the cylinders and sectors that divide the disk surface into manageable sections on which data and programs will be stored. Using the high level formatting command it is necessary to boot up the system with the DOS system disk in drive A. After entering the date and time, the A> prompt will appear on the screen. The format command may now be executed by entering the following instruction:

FORMAT C:/S/V

Two optional parameters have been included in the command. The first, /S, will copy the DOS system files onto the hard disk, and the second, /V, allows a volume label to be placed on the formatted disk. The volume label is displayed when DIR is entered. Note that if the disk has been partitioned it will be necessary to format both logical drives C: and D:. However the /S parameter will only usually be required on one drive which will be the bootable drive.

Having pressed Enter there will be a short delay before the following message is displayed on the screen:

WARNING, ALL DATA ON NON-REMOVABLE DISK DRIVE C: WILL BE LOST

Proceed with format [Y/N] ?

On typing Y (E) the formatting process begins and the word Formatting is displayed.

The format process does several things. It magnetically divides the disk into sections, and sets up some housekeeping areas. The DOS system files that are transferred make the disk a bootable disk.

When formatting is complete the following message will be displayed:

Format Complete
System Transferred

A prompt for the volume label then follows:

Volume Label (11 Characters, ENTER for none)?

The volume label will normally be the name of the user or company, or some other reference that is relevant to the particular machine. The entering of a volume label on the hard disk reduces the risk of accidentally reformatting that disk, as when the format commands is issued the system asks for the volume name to be entered before allowing the format to proceed.

To complete the procedure a summary of statistics about the hard disk are supplied. For example for a 20MB logical disk the following would be typical:

```
21213184 bytes total disk space
   70656 bytes used by system
21142528 bytes available on disk
```

The precise number of bytes shown will vary depending on the size the hard disk and the version of DOS. With a 20MB disk and DOS version 4.01, 70656 bytes are used by the DOS system files that FORMAT copied to the hard disk. The system may now be reset after removing the DOS disk from drive A and will boot up from the hard disk C:

9.3   MAKING AND CHANGING DIRECTORIES

With each logical disk drive on a system likely to have at least 32 million characters of space, and in many instances considerably more, it is very important to structure the way this space is utilised. Within the DOS environment this is achieved through the use of directories.

With a newly formatted disk there is only one directory referred to as the *root* directory and it is from here that all future directories will branch. Figure 9.5 shows a typical disk structure.

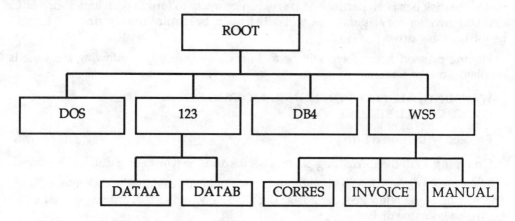

Figure 9.5   A typical directory structure

Notice that from the root directory there are three directories in which software packages are contained - in this example DOS, 123, dBASE and WordPerfect. Within these directories there are additional sub-directories for various uses – these might alternatively be various applications used with the software. It is important to limit files in the root directory to only the essential ones. These include the two DOS system files, COM-MAND.COM, CONFIG.SYS, AUTOEXEC.BAT and any driver files that are required to be in root. All applications and utilities, including DOS, should be stored in separate subdirectories.

To create a new directory the command MD is used. For example, to create a directory for DOS, the following is required:

MD DOS (E)

When the directory has been created, the DOS prompt C> will return to the screen. Keying DIR at this point will list the files in the root directory, plus a reference to the newly created DOS directory.

To access the contents of the new directory it is necessary to issue the Change Directory command, CD:

CD DOS (E)

There is nothing on the screen to indicate the current directory, but by keying DIR a list of the contents of the DOS directory is displayed:

```
        Volume in drive C is TECHTRANS
        Directory of  C:\DOS

    .           <DIR>        8-03-89    5:07p
    ..          <DIR>        8-03-89    5:07p
        2 File(s)    20106254 bytes free
```

Obviously at this stage there are no files in the directory, but notice the presence of two directories called . and .. These are pointers used by DOS to refer to the current and parent directories respectively.

With the C> prompt on the screen the PROMPT command may be executed that will cause the name of the current directory to be displayed every time the prompt appears:

PROMPT PG

On pressing enter, the following is displayed as the DOS prompt:

C:\DOS>

The DOS files can then be copied into this directory using the COPY command. Ensure that the DOS system disk is in drive A and then enter the following:

COPY A:*.* (E)

To return to the root directory from the current DOS directory, either of the following may be entered:

CD \ (E)
CD .. (E)

The first option, CD \, will always make the root directory active from any other directory, whereas CD .. will take control back one level, which in this case will be to the root directory.

To create another directory off the root for 123, it is advisable to first return to root before issuing the MD command. With control at root, a directory called 123 and three data directories could be created as follows:

MD 123 (E)
MD \123\DATAA (E)
MD \123\DATAB (E)
MD \123\DATAC (E)

Control has remained with the root directory throughout the series of commands. Notice the use of the backslash key (\) to indicate a *path* for each directory. The source of all paths in the directory is always the root directory.

To look at the contents of the directory, the following could be entered,

CD \123\DATAC

or

CD 123   followed by
CD DATAC

It is not possible at this stage to directly change the directory to DATAB using CD DATAB because this is not a sub-directory of DATAC, but of 123. In other words there is no path between DATAB and DATAC.

The following is required instead:

CD \123\DATAB (E)

This instructs the system to first return to the root directory and then follow the path down to the 123 directory and from there down to DATAB. Control is now with DATAB, and to give control to the DOS directory, the following must be entered:

CD \DOS

To check which directory is currently in use type

CD (E)

and the current directory name is displayed.

9.3.1 PATH

The creation of sub-directories can cause the duplication of many of the frequently used external commands and utilities. Lotus 1-2-3 may have been placed in its own directory and yet it may be necessary to use the FORMAT command to prepare new data disks. The FORMAT command is currently located in the DOS directory which would have to be active or directly accessed before the command could be used. To overcome the need to duplicate commands and utilities, the PATH command may be used.

The PATH command defines a list of sub-directories through which the computer will search to find a particular executable file.

PATH C:

is used to inform the computer to look in the root directory of disk drive C if the required program is not in the current sub-directory.

If the system is to search through several directories, then each is specified on the PATH command, separated by a semi-colon (;). For example:

PATH C:\;C:\123

informs the computer that it should look in the root directory of drive C to find a program. It the program is not present in the root directory, then it will automatically search through the sub-directory called 123 on drive C.

The path command may only be used to search for directories and executable program files, ie those that have extensions of .COM, .EXE or .BAT.

9.4 CONFIGURING THE SYSTEM WITHIN DOS

Different software packages have different configuration requirements to ensure that they communicate correctly with the various components of the computer system. In some instances this may involve changing hardware settings such as DIP switches or jumpers, but more often software configuration is required by inserting commands into a special file called CONFIG.SYS. When the computer is booted, DOS searches the root directory for CONFIG.SYS and if it is present sets various system parameters according to the specification in this file. If a CONFIG.SYS file is not present, then DOS uses a series of default values instead. If the CONFIG.SYS file is changed during a working session the revised settings will not be apparent until the computer is rebooted.

On the more advanced systems, such as 80386, 80486 and some 80286 based machines, there will be a special program designed to specify the hardware configuration of the machine. This is often called SETUP.COM, although it may have another name (eg TEST3.COM for Toshiba laptops). In certain systems (eg Tandon 80386 machines) the program has been placed in ROM and is initiated by simultaneously pressing a certain combination of keys, such as [Ctrl]+[Alt]+[Esc] whilst the computer is booting up.

The setup program displays the configuration of the system on the screen, and allows the user to change certain items if required. Different systems allow different things to be specified. However, there are normally at least six items:

- Date and time
- Language
- Keyboard configuration
- Country
- Display type and mode
- Diskette types.

Some systems allow other factors to be altered, including processor speed, type of hard disk installed and the configuration of the memory. To determine exactly how the setup program can be executed for any particular machine, and what factors can be changed, it is necessary to consult the system manual.

Note: Even though the country, keyboard and language are specified in the setup program, it may still be necessary to include the appropriate drivers in the CONFIG.SYS and AUTOEXEC.BAT files (see below). This is because setup only configures the hardware, any applications software may require the use of the software drivers. Only trial and error will determine which applications programs use the hardware configuration information, and which use the software drivers.

9.5   CONFIG.SYS

CONFIG.SYS may be used for a number of procedures, including:

- Set the Ctrl-Break
- Specify the number of buffers in use
- Specify the country date and time format
- Install device drivers
- Specify the number of files that can be opened by file control blocks
- Specify the number of files which can be opened at one time
- Specify the maximum disk drive letter which can be addressed
- Specify the name of a top-level command processor.

CONFIG.SYS is created using a text editor. This could be the DOS files EDLIN or COPY CON or may be a word processor such as WordStar. The following explains the options available in CONFIG.SYS in more detail.

9.5.1   BREAK

This command allows the user to activate or deactivate the Break Key. The Break may be set On or OFF.

The format of the command is:

BREAK = [ON or OFF]

The default for this command is OFF. This means that DOS only checks for Ctrl-Break being entered during:

- Standard output operations
- Standard input operations
- Standard print operations
- Standard auxiliary operations.

By setting BREAK=ON DOS will check Ctrl-Break whenever requested.

9.5.2   BUFFERS

A disk buffer is a block of memory which has been set aside for the reading from and the writing to memory of data.

The format of the command is

BUFFERS = X

where X is a number between 1 and 10000. The number of available buffers is a function of the hardware and DOS version in use. With DOS versions up to and including 3.3, between two and 255 buffers are allowed. With DOS 4 the maximum is 10000. Furthermore, in DOS 4, buffers can be held in expanded memory which allows for more efficient use of main memory. Each buffer is normally 528 bytes, but with DOS 4 it is possible to have larger buffers when working with a disk partition larger than 32MB.

The buffer facility works as follows:

- If a program requires data in 128 byte records, DOS will read an entire sector into a buffer and then move the required data from there into the application area of the machine's memory. The buffer is then marked as having been used.

Applications which use random accessing techniques may benefit substantially in speed by using a large number of buffers. Database applications are good examples of this. Sequential applications will benefit little and a smaller number will be adequate.

For database applications it is necessary to experiment to find the optimal number of buffers, and most software packages will recommend a setting for optimising performance with that system. The problem is that different systems may have different requirements and thus optimising the setting for one application can reduce performance in another.

The optimum number of buffers may be determined by balancing the following:

- The types of applications most frequently used
- The memory available in the computer
- The results of experimentation with different numbers of buffers.

9.5.3   COUNTRY

This command is used to set the date and time format, currency symbol, decimal separator, accented characters and capitalisation conventions for a specific country.

The format of the command is,

COUNTRY = XXX

where XXX is the three digit international country code for long distance telephone calls.Therefore the command required to set the date and time format for the UK would be,

COUNTRY = 044

The COUNTRY commands gets its information from the file COUNTRY.SYS, and this file should be stored in the root directory.

9.5.4   DEVICE

This command allows the name of a device drive file to be specified.

The format of the command is

DEVICE = [d:][path]<filename>.<extension>

DOS also automatically loads a series of device drivers for standard input, standard output, the diskettes and hard disk, as well as a clock driver. It is not necessary to specify device commands to support any of these.

The following device driver files are included with DOS:

- ANSI.SYS (all versions) gives access to extended screen and keyboard functions.
- DISPLAY.SYS (version 3.3 and later) configures a monitor for displaying alternative national character sets on EGA and VGA screens.
- DRIVER.SYS (version 3.2 and later) allows additional logical drives to be created, and allows the system to address external disk drives.
- PRINTER.SYS (version 3.3 and later) is used with the IBM ProPrinter II Model 4401, or IBM QuietWriter III Model 5202 printers to configure the system to print characters in one or more alternative language character sets supplied with DOS.
- VDISK.SYS (version 2.1 and later) creates a RAM disk which means an area of memory may be treated as a disk. On 286 and 386 systems this can be placed in extended memory.
- XMAEM.SYS (version 4 and above) is used with PS/2 computers to allow the 80386 processor to take advantage of extended memory.
- XMA2EMS.SYS (version 4 and above) manages expanded memory when used in conjunction with the IBM 2MB expanded memory adapter, the PS/2 80286 memory expansion option or the 80286 expanded memory adapter.

The VDISK.SYS driver is especially useful. It is a device driver which simulates a very fast disk drive by using a portion of the computer's random access memory (RAM) as an intermediate storage area. This simulated disk storage is usually referred to as a Virtual Disk. Virtual Disks have the following characteristics:

- Reading and writing to virtual disks is very fast as they function at the speed of RAM.

- More than one virtual disk may be installed at a time. Thus the first virtual disk could be addressed as D and the second virtual disk as E.
- With each virtual disk the amount of memory used, the sector size and the number of permissible entries in the directory are specified.
- A volume label may be created for each virtual disk in use.
- The VDISK.SYS device driver requires 800 bytes. In addition the size of the virtual disk itself must be taken into account.
- The contents of the virtual disk will be lost when the power is switched off.
- It is not possible to format a virtual disk. Each VDISK is installed in a formatted form.

In order to install a VDISK driver the following command should be included in the CONFIG.SYS file.

device=[d:][path]VDISK.SYS [bbb] [sss] [ddd] [/E]

where bbb is the virtual disk size in KB, sss is the sector size in bytes, ddd is the number of directory entries and /E informs VDISK to use extended memory. Extended memory is memory at or above 1MB.

A typical VDISK installation command is,

DEVICE=C:\DOS.DIR\VDISK.SYS 128 512 16

9.5.5 FCBS

This command allows the number of file control blocks which can be concurrently open by DOS to be specified. The format of the command is,

FCBS=m,n

where m specifies the total number of files opened by FCBs that can be open at one time. The default value is 4. The range of values for m is 1 to 255. n represents the number of files opened by FCBs that cannot be closed automatically by DOS.

This command is not required by many software packages today and is a hangover from the way files were structured with the early versions of DOS. Therefore it will only rarely be encountered in CONFIG.SYS files.

9.5.6 FILES

The FILES command allows the maximum number of files that can be open concurrently to be specified. The format of the command is,

FILES = X

where x is a number between 8 and 255. The default value is,

FILES = 8

If FILES= is specified in the configuration file, the size of the resident portion of DOS increases by 48 bytes for each additional file above the default value of 8. As a result of this the memory available to the application in use is reduced by the same amount. Most software packages recommend the optimal number of FILES that should be specified. Values of 20 or 30 are quite common.

Note that the number specified in a FILES= command represents the maximum number of files which can be opened for the entire system. This includes file handles in use by currently running foreground tasks (programs like COMP and CHKDSK), and background tasks like PRINT and a network.

9.5.7   LASTDRIVE

This command sets the maximum number of drives that may be accessed. The format of the command is,

LASTDRIVE=X

where X can be any alphabetic character A through Z. It represents the last valid drive letter that DOS may accept. The default value for a standalone system is E because DOS allows access to drives A through E. When using a network the default is N, allowing access to drives A through N.

9.5.8   SHELL

The SHELL command allows the name and location of a top-level command processor to be specified. In versions of DOS up to 3.1 this would replace COMMAND.COM at DOS initialisation. The format of the command is,

SHELL=[d:][path]filename[.ext][param1][param2]

In later versions of DOS, the SHELL command can be used to select certain options for COMMAND.COM. This is especially important on networked systems, and when working with environments such as Windows.

9.5.9   A CONFIG.SYS FILE

A typical example of a CONFIG.SYS file may be seen in Figure 9.6.

```
BUFFERS=15
FILES=20
LASTDRIVE=G
DEVICE=GMOUSE.sys
DEVICE=BRIDGE.DEV 1
DEVICE=C:\DOS\VDISK.SYS
DEVICE =C:\DOS\ANSI.SYS
COUNTRY=044
BREAK=ON
```

Figure 9.6   A typical CONFIG.SYS file

– **BUFFERS=15**

This command sets 15 units of RAM (each of which is 528 bytes) to act as an intermediate storage area between the main memory and the disk storage. This will enhance the performance of the system.

- **FILES=20**

  This command allows up to 20 files to be open at any given time. It is necessary to set this command when using multiple file systems such as dBASE III/IV or WordStar.

- **LASTDRIVE=G**

  This command allows 7 disk drives to be active on the system at any one time. Drives will be labelled A through G.

- **DEVICE=GMOUSE.SYS**

  This command informs the system that a device driver called GMOUSE is to be executed. This allows the system to recognise the presence of a mouse.

- **DEVICE=BRIDGE.DEV 1**

  This device command informs the system that a device driver called BRIDGE is to be executed. This is a communications driver which establishes a link between two separate computers.

- **DEVICE=C:\DOS\VDISK.SYS**

  This device command informs the system that a device driver called VDISK in the DOS directory of drive C is to be executed. VDISK, which is an abbreviation for virtual disk, allocates part of the RAM (64K by default) as a temporary storage area which functions exactly like a disk drive, except at a much higher saving and retrieval speed. The VDISK is composed of sectors of 128 bytes and allows 64 directory entries to be stored. However, items filed to VDISK must eventually be transferred to the hard disk at the end of a working session or they will be lost when the system is switched off.

- **DEVICE=C:\DOS\ANSI.SYS**

  This device command executes the device driver ANSI.SYS in the DOS directory of drive C. ANSI.SYS, which is supplied by DOS provides greater control over the presentation of information on the screen when creating batch files.

- **COUNTRY=044**

  This command establishes the keyboard layout and the date and time format for a particular country. The number corresponds to the international dialling code for the country.

- **BREAK=ON**

  This command sets the break key on.

9.6 THE AUTOEXEC.BAT FILE

The final step in making a new computer installation ready for use is the creation of another special file called AUTOEXEC.BAT. As the name suggests, the instructions in this file are automatically executed when the computer system is booted. The execution of this file usually follows the CONFIG.SYS file. The extension .BAT refers to batch, and there will normally be a number of batch files which help to control the system as will be seen in the next section.

A batch file is a file of readable text containing a series of DOS commands. Figure 9.7 is typical of the type of commands that may be contained in the AUTOEXEC.BAT file.

```
CLS
DATE
TIME
PROMPT $P$G
PATH C:\DOS;123_2;C:\WS4;C:\DB3;C:\SYM
MODE COM1:9600,N,8,2,P
MODE LPT1:=COM1
PAUSE
CLS
ECHO OFF
CD BATCH
TYPE MENU
```

Figure 9.7   An example of an AUTOEXEC.BAT file

The following explains the purpose of each line.

–   **CLS**

This command clears the screen.

–   **DATE and TIME**

These two commands cause the computer to pause in order that the user may enter the current date and time. If there is a real-time clock built into the system then these commands are not required.

–   **PROMPT PG**

By default the computer will only prompt the current disk drive letter that is active. Especially in the case of hard disk systems it is useful to have more information on the prompt line such as the directory path. The above prompt command displays the drive letter and the directory path. For example C:\DOS>

–   **PATH C:\DOS;123R3;C:\WS6;C:\123R2;C:\DB4**

This command sets the path that the computer is to search for files.

–   **MODE COM1:9600,N,8,2,P**

This mode command sets the communications protocol necessary for the installed serial printer.

–   **MODE LPT1:=COM1**

If a serial printer is the primary printing device the lpt1 mode command must be directed to the first communications port which is referenced as COM1.

–   **PAUSE**

This command causes the system to wait in order that the user may read the information currently displayed on the screen. Pressing a key will continue execution of the batch file commands.

- **CLS**

    The screen is once again cleared of information

- **ECHO OFF**

    This command prevents the execution of the batch file being viewed on the screen as each instruction is processed.

- **CD BATCH**

    The directory is changed to the BATCH directory

- **CLS**

    The screen is once again cleared

- **TYPE MENU**

    A text file called MENU is displayed on the screen.

This completes the execution of the AUTOEXEC.BAT file and will leave the user looking at a menu of options on the screen. Each menu option will have its own batch file which will be executed when a selection is made.

9.7 MODIFYING THE SOFTWARE CONFIGURATION

Whilst hardware and software manuals will provide guidelines for configuring the system, in many cases the only way to determine exactly what is required in CONFIG.SYS and AUTOEXEC.BAT is to try different combinations of commands. This process can be time consuming, but invariably produces the best results.

IMPORTANT

> *Before making ANY changes, rename the existing CONFIG.SYS file C.C and the existing AUTOEXEC.BAT file A.A. If problems are encountered, the originals can be reinstated.*

9.8 BATCH PROCESSING

Although DOS is most frequently used in *interactive mode,* which means that a command is entered and executed immediately, the real power lies in the fact that it may also be used in *batch mode.* This is a method of entering DOS commands so that they are not executed immediately but rather stored on disk to be subsequently executed when required. This technique is referred to as *batch processing,* the main characteristic of which is that a series of commands contained in a file may be executed again and again on demand.

9.8.1 CREATING A BATCH FILE WITH COPY CON

An example of a simple batch file is one which will change directory and execute a program. The DOS BATCH file to do this could contain the following commands:

```
CD \123
LOTUS
```

Batch files are text files and may be created by using either the COPY CON: command, the DOS editor known as EDLIN, or any word processor.

The COPY CON: command works by copying from the screen or console (CON:) into a file on the disk. It is a very useful technique for quickly creating short batch files, but as COPY CON: cannot be used to edit files it is not much use in dealing with longer files.

All batch files are identified with a filename and must have an extension of .BAT. Thus the COPY CON: command to create a batch file called LOT123.BAT would be as follows:

COPY CON: LOT123.BAT (E)

On pressing Enter the cursor will be positioned on the next line. There is no prompt or message, but each command required in the batch file may be entered. Each command should be on a separate line as follows,

CD \123 (E)
LOTUS (E)

To indicate the end of the file, an end of file marker is required, which is obtained by pressing [CTRL] Z, (hold the CTRL key down and press Z). Finally, pressing (E) will complete the COPY CON: command and return the operator to the DOS prompt.

To execute the commands in the LOT123.BAT batch file the operator enters the filename, in this case LOT123. Note that it is not necessary to enter the .BAT extension. Each of the commands will be executed in turn.

Although the COPY CON: command is useful to create small batch files it does not allow the operator to make corrections easily. One of the utilities available in DOS is a line editor. The line editor operates in a similar way to that of a simple word processor. The DOS line editor is called EDLIN.

9.9   EDLIN

EDLIN is a DOS file and the term refers to *line editor*. It is used to create text files on a line by line basis. All functions within EDLIN are carried out through the use of single character codes. A list of the commonly used codes is shown below

D   Delete lines of text.

E   End the edit saving the changes made.

I   Insert new lines of text.

L   List the contents of the file on the screen.

Q   Quit the edit without saving the changes made.

Editing an existing line to make a change is achieved by entering the line number. The first six function keys [F1] to [F6] may also be used to speed up the editing process.

[F1] Copy and display one character from the retained line.

[F2] Copy all characters up to a specified character.

[F3] Copy all of the remaining characters from the retained line.

[F4] Skip (delete) all characters to a specified character in the retained line.

[F5] Re-edit the current retained line.

[F6] ^Z. Used to exit insert mode.

Using EDLIN to create the 123LOT.BAT batch file the following is required,

EDLIN 123LOT.BAT (E)

As EDLIN is an external DOS file, either the DOS directory must be active or there must be a path to it. Once EDLIN is running, a " * " will be displayed on the next line. This is the EDLIN prompt. The following commands are required to complete the file.

      I (E)   Insert new lines into the file.

Even though there are no instructions in the file the Insert command is used to start entering information. The first available line is presented on the screen which in this case would be line 1.

      CD \LOTUS (E)   First command
      LOTUS (E)   Second command
      ^C   The ^C is used to signify the end of inserting.

The * prompt will reappear. The L command will list the contents of the file on the screen as follows,

      L (E)
      1: CD \123
      2: LOTUS
      *

To Insert or delete lines in the file the appropriate command is preceded with an appropriate line number concerned. For example, to add a line to the LOT123.BAT file the following is required,

      3I (E)   Insert a new line 3
      CD \ (E)   Change the current directory back to
                          root after LOTUS has finished running.

      ^C (E)   Finish inserting.
      L (E)   List the amended file
      1: CD \LOTUS
      2: LOTUS
      3: CD \
      *

      E (E)   Leave EDLIN saving file

The batch file may now be executed by typing LOT123.

9.10   BATCH FILES FOR MENUS.

A useful application for batch files is the development of user menus. Menus are used in many application packages as a means of making the system easier to use by non-computer experts. The choice from a menu substitutes a command.

The menu technique can be used for making the execution of DOS commands a matter of selection from a predetermined list, as opposed to entering the command in full.

9.10.1   DEVELOPING TAILORED MENUS

There are several different ways or approaches to developing a user defined menu system in DOS. The approach used depends upon how large and complex the required system is, how many options are required to be displayed on the menu and how sophisticated the programmer wishes to be.

Most DOS menu systems require the involvement of the AUTOEXEC.BAT file to initiate the listing of the menu. This means that whatever other commands are included in AUTOEXEC.BAT, it should end with the instruction to put the menu options on the screen.

The instructions required to initiate the menu from the AUTOEXEC.BAT file are:

CLS
TYPE MENU

The menu or list of options are held in a separate text file which is usually called MENU. Care must be taken with the wording and layout of this file because the computer will simply display the text on the screen in the format it is written.

For each menu option there must exist a batch file with the same name as the option in the menu. Thus if the menu options on the screen are 1, 2, 3 etc then there must be files 1.BAT, 2.BAT, 3.BAT etc. The function of these batch files is to execute the instructions required by each option.

9.10.2   CREATING A MENU DRIVEN SYSTEM

When there are less than 10 menu options required a simple list menu system is usually suitable. In such a case the text file MENU would appear as follows:

```
            ------------
            Opening Menu
            ------------


        1 .......... WordStar
        2 .......... Lotus 1-2-3
        3 .......... dBASE
        4 .......... DOS v4.01

        Please make your selection :-
```

This file is a straightforward text file which can be created using COPY CON:, EDLIN or a word processor. As the format and layout of the file on the screen is the key to this file, it is advisable to use a word processor. If the word processor used assigns an extension to files by default then the instruction in the AUTOEXEC.BAT file TYPE MENU must include the extension. For example TYPE MENU.DOC.

| NOTE |

If using a word processor to create batch files, ensure a straight ASCII file is created without any of the control characters from the word processing package.

The commands required for the options described above are contained in four separate batch files which are listed below. It is assumed that the hard disk drive C: will be divided into a series of directories and that there will be a separate directory for each of the options displayed in the menu.

9.10.2.1 Batch file 1.BAT

This batch file is used to execute the WordStar program, which is located in a subdirectory called WS. The code is as follows:

```
echo off
cls
rem ** Change to WordStar directory, and Run **
cd \ws
ws
rem * Return to root directory, and invoke menu *
cd \
type menu
```

9.10.2.2 Batch file 2.BAT

This batch file is used to execute the Lotus 1-2-3 program, which is located in a subdirectory called 123. The code is as follows:

```
echo off
cls
rem ** Change to Lotus 123 directory, and Run **
cd \123
123
rem * Return to root directory, and invoke menu *
cd \
type menu
```

9.10.2.3 Batch file 3.BAT

This batch file is used to execute the dBase IV program, which is located in a subdirectory called DB4. The code is as follows:

```
echo off
cls
rem ** Change to Dbase IV directory, and Run **
cd \db4
dbase
rem * Return to root directory, and invoke menu *
cd \
type menu
```

9.10.2.4 Batch file 4.BAT

This batch file is used to display the DOS version number. This entails changing into the

DOS directory and running the VER utility. This could easily be adapted to allow the user to choose which utility they wished to execute, thus simplifying the interface to DOS.

```
cls
rem ** Change to DOS4 directory, and show version **
cd \dos4
ver
rem * Return to root directory, and invoke menu *
cd \
type menu
```

Batch files are extremely convenient and useful DOS tools. They provide for the automation of repetitive or long instructions, and the chance of mistyping a command is reduced.

Many software manufacturers include batch files with their programs and these can make the installation of a system simple for the end user.

9.11 SUMMARY

A good understanding of how DOS is used to control the operation of the system is an essential knowledge base that all troubleshooters should gain.

It may well be necessary to configure hard disks from scratch when new systems are purchased, a process that involves low-level formatting, partitioning, high-level formatting, directory construction and software configuration.

The last issue in the above list refers to the creation of the CONFIG.SYS and AUTO-EXEC.BAT files. These control the allocation of memory to devices, tell the system what equipment is connected, and perform routine tasks such as setting date and time formats. Many software problems can be traced to errors or incompatibilities in either of these files, so a thorough understanding of the commands is essential.

10   Debug

10.1   WHAT CAN DEBUG BE USED FOR?

DEBUG is a special tool that allows the computers memory to be examined and, if required, altered. It also has a variety of other facilities: it can execute a program one step at a time, allowing the user to check that it is operating correctly; it can trace the execution of a program, compare values before and after an instruction, and compare, move and fill sections of memory. In addition to working with memory, DEBUG can also be used to manipulate information stored on the computer's disks, either in the form of files or on a sector-by-sector basis.

Many of these facilities will be of use only to assembly language programmers and those who wish to 'poke about' inside the system. However, DEBUG can be used by nonprogrammers for a wide variety of tasks, including the following:

- Patching program files
- Examining memory
- Exploring the contents of disks
- Altering directory entries, such as file attributes and sizes
- Creating short .COM files to perform simple tasks
- Undeleting short files
- Recovering files that are stranded in memory
- Repairing damaged files.

Some of these tasks will be more efficiently performed with proprietary software, particularly those involving writing directly to the disk. However, if software is unavailable, then DEBUG is a safeguard against total disaster.

To use DEBUG requires at least a basic knowledge of how computer data is stored. All data is treated as a series of *bytes*, a byte being a value between 0 and 255. Most applications software displays the data by converting each byte to its ASCII character equivalent. Thus the value 65 represents the letter A, 66 represents B and so on. Each value has a different character associated with it, although some cannot be displayed on the screen. However, since DEBUG works with the data in its simplest form, it uses another notation known as hexadecimal format.

In hexadecimal format the decimal value is converted to base 16. Hexadecimal numbers use the digits 0 to 9 as normal, but additionally use the letters A through F for the values 10 to 16. Thus any decimal value up to 255 can be represented by a two digit hexadecimal number. The following are some examples of hexadecimal numbers and their decimal equivalents.

Dec.	Hex.	Dec.	Hex.
0	0	25	19
9	9	26	1A
10	A	27	1B
11	B	32	20
15	F	128	80
16	10	254	FE
17	11	255	FF

DEBUG always displays data in hexadecimal format, but will also display it in the form of ASCII characters if the value is between 32 and 126. This means that when DEBUG displays the data, the screen generally shows it as hexadecimal (in which the value of all bytes can be seen) and ASCII (in which the printable characters are displayed). Figure 10.1 shows an example of the display produced by DEBUG when working with the COMMAND.COM file.

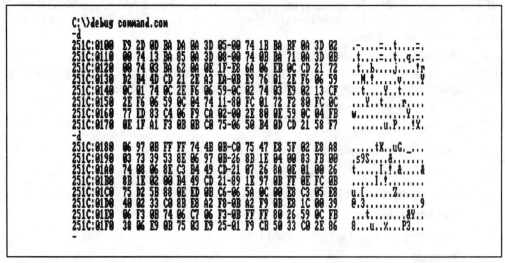

Figure 10.1   DEBUG display showing COMMAND.COM

10.2   DEBUG COMMANDS

There are 22 basic commands available within Debug, as shown below. They consist of one or two letters, and are entered at the keyboard in response to the prompt. Any command shown in several different formats indicates that any one may be used.

A
A [start-address]
    Assembles machine language assembler statements into memory as binary machine code

C [start-address] [end-address] [start-address2]
C [start-address] L [length] [start-address2]
    Compares the contents of two blocks of memory

D
D [start-address]
D [start-address] [end-address]
D [start-address] L [length]
> Displays the contents of a specified area of memory

E [start-address] [data-list]
E [start-address]
> Enters a list of byte values or characters into memory. The second command causes each byte in turn to be displayed and changed as required

F [start-address] [end-address] [data-list]
F [start-address] L [length] [data-list]
> Fills a block of memory with a list of byte values or characters. If the block is larger than the list then the list is repeated until the block is filled

G
G=[start-address]
G=[breakpoint(s)]
G=[start-address] [breakpoint(s)]
> Begins execution of a program in memory (Stands for Go)

H [number1] [number2]
> Adds and subtracts two hexadecimal numbers

I [port-address]
> Reads and displays a byte from one of the PC input/output ports

L
L [start-address]
> Loads a file into memory

L [drive] [sector-number] [sector-count]
L [start-address] [drive] [sector-number] [sector-count]
> Loads specified sectors from the disk into memory

M [start-address] [end-address] [start-address2]
M [start-address] L [length] [start-address2]
> Moves a block of data from one memory location to another

N [filespec]
N [parameter-list]
> Names a file or a list of parameters that must be specified when the file is executed

O [port-address] [byte]
> Sends a byte value to an input/output port

Q
> Quits from Debug

R
R [register-name]
RF
> Displays the contents of the machine registers and status flags, allowing them to be changed if required

S [start-address] [end-address] [data-list]
S [start-address] L [length] [data-list]
  Searches a block of memory for a specified list of values

T
T=[start-address]
  Traces program operation, by executing one or more instructions

U
U [start-address]
U [start-address] [end-address]
U [start-address] L [length]
  Unassembles machine code into assembly language

W
W [start-address]
  Writes a file to disk

W [drive] [sector-number] [number-count]
W [start-address] [drive] [sector-number] [number-count]
  Writes one or more sectors to disk

XA
  Allocates EMS pages

XD
  Deallocates EMS

XM
  Maps an expanded memory page into the page frame

XS
  Displays the status of expanded memory

Note that all data that is entered using any of the commands, and all data that is displayed, must be in either hexadecimal format or the ASCII equivalent character.

10.3 A WORKED EXAMPLE USING DEBUG

This chapter is not intended to be a tutorial on the full use of Debug, but rather it is intended to provide examples showing how such tools can be used to to assist the troubleshooter. It should always be remembered that no single tool will solve all problems, and therefore the user should appreciate just how far they can go in using Debug for data recovery.

Debug is one of the most user-unfriendly programs available, due mainly to its poor command set. As some of these commands are very complex, care should be taken to ensure that they are fully understood before modifying important files.

Generally speaking, it is unwise to attempt to modify important program files, and on no account should untrained staff use Debug unsupervised. Debug can be used for modifying system information, and also for exploring memory. It is even possible to change the SETUP information through the use of Debug, and to low-level format the entire hard disk. Thus Debug should be treated with a great deal of care.

10.3.1 GROUND RULES

Before attempting to make any changes at all, it is essential that a copy is made of the data, and any work then carried out on the copy. If anything then goes wrong, it is a simple matter to make another copy from the original.

Whilst this is relatively simple with single files, it becomes noticeably more difficult when considering entire floppy disks, and almost impossible in the case of an entire hard disk. The following are some hints on the production of such a copy:

- Single files can be copied using the DOS copy command, although it is more than likely that this will not copy any lost data as well.

- Floppy disks can be copied using a product such as COPYIIPC or COPYWRIT. The DOS DISKCOPY command is not recommended as it can in some cases introduce unwanted problems of its own.

- Entire hard disks can be copied across a network or by attaching a second hard disk to the computer. A special program will have to be used to accomplish the actual copying.

- **Above all, the copy should always be made onto a different device to the original. ie, use a separate floppy or hard disk. Changes should NEVER be made to the original data.**

10.3.2 PATCHING A FILE

As explained above, Debug can be used to patch files on disk. This may be necessary due to data loss or some other factor. This example considers the situation in which a memo has been written in WordStar, to which it is necessary to attach a list of filenames from a specific directory. The simplest way to obtain the list is to use the DOS redirection facility which allows the output from any command to be diverted to a printer, or alternatively a file. To redirect the output from the DIR command to a file, issue the command:

DIR >[filename]

To append the output from the DIR command to the end of an existing file, issue the command:

DIR >>[filename]

Thus if WordStar is used to create a file called MEMO.TXT, the directory listing can be appended to the file by entering:

DIR >>MEMO.TXT

It would be reasonable to assume that if the memo file was now loaded back into WordStar, then the directory listing would be appended to it. However, this is not the case, as WordStar uses a special character to indicate the end of the file. Although MS-DOS has appended the list of files to the end of MEMO.TXT, it has not removed the special characters, and so WordStar does not recognise that there is more data in the file. Debug can be used to remove these special characters, and thus correct the file.

The memo should be created to read as follows:

```
John,
        Here's a floppy with the files for the newsletter that you
    wanted. See the directory listing below:
```

The size of this file is 256 bytes, as can be seen from the directory listing. The DIR command can then be used to list the files:

DIR >>MEMO.TXT

The size of the file will now have changed to reflect the additional data. This can be verified by checking the value returned by the DIR command, which is 769 for the listing of the files used here.

Debug is then invoked, specifying the name of the file so that it is automatically loaded:

DEBUG MEMO.TXT

The screen then displays the debug prompt, shown as a hyphen (-). Entering the D (display) command causes the first few lines of the file to be displayed on the screen, as shown in Figure 10.2. If D 100 L 120 is entered, then the subsequent lines are also displayed, as shown in Figure 10.3.

```
C:\NEWS>debug memo.txt
-d
2502:0100  1D 7D 00 00 55 48 50 00-00 00 00 00 00 00 00 00   .}..UHP.........
2502:0110  00 01 00 00 00 00 00 00-00 00 00 00 00 00 00 00   ................
2502:0120  00 00 00 00 00 00 00 00-00 00 00 00 00 00 00 00   ................
2502:0130  00 00 00 00 00 00 00 00-00 00 00 00 00 00 00 00   ................
2502:0140  00 00 00 00 00 00 00 00-00 00 00 00 00 00 00 00   ................
2502:0150  00 00 00 00 00 00 00 00-00 00 00 00 00 00 00 00   ................
2502:0160  00 00 00 00 00 00 00 00-00 00 00 00 00 00 00 00   ................
2502:0170  00 00 00 00 00 00 00 00-00 00 00 00 00 7D 00 1D   .............}..
-
```

Figure 10.2   Listing of the first 128 bytes

```
2502:0130  00 00 00 00 00 00 00 00-00 00 00 00 00 00 00 00   ................
2502:0140  00 00 00 00 00 00 00 00-00 00 00 00 00 00 00 00   ................
2502:0150  00 00 00 00 00 00 00 00-00 00 00 00 00 00 00 00   ................
2502:0160  00 00 00 00 00 00 00 00-00 00 00 00 00 00 00 00   ................
2502:0170  00 00 00 00 00 00 00 00-00 00 00 00 00 7D 00 1D   .............}..
-d 100 l 120
2502:0100  1D 7D 00 00 55 48 50 00-00 00 00 00 00 00 00 00   .}..UHP.........
2502:0110  00 01 00 00 00 00 00 00-00 00 00 00 00 00 00 00   ................
2502:0120  00 00 00 00 00 00 00 00-00 00 00 00 00 00 00 00   ................
2502:0130  00 00 00 00 00 00 00 00-00 00 00 00 00 00 00 00   ................
2502:0140  00 00 00 00 00 00 00 00-00 00 00 00 00 00 00 00   ................
2502:0150  00 00 00 00 00 00 00 00-00 00 00 00 00 00 00 00   ................
2502:0160  00 00 00 00 00 00 00 00-00 00 00 00 00 00 00 00   ................
2502:0170  00 00 00 00 00 00 00 00-00 00 00 00 00 7D 00 1D   .............}..
2502:0180  4A 6F 68 6E 2C 0D 0A 20-20 20 20 20 48 65 72 65   John,...    Here
2502:0190  27 73 20 61 20 66 6C 6F-70 70 79 20 77 69 74 68   's a floppy with
2502:01A0  20 74 68 65 20 66 69 6C-65 73 20 66 6F 72 20 74   the files for t
2502:01B0  68 65 20 6E 65 77 73 6C-65 74 74 65 72 20 A0 74   he newsletter .t
2502:01C0  68 61 74 20 8D 0A 79 6F-75 20 77 61 6E 74 65 64   hat ..you wanted
2502:01D0  2E 20 53 65 65 20 74 68-65 20 64 69 72 65 63 74   . See the direct
2502:01E0  6F 72 79 20 6C 69 73 74-69 6E 67 20 62 65 6C 6F   ory listing belo
2502:01F0  77 3A 1A 1A 1A 1A 1A 1A-1A 1A 1A 1A 1A 1A 1A 1A   w:..............
2502:0200  0D 0A 20 56 6F 6C 75 6D-65 20 69 6E 20 64 72 69   .. Volume in dri
2502:0210  76 65 20 43 20 69 73 20-54 45 43 48 54 52 41 4E   ve C is TECHTRAN
-
```

Figure 10.3   Listing of the first 288 bytes

It can be seen from this display that the memo does not actually begin until some way into the file. In fact the first few bytes of the file contain special control characters and information used by the WordStar program. However, it is easy to see where the memo ends, and the list of file names begins. The space between the two sections is filled with values of 1A. This is the hexadecimal value for the end-of-file characters used by WordStar, and is the numeric equivalent of pressing [Ctrl]+[Z].

To correct the file, these need to be replaced with spaces. The simplest way to do this is to use the F (fill) command. However, before this can be accomplished, it is necessary to establish the addresses of the locations containing the end-of-file markers. This is achieved by searching a section of the file for the 1A value. The S (search) command can be used for this by entering the following:

S 100 L FF 1A

This translates into search the data, starting at location 100h and continuing until 256 bytes have been checked, noting any locations that contain the value 1Ah. When this command is executed, the display will appear as shown in Figure 10.4.

```
2502:01A0  20 74 68 65 20 66 69 6C-65 73 20 66 6F 72 20 74   the files for t
2502:01B0  68 65 20 6E 65 77 73 6C-65 74 74 65 72 20 A0 74   he newsletter .t
2502:01C0  68 61 74 20 8D 0A 79 6F-75 20 77 61 6E 74 65 64   hat ..you wanted
2502:01D0  2E 20 53 65 65 20 74 68-65 20 64 69 72 65 63 74   . See the direct
2502:01E0  6F 72 79 20 6C 69 73 74-69 6E 67 20 62 65 6C 6F   ory listing belo
2502:01F0  77 3A 1A 1A 1A 1A 1A 1A-1A 1A 1A 1A 1A 1A 1A 1A   w:..............
2502:0200  0D 0A 20 56 6F 6C 75 6D-65 20 69 6E 20 64 72 69   .. Volume in dri
2502:0210  76 65 20 43 20 69 73 20-54 45 43 48 54 52 41 4E   ve C is TECHTRAN
-
-s 100 l 256 1a
2502:01F2
2502:01F3
2502:01F4
2502:01F5
2502:01F6
2502:01F7
2502:01F8
2502:01F9
2502:01FA
2502:01FB
2502:01FC
2502:01FD
2502:01FE
2502:01FF
-
```

Figure 10.4   Results of the fill command

The first and last addresses that are listed give the start and end of the range containing the end-of-file markers. The fill command can now be used as follows:

F 01F2 01FF 20

This means fill locations 01F2 to 01FF with the value 20, which is the hexadecimal equivalent of the space character. Thus all of the end-of-file characters are replaced with spaces. The write command is then issued to write the changes to the disk, and Debug may then be exited:

W

Q

If the memo is then loaded into WordStar, or displayed on the screen, it includes the directory listing, as shown in Figure 10.5.

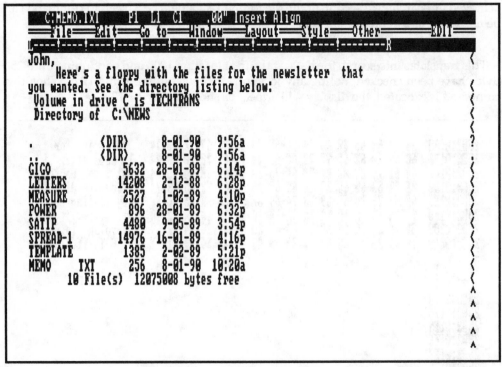

Figure 10.5   The patched memo file

Although this is only a simple example of the facilities offered by Debug, it does show how powerful the program can be. This form of patching and modification could not be accomplished in any other way, although the final result of the directory listing appended to the memo could perhaps have been achieved more easily by creating two files, then reading one into the other within WordStar.

However, one area in which the file patching feature is particularly important is that of damaged file recovery. For example, if the power to the system is removed while a file is being saved, then the operation will not be completed, and this in turn will cause errors if the file is later read. The reason for this is that the end-of-file marker is not in place. Using the above method, the end-of-file marker can be inserted so that at least some of the file is recoverable.

10.4 SUMMARY

This brief examination of Debug has shown it to be a powerful and versatile utility, although the way in which commands are issued and data displayed tend to make it difficult for the inexperienced to come to terms with. Debug is by far the most powerful DOS utility, and allows the user to do almost anything from examining and modifying the computers memory to writing directly to the disk. Thus it can be used for repairing damaged files, making alterations to data from proprietary software packages that could not be made in any other way, and creating small programs, to name only a few of its many applications.

However, it should always be remembered that some tasks are more efficiently performed with proprietary software such as The Norton utilities or PCTools. Thus when faced with a problem situation, it is up to the troubleshooter to determine the best tool for the job.

11 Hardware, Software and Data Security

11.1 INTRODUCTION

The issues of hardware, software and data security are inclined to be grouped with the security of the main office premises, and the equipment stored therein. However, the problems that affect computer systems can be very different from those encountered in ordinary security operations.

11.1.1 HARDWARE SECURITY

The value and portability of computer systems and peripherals means that they are very attractive for the common thief. Offices in which previously the most valuable item was a typewriter are now having to face the fact that their computer systems are of great value, both financially and in terms of the amount of work that would be required to reinstate them. With computers becoming ever smaller, it is apparent that it is now easier than ever for thieves to steal valuable equipment.

11.1.2 SOFTWARE SECURITY

Software is open to even more threats. It is normally supplied on floppy disks, which are small and easily concealable, thus increasing the chances of their being stolen. Additionally, software can often be copied onto other diskettes which may then be removed. Although this does not prevent the company from using the product, there may be the possibility of staff or directors being prosecuted under the Copyright Act.

11.1.3 DATA SECURITY

Most corporate computer systems, whether they are WANs, LANs or standalone PCs, will contain data vital to the ongoing business of the company. It may be of particular importance to the company itself, such as order processing information, or it may be of interest to other companies, such as design data. In either case, it is important that no unauthorised personnel gain access to the information, as this will allow them to read, copy, modify or destroy it.

Despite the value of computer systems and the information they hold, many companies have no formal procedures or safeguards to ensure the security of their systems. This means that hardware and software may be stolen, and data mis-used, a situation that may produce many undesirable consequences for the organisation concerned.

11.2 PROTECTING THE HARDWARE

Hardware must be protected against theft, either by securing the devices so that they cannot be removed, or by making them unattractive to the thief. To ensure that these measures are effective, it is necessary to introduce policies and procedures into the firm which must be followed by all staff. This will reduce the risks and also enable an up-to-date register to be kept of all devices.

The measures to be taken are as follow:

– Mark all system boxes, so that they cannot easily be sold by the thief without considerable effort to disguise their origins. This may be done in two ways:

• Brand boxes with identification marks, preferably several, including the full name and postcode of the company. This should be done in a prominent position, and should not be easily removable. Soldering irons are effective for marking plastic parts.

• Spray boxes with permanent paint. Paint is available which is "graffiti-proof", meaning that it cannot easily be removed or sprayed over. Either the entire system box can be sprayed a particular colour (bright red is popular) or appropriate stencil images can be sprayed to indicate ownership. These should be in prominent positions.

– If there is no need to move systems on a regular basis then bolt them to the desks on which they are situated. The bolts should go through the case of the computer and through the desk. Thus to remove a PC it will be necessary to dismantle it to a considerable degree, a task which a thief will unlikely be prepared to do.

– Appoint a PC security supervisor to be responsible for the overall security of hardware and software. They should be vetted to ensure that they are reliable and honest, and should be empowered to have overall control over the placement and usage of all computer systems. Before any system may be altered or moved, express permission must be obtained from the supervisor.

– Each departmental head should be made responsible for the equipment used within their department. They should report directly to the PC security supervisor. This policy will have the effect of making management take an interest in what equipment is in use, where it is and who is using it. This may produce additional benefits in that these observations will reveal if any systems are extraneous, or if further systems are required.

– Create an asset register, detailing each machine, its location, its most regular users and any other appropriate details. If any changes are made to the machine specification, or if a machine is moved to a new location, the new details should be recorded immediately in the register.

– Laptop computers and portables should be treated with special care. Their use should be limited to senior management, or if necessary, a few individuals whose work requires them. The user of the system should be made responsible for its security.

If these measures are implemented, then there should be a minimal risk of computer systems being mis-placed or stolen. It should be remembered that these procedures must be followed in addition to the standard security techniques implemented in any modern organisation.

11.3 PROTECTING THE SOFTWARE

As stated before, the threats to software are considerably more complex than those facing the hardware. The two most common problems are that the original disks for a software product are stolen or mis-placed, or that the software is illegally copied.

– The initial problem of software being stolen can be overcome by ensuring that the original disks are locked in a strongroom after the product has been installed onto the hard disk of the appropriate machine. The PC security supervisor should be responsible for the safe keeping of these disks, and should be the only person to handle them from the time they are purchased. This ensures that the location of the software is known at all times. However, further measures can be taken to minimise the risks:

- Disks can be tagged with special labels, similar to those used within clothing in department stores. These labels are used in conjunction with detectors at all exits to the building. If one of the disks with a special label is carried through a detector, an alarm is triggered. As these labels are quite small, they can be hidden under a standard disk label,

- An asset register can be kept to detail all software owned by the company. This is treated in the same way as the hardware register, and is also of use in determining whether the company is using unauthorised copies of software.

– The problem of preventing unauthorised duplication can become very complex, and the effective solutions vary between organisations, depending largely on the usage of the computer systems.

- Some security products offer a facility to prevent programs from being copied (see later section), but this can often be overcome by a determined programmer.

- If original system disks are kept in a safe place then the only way that software can be duplicated is by copying it from the hard disk of a system to a floppy. An obvious way of preventing this is to make systems into hard-disk only installations. This is particularly easy when a LAN or WAN is implemented as new software can be loaded onto the server which can be situated in a secure room, and data can be downloaded to the server for backup purposes. However, with standalone PCs, it will be necessary to plug in a floppy disk drive to load new software or data.

Note that once programs have been copied onto floppies that are not tagged, it is impossible to detect their removal from the premises. Thus in this case, prevention is not just better than cure, it is the only effective measure that can be taken.

An organisation offering advice and help in preventing the unauthorised duplication of software is FAST, the Federation Against Software Theft. Chapter 12 deals in detail with this subject, and gives more information about FAST.

11.4 PROTECTING THE DATA

Data is perhaps of more value to an organisation's competitors than either the hardware or software involved. Data is also essential to the organisation itself, as it ensures the continued success of the business operation. However, computer data is open to mis-use, perhaps even more so than hardware and software, due to the fact that it must be made available to the legitimate users of the computer systems.

It sometimes happens that the threat to the computer data comes from an employee, either by accident or maliciously. A solution adopted by many organisations is to include in the employees contract of employment a statement to the effect that all data used in the employees every day work, and all data produced in conjunction with that work is owned by the company, and that the employee has no legal right to distribute, modify or destroy that data. This does not however prevent the data from harm, it merely seeks to deter the vandal from committing the act. If data is destroyed, then it may be no consolation to the company to know that they can sack the person concerned, they are probably more interested in retrieving the lost information.

To counter these risks, many suppliers have produced devices and programs to improve the security of a computer installation. These range from simple, inexpensive programs requiring the user to enter an identification code and a password before they can use the computer, to sophisticated hardware devices that require a special key to be inserted before the computer will boot up. The latest devices use *biometric* techniques, ie the measurement of biological data. These systems normally use fingerprints as an identification, but some other systems scan the vein pattern on the retina, or analyse the users signature. Some systems do not restrict access to the machine, but rather restrict access to the data. This is most commonly achieved by *encrypting, encoding,* or *scrambling* the data before it is written to the disk. All of these terms have the same basic meaning - that the information is re-written in a different form so that it would appear meaningless to the casual reader. The data can only be translated back to a usable form by supplying the program with the same code with which it was originally encrypted.

11.5 ANALYSING REQUIREMENTS

Before selecting a security product it is important to determine a variety of factors relating to the use of the system concerned:

- How safe should the system be ?
- Is it to be protected against unauthorised access, malicious damage or accidental data corruption or loss ?
- How computer literate are the users of the system ?
- How many users are likely to require access ? Is it just one, or are there several people sharing the same computer ?

11.5.1 HOW SAFE SHOULD THE SYSTEM BE ?

Initially most organisations feel that they need their systems to be as safe as possible, within a limited budget. This approach can pose problems as there are some products available on the market which not only prevent unauthorised access, but also in some cases prevent legitimate users from gaining access. Therefore it is necessary to determine how important the data is, and just how secure it needs to be made.

Generally speaking, the more sensitive the data, the more secure it needs to be. For example, banks and financial institutions with electronic funds transfer capabilities will require a greater level of security than a word processing department. Similarly, military and government systems will require better security procedures and safeguards than almost any other systems.

As the system is protected more and more, there will be a greater number of checks and keystrokes required to gain access. All of the correct routines, identification codes and passwords have to be learnt by all users, which in turn means implementing a system that is too secure for the chosen application may have the effect of reducing productivity.

It is also important to realise the possibility of data loss due to forgotten passwords. In many cases the systems are so secure that neither the system administrator nor the product supplier will be able to retrieve it if the relevant password or key is lost.

11.5.2   WHAT IS THE DATA TO BE PROTECTED AGAINST ?

There are three possible threats to data held on a computer system:

- Unauthorised access
- Malicious damage
- Accidental damage.

The majority of security systems protect against unauthorised access, by using a combination of passwords, identification codes, hardware keys, or biometric techniques.

Many also protect against malicious damage, by allowing only selected users to write or modify data in a file.

However, few security systems address the problem of accidental damage. One of the more recent additions to this category is the Opus Datasafe. This is a computer system designed with security in mind:

- It has an integral high-security lock, the keys for which are unique to each machine. This lock keeps intruders out of the system box (so it cannot be bypassed) and has options to prevent booting from the A: drive or the hard disk.

- There are sophisticated log-on procedures and password protection facilities supplied with the machine. These cannot be bypassed as the break key is disabled until they have been correctly executed.

- It has two hard disk drives. They are mechanically separate from each other, and one is kept as an exact copy of the other. Thus if one crashes, no data is lost as it can be retrieved from the other.

The Datasafe has very high performance figures for disk-intensive applications, as Opus have rewritten the disk I/O routines. All disk read operations now look at whichever disk has the information most readily available.

11.5.3   HOW COMPUTER LITERATE ARE THE USERS ?

The experience of the regular computer users is an important factor when considering security systems. Some offer a menu-type front end, from which applications can be selected. These systems are generally much easier to use, prompting for passwords and identification codes etc before access is permitted. Other systems act only as a shell around DOS, allowing all DOS operations to be carried out as normal once the initial security procedures have been performed. These systems require the user to be more experienced with DOS commands, and may not prompt for passwords and codes, but rather expect the user to enter them automatically.

The exact choice of system thus depends on how experienced the users are. If they are not familiar with DOS, it may be better to consider a menu based system. If however they are regular computer users with a good knowledge of DOS then a DOS based system may be more suitable.

11.5.4   HOW MANY USERS WILL REQUIRE ACCESS

Different systems cater for different numbers of users. Some systems allow only a single user to access the data, whilst others can keep passwords and identification codes for unlimited numbers.

If data is being shared among several users, then a single user system cannot be implemented, and a more sophisticated multi-user system must be used. However if the computer is to be used by only one person, then the increased complexity of the multi-user system will be an unnecessary waste of time.

For a single user system, there is a very simple form of security; lock the computer in a strong room when it is not in use. This is particularly relevant to laptops and luggables which can be easily transported, although ordinary PCs can be placed on a movable trolley to make transport easier, and thus more vulnerable to theft.

11.5.5   LEGAL REQUIREMENTS

Data held on a computer system is subject to the Data Protection Act (1987). This states that companies are required to take steps to prevent information held on a computer from falling into the wrong hands. Individuals can claim compensation from companies who allow leaks to occur.

The Act states that *"Appropriate security measures shall be taken against unauthorised access to, or alteration, disclosure or destruction of personal data, and against accidental loss or destruction of personal data."* It is the company holding the data who is responsible for taking appropriate steps to prevent unauthorised access. In the event of a leak, the company must be able to show that it took reasonable measures to prevent a breach of security. Furthermore, security should be at a level appropriate to the information. For example, details of bank accounts should be more secure than details of magazine subscriptions.

The Act also says that it is not sufficient to have password protection on its own. Rather, it is necessary to have different levels of access for different staff. Companies must also take suitable backup measures to ensure that data is not lost. Any data that is no longer required should be disposed of properly, so that it cannot be retrieved.

Although the above statements tend to indicate that software and hardware are of fundamental importance, it is also necessary to protect the area in which the data is located. This may be achieved with entry restrictions to the computer room, and by taking steps to minimise the risk of burglary. Employees in contact with the data should be vetted to ensure that they are reliable and honest. All data processing personnel should be properly trained to know their responsibilities and the procedures they must follow.

If the above measures are not taken, then the company may be considered to be in breach of the Data Protection Act. Any loss, distress or embarrassment caused to an individual by a data leak from the company will render them liable for compensation, as well as open to prosecution. Note that none of these restrictions currently apply to information held on paper.

11.6   SECURITY METHODS

Security systems can be software or hardware based.

11.6.1   SOFTWARE SYSTEMS

Original security products simply prevented the user from gaining direct access to DOS, by routing all commands through their own programs. These could be circumvented by interrupting installation at boot-up time, booting from the A: drive or otherwise escaping from the program shell.

More recent products attack the problem in a different way, by re-writing sections of the system area on the hard disk. Thus it is no longer possible to bypass the system as all requests to access the disk must be routed through these areas. This form of control is offered in several forms. One such example is an alternative operating system for PCs called DR-DOS, which is produced by Digital Research. DR-DOS allows passwords to be set for individual files and directories to prevent unauthorised access. However, even these methods can be bypassed by using absolute disk control routines from the A: drive.

The most secure form of software protection is to encrypt the entire contents of the hard disk. This means that although information can be read from the disk, it is meaningless unless it is first decoded which requires the user to know the appropriate encryption key. System performance can suffer in this area as the routines used for the encryption of data can be extremely long-winded and time consuming.

11.6.2   HARDWARE SYSTEMS

Hardware systems are not necessarily more expensive than software systems, and generally offer greater protection. They often take the form of a plug-in board that occupies a standard expansion slot, or ROM chips that fit directly into sockets on the motherboard. These systems intervene as soon as the system is powered up, before DOS can boot.

The normal form of protection is for the system to ask for a user name and password before allowing access. Hardware systems are obviously only effective if access to the system box is restricted, to prevent removal of the board or chips.

Hardware systems that scramble the hard disk offer the greatest protection. The encryption routines tend to be stored in the form of ROM chips, which allow them to be executed at great speed. These systems ensure that the computer remains secure even if the board or chips are removed as the data cannot be unscrambled.

Many hardware devices support the use of *tokens* or *keys* as identification. The system cannot be accessed until the correct token or key is inserted into a special device. Therefore users must have their own key or token to gain access to the computer. These keys and tokens take many forms, including credit-card style items, small plastic keys and electronic devices that supply a special code sequence. Most token based systems will also require the user to enter a password, to guarantee that the user is genuine.

It is important to consider how easily additional keys can be obtained, and how much they will cost. If the keys are unique to each client then the supplier may charge a high price for replacements. If not, users of similar systems may be able to gain access by using their own keys.

11.7   SELECTING A SYSTEM

Once the requirements have been analysed, the security system can be chosen. There are many different systems on the market, of which seven are compared in the table shown in Figure 11.1.

	Kinetic Access II	PC Boot	PC-Guard	Protec	Stoplock IV	Trispan	Triumph
Product Type							
Software	■	■	■	■	□	■	■
Hardware	□	■	□	□	■	■	■
Number of users	16	10	U/L	52	33	64	8
System Access							
User ID	■	■	■	■	■	■	■
Password	■	■	■	■	■	■	■
Min. length	5	1	1	1	1	1	1
Case sensitive	□	■	■	■	■	■	■
Number of access attempts allowed	3	V	V	V	V	3	3
Token	□	□	□	□	□	■	■
Boot protect	■	■	■	■	■	■	■
Independent clock	□	■	□	□	■	■	□
Peripheral control	■	■	■	□	■	■	□
Time-slotting	□	■	□	□	■	■	□
Timeout	■	■	■	□	□	■	■
File Access							
DES encryption	□	□	□	■	■	□	□
Proprietary encryption	□	■	■	■	□	■	■
Execute protect	■	■	■	■	■	■	■
Secure delete	□	□	■	□	■	■	■
System Management							
Group permissions	□	■	■	□	■	■	□
Audit trail	■	■	■	■	■	■	■
Audit filter	■	□	■	■	□	Opt	Opt
Variable lockout time after failed access	■	■	■	■	■	■	■
Price	£295	£295	£195	£195	£500	£695	£145

■ – Yes   □ – No   U/L – Unlimited   Opt – Optional
V – May be varied by system administrator

Figure 11.1   Features of leading security products

Security systems such as these generally offer many different features, as can be seen from Figure 11.1. The following features are among the more important.

11.7.1   AUDIT LOG AND FILTER

Some products can be configured to collect information about usage or attempted usage of the PC. The Audit facility provides statistics on each user or on the PC as a whole. It can also highlight attempted security violations. This information is stored in the audit log, normally in the form of a file on disk. This can quickly grow very large, meaning that the task of examining the log becomes extremely time consuming, and is therefore not regularly performed. The Filter is designed to extract certain information matching chosen criteria, so that it is much easier to examine the log. These criteria may include time periods, user names or event types.

11.7.2   ENCRYPTION

Data can be encrypted either to a known and officially sanctioned standard, such as DES, or by a proprietary algorithm. The first method is generally much more secure, and is guaranteed to be recoverable. The latter method relies heavily on the quality of the product, as the data is at the mercy of the supplier. If something goes wrong with the program then it may not be possible to decode the information.

11.7.3   TIME-SLOTTING

It may be useful to limit access for some users to particular times of the day, such as when supervision is available. Some packages allow different time-slots to be created for each user, possibly with different times for different days of the week.

11.7.4   MAXIMUM ACCESS ATTEMPTS

Attempted security violations can show themselves in the form of a number of tries at logging on under the same identification code. Some packages allow the maximum number of tries to be limited, and access denied when this limit is exceeded. The identification code cannot then be used until it is reset by the system administrator.

11.7.5   TIMEOUT

Users who forget to log out, or who leave their machines unattended while they go for a cup of coffee provide the perfect opportunity for unauthorised access. Therefore, many programs automatically lock the keyboard after a specified period of inactivity. The system is reset by entering the users password.

11.7.6   MAXIMUM USERS

As discussed above, different products allow different numbers of users. Always choose the product allowing the maximum number of users that is likely to occur in the future.

11.7.7   GROUPS

Users can be categorised into groups or project teams to allow access permissions to be quickly assigned. This also helps with analysing system usage or collating billing information.

11.7.8 SECURE DELETION

The DOS DELETE command simply marks the space used by a file as re-usable, it does not overwrite the data. When the legal obligations of the company are remembered, it will be realised that this is not satisfactory as the data can be retrieved with any good utility program. Therefore several programs offer a secure delete facility, whereby the data is overwritten so that it cannot be retrieved.

11.7.9 EXECUTE PROTECTION

All versions of DOS prior to 3.0 required program files to have read access before they could be executed. However, since DOS 3.0 was introduced, programs can be executed without this, and some products exploit this to prevent illegal copies of the software to be made. This allows users to run the programs, but not to copy them.

11.8 A SUMMARY OF POPULAR SECURITY PRODUCTS

Figure 11.1 indicates the features offered by seven security products. Of these, PC-Guard was considered to be the best buy as it provided the majority of features that would be required in most situations. Trispan is as good a product, but it also has a higher price tag. However, Trispan does have a hardware based encryption system, and so offers greater performance. Protec is the best option for those who require a DES encryption algorithm, and is marketed at the same price as PC-Guard.

It is difficult to determine a clear winner in terms of the security levels offered by these products. Those systems based purely upon software techniques offer a lower level of security to those that employ hardware, primarily because any changes introduced by the software system can be reversed by a determined intruder. However, those products using hardware methods are not perfect either, as they must be based on plug-in option boards or ROM chips. These can very easily be removed, thus circumventing the security altogether. The best way to ensure that data is secure is to encrypt it as it is written to the disk. Thus it is necessary for an observer to know the encryption key or password before the data can be recovered. The most secure technique for encryption is the DES algorithm, which is used by *Protec* and *Stoplock IV*.

11.9 SUMMARY

The issues of computer security must be addressed in every organisation, whether the data is essential to the ongoing success of the enterprise or not. Legal requirements alone mean that firms must take appropriate steps to ensure that personal data is not disclosed to unauthorised personnel.

There are a wide variety of security products available to aid in this task, each offering different levels and facilities. However, even the best of these will not solve the problem on its own. The solution also involves training the users, and adopting security policies within the organisation. A badly installed or mis-used security system is more dangerous than none at all, as there is a real possibility that important data will be irretrievably lost.

To ensure that there is as little chance of this as possible, it is important to make regular backups of the information held on hard disks. Even with the best security procedures available, it is of little comfort when the hard disk crashes to know that the data was secured by encryption.

12 Internal Control of Your Software

12.1 INTRODUCTION

Personal computer software has been used in the business environment for around ten years. During this time there have been many debates and discussions to determine how much protection is offered to software developers and publishers by the law, especially with reference to the problem of unauthorised duplication. This situation was finally clarified in 1985, with the enactment of the Copyright (Computer Software) Amendment Act, which stated that money paid for a software product represents a licence fee for the use of a specific number of copies of that product. In no way does it represent an authorisation to make further copies of the product.

This act was put through in record time, thanks largely to the efforts of an organisation called the Federation Against Software Theft (FAST). FAST is an industry based organisation, set up in 1984 to provide a solution to the problem of software duplication. Its initial aim was to force an amendment to the law governing copyright, to clarify the position and offer more protection to the industry. After achieving this, FAST has gone on to investigate other methods of software protection and reduce the amount of software theft which occurs in this country. It is doing this by means of two main approaches:

- FAST supports software developers and law enforcement agencies in preventing, detecting and prosecuting offenders.

- FAST is actively promoting a public-awareness campaign, highlighting the issues of software theft.

Software theft has been a problem to developers almost from the date that the first IBM PC was installed. The industry is no longer prepared to sit back and watch revenues fall due to illegal duplication of their products. To this end, FAST is actively supported by many major software developers, education and training organisations and consultants.

12.2 FORMS OF SOFTWARE THEFT

Most people think of theft as the act of walking into a store, office or house, picking up something that was not legally owned, and walking out again with the aim of not paying, returning or compensating for its loss. Under this definition, there would be very few people who would likely consider committing a theft.

However, the act of copying a software product is just as much theft as the above

187

example, and is condoned and performed by many people. This may be because they genuinely believe that there is nothing wrong, or they know it is wrong and choose to ignore the law, or they consider that the software developers make enough money from the legitimate copies of the product that are sold. No matter what the reason, software theft is illegal and carries the same possible penalties for the offender.

There are several circumstances in which software theft commonly occurs:

- Making a copy of a corporate software package to use on a private machine at home

- An organisation buying a single copy of a product and then making sufficient copies to use on all the machines that are owned

- Copying software for a friend or colleague, often so that they can use data prepared by the owner of the product.

There is also a further class of software theft, which may be placed under the broad title of plagiarism. This involves a software developer directly using ideas and techniques in their own product which were originated by some other organisation. This form of theft cannot take place unwittingly, but is also quite difficult to prove and obtain a successful result from a prosecution.

Some developers now include a licensing agreement with their products which states that it *may be used in the same way as a book, ie be in use by one person, on one machine, at any one time.* Subject to this restriction, users are permitted to make any number of copies, and to install them on any number of machines. If this form of licence is supplied with a product, it is essential that it is followed exactly if there is to be no infringement of the copyright laws. It is particularly important to delegate someone to take responsibility for the product, ensuring that it is used in line with the agreement. In general, this form of licence is designed to cater for situations in which a single user has sole access to two separate machines, perhaps in separate offices. If there is any likelihood of both machines being in use at the same time, then two copies of the product must be purchased.

A similar problem surrounds the issue of backup copies. As a general rule, only one backup copy should be made of the product, and this should be kept in a secure place, under the responsibility of one individual. The backup should only be used if the original is corrupted, and should then be returned to storage.

To prevent unauthorised duplication of software, many developers are now introducing protection methods for their products. These vary from routines within the program that ask the user to enter a particular word or statistic from the manual to sophisticated hardware devices known as *dongles* which plug into the PC. Without the dongle the software will not run. These methods rely on the appropriate item (ie the manual or the dongle) being too expensive or too difficult to copy.

As a contrast to this, some manufacturers (including Lotus Development Corporation) have adopted a method whereby the licensee (ie the purchaser) of the product is asked to enter their name and the name of their company when the software is first used. These details are then displayed whenever the program is executed. Thus if an unauthorised copy is made, the original licensee's details will still be shown, allowing the culprit to be traced.

12.3   POSSIBLE CONSEQUENCES

There are several obvious consequences of committing theft:

- The company using illegal copies of the product can be prosecuted for civil damages. These can be very substantial indeed.
- The individual committing the act can be prosecuted under the Copyright Act. The penalties for this include significant fines and imprisonment. Additionally, anyone found guilty will have a criminal record kept on them for the rest of their life.
- Police have search-warrant powers to allow them to enter any building in which they have reason to believe there has been a breach of the Copyright Act. If there are clients etc on the premises at the time, then the cost of the lost business will be far greater than the punitive savings made by copying the software.

In addition to these, there are many hidden effects which do not become immediately apparent, including the following:

- Only successful computer software is stolen; This reduces the market forces which would normally cause the price of the product to fall, as there are fewer copies being legitimately sold.
- Investors are less likely to back new projects, as they may feel that there is no guarantee of a good return on their investment. Thus development of new, perhaps more inventive products is stifled. This point also applies to the developers themselves; they are unlikely to spend time and money developing new products if they are unsure that they will make a profit.

These hidden effects have the overall result that development of new products is reduced, and the prices of existing ones are kept high. Thus the purchasers of legitimate copies are effectively paying for software theft in the same way as the developers.

12.4   COMBATTING SOFTWARE THEFT

Reducing, and ultimately eliminating software theft will benefit all users. New development will be encouraged along with improved support for existing products. Prices of established products will fall as the developers will be able to recoup their investment more quickly. Better services will be offered, as the developers know that it is only by providing backup for their products that they will keep existing customers and attract new ones.

To achieve these benefits it is necessary to take steps to prevent software theft. In general, most people confronted with the consequences of their actions will stop, although there are some who will blindly ignore all protests. In such cases it may be necessary to take formal action. Offenders can be divided into two categories;

- those within the company
- those outside the company offering software for sale, or perhaps for free.

12.4.1   WITHIN THE ORGANISATION

Software theft occurring within the organisation can be difficult to detect if appropriate procedures are not followed. However, these are quite simple. FAST have produced guidelines showing that the necessary action may be broken down into three steps:

- The first is a self-audit to determine what software was originally purchased and what is currently in use.
- The second is the distribution of a memorandum to employees stating the effects of software theft.
- Finally, an employee agreement is produced to be signed by all staff, stating that they appreciate the problem and agree to abide by the copyright law.

12.4.1.1 Self-audit

FAST have produced the following ten point guide to performing a self-audit to determine the degree to which software theft is prevalent among staff. This should be performed on a quarterly basis thus:

1   Collect and review all purchase records.

2   Collect and review all licence agreements.

3   Select a date for the audit to take place. Evenings/weekends are the least disruptive.

4   Decide whether employees will be notified in advance:

  - If employees are to be notified, send an explanatory memorandum
  - If employees are not to be notified, be respectful of property. It is always possible that a program may be found that does not belong to the company, but is an employee's legitimate property. No software should be erased without first consulting the employee on whose PC the program is found.

5   Determine who is to be involved in the audit:

  - Information technology manager
  - Senior management/legal department
  - Department heads
  - Outside lawyers/auditors.

6   Search procedures:

  - Locate all PCs
  - Include portable computers
  - If the organisation is large, mark locations on a floor plan to ensure that all machines are included
  - If a machine is unavailable, its identification and owner should be noted and the hard disk searched at a later date
  - Print a list of directories for each hard disk
  - There may be several hard disks on a single machine, ie C, D, E and F
  - With Macintosh machines, it may be necessary to open folders within other folders to find all applications
  - Programs often use abbreviations for their directory and file names, such as WP for WordPerfect, Lotus or 123 for Lotus 1-2-3, WS for WordStar
  - Entertainment software is frequently held in a subdirectory called GAMES
  - If software is not stored on hard disks, make inventories of floppy disks and documentation.

7   Compare software found on the disks to the purchase records. Alternatively locate authorised disks or documentation for each program listed.

8   If the organisation has a LAN, determine if the software can be downloaded onto a hard disk.

9   Review company policies with respect to the use of corporate software on private machines.

10   Do not destroy software for which there are no records or disks without first consulting the employee on whose machine it was found. It may be that they are using their own legitimate copy of the program on the office computer. The employee should be asked to demonstrate the legitimacy of the product in question. Any software found that is known to be pirated or unauthorised should be immediately destroyed.

To assist in the above procedure, FAST have produced a checklist which can be used to determine the validity of any particular product. This is shown in Figure 12.1.

FAST
Federation Against
Software Theft

132 Long Acre
London WC2E 9AH

AUDIT SUMMATION SHEET

A PRODUCT	B PUBLISHER	C # OF COPIES FOUND	D # OF COPIES PURCHASED	E (C-D) SHORTFALL	F RETAIL PRICE	G (E X F) VIOLATION

Figure 12.1   The FAST audit summation sheet

FAST has also produced examples of a memorandum and an employee agreement which can be used to inform and educate employees who use proprietary software in their everyday work. These are shown in Figures 12.2 and 12.3.

SUGGESTED MEMORANDUM TO EMPLOYEES

TO: (Specify Distribution)

FROM: (Senior Management Official)

SUBJECT: PC Software and the Copyright, Designs and Patents Act 1988

DATED: (Insert)

This memorandum is to remind you of the Company policy on software duplication. Any duplication of licensed software without the copyright owner's permission is an infringement under copyright law. Each software program, such as Lotus 123 or WordPerfect, that the Company licenses is to be used on only one computer at a time. If the computer has a program loaded on its hard disk, then that particular program, which is serially numbered, should not be loaded on any other hard disk. This means that if a department has 10 computers, with Lotus 123 installed on each, then that department should also have 10 sets of original documentation and system disks.

All computers purchased by the company are being supplied with newly licensed copies of [insert name(s) of software program(s)] installed on them. (Insert name of employee) is responsible for ensuring that each program is properly registered with the software publisher.

The company will not tolerate any employee making unauthorised copies of software. Any employee found copying software is subject to disciplinary action by the Company. Any employee giving software to any outside third party, including clients or customers, is also subject to disciplinary action. [If you want to use software licensed by the Company at home, you must consult with (Insert name of employee) before removing the system disks from the premises.] This policy may seem harsh, but unless we enforce a strict policy on software use, the company will be exposed to serious liability.

(Insert name of employee) will be visiting the departments over the next week to make inventories of hard disks and to check that original documentation and system disks for each copy of a software product resident on a hard disk. If documentation and/or disks are not present then they will be ordered and charged to that office. Please organise your documentation and system disks for (insert name of employee's) review.

If you have any questions, please do not hesitate to contact me.

Figure 12.2   Suggested memorandum to employees

SAMPLE CORPORATE EMPLOYEE AGREEMENT

COMPANY POLICY REGARDING THE USE OF PERSONAL
COMPUTER SOFTWARE

1. (Company) licenses the use of computer software from a variety of outside companies. (Company) does not own this software or its related documentation and, unless authorised by the software developer, does not have the right to reproduce it.

2. With regard to use on local area networks or on multiple machines, (Company) employees shall use the software only in accordance with the licence agreement.

3. (Company) employees learning of any misuse of software or related documentation within the company shall notify the department manager or (Company's) legal department.

4. According to UK Copyright Law, persons involved in the illegal reproductions of software can be subject to unlimited civil damages and to criminal penalties, including fines and imprisonment. (Company) does not condone the illegal duplication of software. (Company) employees who make, acquire or use unauthorised copies of computer software will be disciplined as appropriate under the circumstances. Subject to (Company's) disciplinary procedures, this may include termination of employment.

I am fully aware of the software use policies of (Company) and agree to uphold those policies.

_____

Employee Date and Signature

Figure 12.3   Sample corporate employee agreement

12.4.2 OTHER SOURCES

Some unauthorised copies of software are acquired from outside the company, either from friends and colleagues in other organisations, or from professional suppliers often initially contacted through a mail order advertisement. In such cases it is difficult to decide how much action should be taken.

In the first example, where software is supplied by a friend or colleague, a friendly explanation of the consequences of software theft will normally change their attitude and prevent them from providing further copies for anyone else. It is often found that a copy of a program was originally supplied for a particular purpose, and that it is no longer used. There are few individuals who blatantly abuse the copyright laws by giving copies to all and sundry.

In the second example, software may have been purchased under the belief that it was a legitimate copy, but at a much reduced price. In practice, this does not happen, as the distributors must pay a hefty price for software themselves, and thus must normally come close to matching the developers price when they retail it to the public. Software bargains offered at around 10 percent of the manufacturers price are almost always illegal copies. These sources of software should be ignored, as no support will be offered by the developers for any products purchased in this way. Additionally, possessing unauthorised copies of software is as unlawful as making them in the first place, so the organisation is making itself open to prosecution. The best way of ensuring that software is legitimate is to purchase it from registered dealers. Any software developer will be able to supply a list of registered dealers who market their product.

12.5 SUMMARY

It is essential to eliminate software theft, for both the good of the software industry and the consumer. The consequences of this illegal act will be felt both by the producers of the product and by the legitimate users, in the form of increased costs and reduced development and support.

The best way to achieve results is felt to be through a public education campaign, which may be greatly aided by organisations taking their own actions to ensure that all of the software they use is legitimate. FAST has been pioneering solutions to these problems for the past six years, but still has a long way to go in eliminating all forms of software piracy.

For further details or questions on software protection, FAST may be contacted at 2 Lake End Court, Taplow, Maidenhead, Berkshire. SL6 0JQ. Telephone 0628 660377.

13   Computer Networks

13.1   WHAT IS A COMPUTER NETWORK?

A computer network is a configuration that will allow the transfer of information through cables or modems between separate computers. There are two main types of computer network referred to as WANs and LANs. The most common type of network in the personal computer environment is a LAN or Local Area Network. As the name implies the LAN is usually restricted to one building or a complex of buildings, although there are exceptions to this. A WAN or Wide Area Network usually involves very powerful computers and controls the communication between such machines over long distances.

A personal computer LAN consists of a number of standard PCs which could be operated as standalone systems away from the LAN. Each computer can have a variety of different peripherals including disk drives, monitor, printer etc. The LAN is formed by linking the computers with a high speed data communications link. The sophistication of the PCs on the LAN can vary, but if establishing a PC LAN today a minimum of 80286 processors would be recommended and 80386 machines will give substantially improved performance.

There are many advantages to working with a LAN, but three specific areas worth mentioning are:

- Sharing information
- Sharing peripherals
- Electronic mail.

Through the efficient application of a LAN environment the collective productivity of PC users be increased, and the operating costs can be substantially reduced:

13.1.1   SHARING INFORMATION

Information can be exchanged far more easily through a LAN. Reports can be copied from one user's directory directly into another user's, without the need to print out a hard copy or put the information onto a floppy disk. Because of the faster and more direct access to information that a LAN offers, it is likely that the quality and number of business decisions will improve. Furthermore a network can facilitate easier access to up-to-date versions of software and data due to the increased control offered by the network.

13.1.2   SHARING PERIPHERALS

Although each PC on the network can have its own full compliment of peripherals, costs can be considerably reduced through the ability to share large disk drives and high quality printers.

13.1.3 ELECTRONIC MAIL

Messages can be sent from one user to any other user or number of users on the network. The recipient of the message need not be at his/her PC as it will be stored in an electronic mailbox in the file server for later reading. This speeds up interpersonal communication by decreasing paperwork and reducing time and money wasted waiting for replies to written memos or telephone messages.

13.2 WHAT CONSTITUTES A LOCAL AREA NETWORK

There are six main elements that are important in understanding the concept of a LAN.

13.2.1 DISTANCE

The personal computers in the LAN will normally be located in the same building, but will seldom cover more than five kilometres. However, it is common to link two or more networks together which would increase the apparent distance covered by the system.

13.2.2 SPEED

The speed at which information is passed around the network will vary substantially with some LANs being as slow as 1Mbit/second. Many LANs operate at speeds between 4-20Mbits/second and there are some high speed LANs which function at speeds up to 13.2Gbits/second. The function of speed is usually dependent on the data transmission medium with high speed LANs requiring fibre optic cabling.

13.2.3 ROBUSTNESS

The reliability of data transmission around a network must be high with no single point of failure. This is sometimes described as no SPOF.

13.2.4 DISTRIBUTED DATA PROCESSING (DDP)

A network usually implies that there is no longer a single central source of information, as would have been the case with a mainframe or mini computer (although on some smaller systems the bulk of the information may in fact be on one file server). Typically however in addition to a large file server on the network each user will have his/her own CPU and hard disk of considerable proportions.

13.2.5 INTERMITTENT TRANSMISSION

Most LANs are not designed for continuous data transmission, but rather as tools which allow periodic data transfer. This form of transmission is referred to as asynchronous and is sometimes described as bursty.

13.2.6 USER INVOLVEMENT

A personal computer network implies that the end user is closely involved in the use and maintenance of the system. Each user will retain a certain amount of control over their own PC and the Network Administrator, who will often also be a user, will be responsible for the servers and the overall control of the system. The acronym sometimes used to describe this is COAM – Customer Owned And Maintained.

13.3 NETWORK COMPONENTS

Networks can be either centralised or distributed. A centralised network implies that there is a dedicated machine to do all the network-related processing. This is referred to as the File Server. A distributed network lets each machine on the network do some of the chores. Typically the cheaper PC networks will be distributed, whereas the higher priced products such as Novell NetWare and 3Com 3+ Open are centralised. Mini and mainframe networks will normally be distributed.

Both centralised and distributed networks have their advantages. For example, a centralised network only requires one high cost, high powered PC and all the data is in one location. If this PC fails however, the entire network is likely to collapse. Whilst a distributed network requires all PCs to be intelligent, if one fails the system will carry on.

13.3.1 NETWORK SERVERS

In order for information to be interchanged between the PCs on a LAN it is necessary for one PC to be designated as a server. This server PC has the ability to share its peripherals with other computers. There are different types of server including file servers, print servers and dedicated servers.

A file server provides disk space that is accessible to other PCs on the network. A print server has a printer or other hard copy device that can be used by other users on the LAN. A dedicated server is purely a CPU, often without a keyboard, monitor etc., which simply services the requests of other computers on the network.

13.3.2 FILE SERVERS

File servers control user access to files, ensuring that only one user at a time is able to write to a file – or specified part of a file. In addition the file server will maintain file access control through the use of passwords. The file server will usually be a faster, more powerful PC than others on the LAN and will have a large disk.

13.3.3 PRINT SERVERS

In the same way that PCs on a LAN can share data through the use of a file server, they can also share a printer through the use of a print server. This will typically enable each user to have an inexpensive dot matrix printer attached to his/her machine and for one PC in the LAN to have a high quality laser printer which will be designated the print server machine. This does not necessarily have to be the same PC as the file server. Figure 13.1 shows a typical LAN with a file server and a printer server.

13.3.4 GATEWAYS

In addition to being able to share information between users on a LAN, it is sometimes necessary to access data on another network, or perhaps a mini or mainframe computer.

Although the computer industry has not yet agreed on a data communications standard to cope with the problem of interconnection, it is possible to access data on external devices through the use of special hardware called gateways which are sometimes

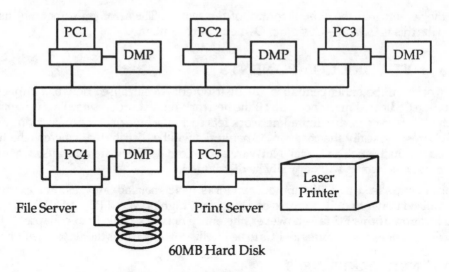

Figure 13.1   A typical LAN configuration

referred to as links or bridges. This might be a PC dedicated to the task of being a gateway or it might be a separate box purchased for the purpose.

13.4   TYPES OF LAN

The way in which the PCs on a LAN are wired together affects the efficiency of the system. There are four main configurations or topologies referred to as:

- Star
- Ring
- Tree
- Bus.

13.4.1   STAR NETWORK

Figure 13.2 shows a typical star network. This LAN will always have a central controller which will be a file server and/or a print server. Any information that is to be passed from one computer in the LAN to another must be routed through the central machine. For this reason a Star topology is excellent for PC intensive applications where only a minimal of host processing is required. The main disadvantage with this type of network is that if the central computer fails then the entire network ceases to function which means that it has a Single Point Of Failure or SPOF. Furthermore, the central computer can become a bottleneck and thus slow processing down to an unacceptable level. Star networks may be joined together to form a Star-burst. This topology has been employed by Arcnet.

13.4.2   RING NETWORK

The PCs in a ring network are wired together in a circle and data may be passed in either direction around the circle. Each PC is recognised in series and information sent from

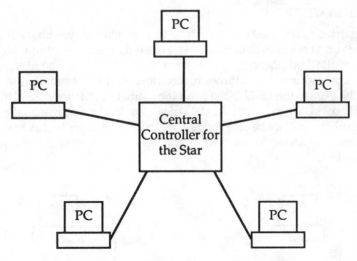

Figure 13.2   The star network topology

one machine to another is passed through the intermediary computers along the circle. For example, in Figure 13.3, if the user of PC1 wanted to send a file to PC3 the data would be dispatched around the ring, first to PC2 which would recognise that the data was not for it, and would retransmit the data to PC3. With this methodology, failure of one PC in the ring would not necessarily mean the complete failure of the system as data can in many cases be redirected around the ring in the other direction, thus avoiding the failed machine. Alternatively the data can sometimes be passed straight along the wire, missing out the failed machine altogether.

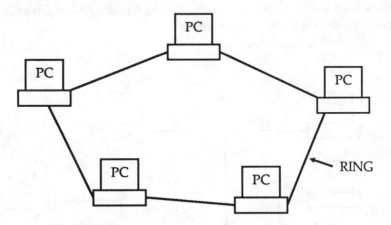

Figure 13.3   The ring network topology

The token ring is the standard adopted by IBM. It works by sending a 'packet' of data around the network ring at a rate of between four and 16 million bits per second. When a workstation wants to send some information it waits for an empty packet to come past, then fills it with data. The advantage is that even under a heavy load, it will perform well. However, for a two station network, it is not as fast as Ethernet.

13.4.3 BUS NETWORK

Generally regarded as the most common implementation today, a bus network configuration depends on a common data 'roadway' referred to as a bus, onto which all the PCs in the LAN are attached. Passage of data on a BUS network can be likened to the way information is passed around a domestic electrical wiring system. Figure 13.4 demonstrates this. The PCs on the LAN listen to all the messages that are passed along the bus, but each one knows only to collect the data meant for it. For this reason if one PC on the LAN fails the others will not be affected and it is therefore described as having no Single Point Of Failure. Bus networks are flexible and easily expandable by addiing additional nodes onto the bus.

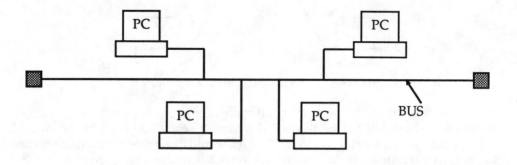

Figure 13.4   The bus network topology

13.4.4   TREE NETWORK

A tree network has a special device which controls the whole LAN, which as can be seen from Figure 13.5 is situated at the root of the tree.

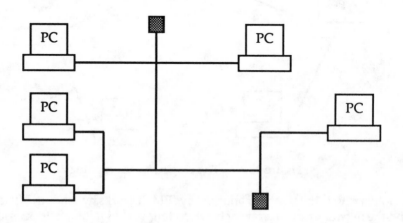

Figure 13.5   The tree network topology

13.5 HARDWARE REQUIREMENTS

All the above terms are ways of describing the technology that is used to send the data. To use any of the methods an add-in driver board is plugged into each computer within the network - including the server - and wired together. Questions often asked are "Why is a board required?" "Why can't the PCs be joined together directly with a cable?" Unfortunately a cable alone is not a stable enough medium for sending large amounts of data across more than a few feet in distance. The digital signal in a PC is only 5V high which leaves itself open to noise and a lack of electrical resistance. In addition it would require a minimum of 12 wires running between each PC. The network add-in boards therefore convert the data into serial form and bundle around it information to ensure it gets to the right place with information as to where it is from and also ensuring that any errors occurring in transmission are corrected. The technology used to convert and send data from the PC along the wire is referred to as low-level protocol. It is called low-level because the software, as opposed to the user controls it.

13.5.1 NETWORK STANDARDS

There are two main standards for network communication referred to as IEEE and ISO/OSI.

- IEEE is an acronym for the Institute of Electrical and Electronic Engineers who formed a special committee called IEEE802 to define guidelines and standards for LAN communications. Because of the definitions laid down by the 802 committee a manufacturer can develop hardware and software that will be able to communicate with another manufacturers products. Networks that have conformed to the IEEE standard include IBMs token ring which is referred to as IEEE802.5 and EtherNet which is IEEE802.3.

- ISO/OSI is an acronym for International Standards Organisation/Open Systems Interconnection and this is based on a seven layer model in which each layer defines a different function in the model. Figure 13.6 shows the definition of the seven layer model.

13.6 POPULAR LOCAL AREA NETWORKS

13.6.1 PC NETWORK (IBM)

This is an attractive LAN option for reasonably small networks of between three and 20 PCs, located within a short range – PCs must not be more than 1000 feet apart. it is easy to install, using coaxial cable and the standard IBM wiring kit. It provides a full LAN service including electronic mail, as well as sharing hard disks, modems and printers.

The following illustrates a typical situation where a LAN such as PC Network would be suitable:

- A 30 person department located on two different floors of a building.

- Each member of staff already has a PC and there are ten printers, two plotters and three modems.

- The applications used in the department feature word processing, accounting and spreadsheets. There is a need, particularly within the word processing and accounting areas, to access the main company database.

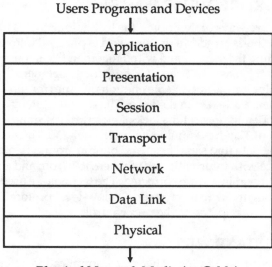

Figure 13.6   The ISO/OSI 7-layer model

The PC Network enables users to access common disk files for both programs and data. This means that when a software package is upgraded, all users will automatically be using the most recent version. The network will enable users to have direct access to the printers, plotters and modems, without having to transfer data from one PC to another. If all the staff in the department were to be supplied with a printer and a modem, installing a network such as this will save 54 devices.

Therefore the benefits to this department include lower costs, faster and easier access to programs and data, as well as good quality printers. In addition, the department has gained the ability to send electronic mail.

In summary, this type of network is appropriate under the following conditions:

–   Small department or business with up to 72 PCs

–   Most computing being PC-based with only occasional terminal access

–   All PCs within 1000 feet of each other

–   Major use of the LAN is resource sharing and electronic mail between users.

13.6.2   TOKEN RING

The term Token Ring is both a generic term for a type of ring network and the name of an IBM network. It is one of the most popular LANs and is particularly useful to companies wishing to connect a large number of PCs together, but also requiring access to mainframe and/or mini computers. The following represents a typical case for a Token Ring LAN:

–   A manufacturing company need a network through which different departments and factories throughout the country, and one branch office in Spain can share information.

- There are currently 320 users and some PCs are in isolated locations on the shop floor - more than 1000 feet from another PC.
- The central mainframe holds data that many users regularly need to access.

A token ring LAN connected with twisted pair wiring would give this company a powerful, well controlled but flexible system. The number of users that can be attached to one ring is a variable figure, depending on how much traffic there is likely to be for what proportion of the time. However, it is generally regarded that having more than about 30 users on any one LAN is unadvisable due to the administration and maintenance that is required to keep the system running. With a Token Ring LAN it is easy to join two or more rings together which in effect removes the barrier as to the number of users that can be installed. In addition to hard wiring, the company will need to use modems to connect users in remote locations. With so many users a number of interconnected rings will be required and it would be possible to isolate one or more rings serving certain parts of the company such as payroll or accounts.

The way in which this type of LAN operates is to constantly pass a 'token' around the ring. When a user wishes to receive or send information they call for the token so that when it is next passing their system they can take control and transmit or receive data. Only one message at a time is passed around the LAN and thus the overall data control is good and the system rarely fails.

This type of network is therefore suitable under the following conditions:

- A large organisation with more than 60-70 users
- PCs spread between different buildings or in excess of 1000 feet apart
- The need to share information between PCs, terminals and mainframes
- Frequent changes in PCs, network configurations or network resources
- Unplanned growth.

13.6.3 ETHERNET

EtherNet LANs are the main competitors to the Token Ring and are also a popular choice in the current market. Traditionally EtherNet LANs have used the BUS topology, but there are now EtherNet rings available from suppliers such as Novell.

The main difference between the EtherNet and Token Ring LANs is that an EtherNet network passes information directly from one PC to another via the bus. This means that the transmission and retrieval time can be much faster than with the Token Ring. However, if information is being transmitted and received by the same PCs at the same time a collision can occur which causes the data to be returned to the originating machine and for it to then be retransmitted. When a collision occurs the system will generate a random number to represent the length of time it will wait until the message is retransmitted. The result is that with a large network carrying a lot of traffic the wait time can be considerable and the LAN can be prone to suffering unacceptable periods of downtime.

Another advantage of EtherNet is its ability to relatively easily link hardware from a number of different manufacturers. Mainframes and mini computers can also be included in the LAN and can act as file servers if required.

13.7 THE COST OF A LAN

As might be expected, you get what you pay for. However, PC networks can be divided into three broad categories:

13.7.1 LOW-COST NETWORKS

This would imply a cost of below £150 per user and the network would be expected to offer basic facilities such as electronic mail, password protection and resource sharing. There would not normally be a central server, it being a distributed network. Cabling will normally be twisted pair and not particularly fast. A maximum of between eight and 64 can be linked - but response time for more than eight would probably be unacceptably slow.

13.7.2 MEDIUM-PRICED NETWORKS

Requiring a central server, this category would normally be limited-user versions of big networks, offering between eight and ten users, but offering all the benefits of a system based on Ethernet or Token Ring. A 286 or 386 would be required for the server in order to produce a decent response time. The server need not be dedicated which means it can function as a workstation as well as provide server tasks. Facilities should include good security, password protection and audit trails, as well as the usual electronic mail, printer and resource sharing facilities.

13.7.3 HIGH-END NETWORKS

A minimum of a fast 386 machine is required as a dedicated server with a fast hard disk. The software will probably cost in the region of £3000 to £4000, but such a set up will support up to 255 users without considerable loss of performance. Several networks may be connected together in order to expand the system or increase computing power. There should be facilities for disk mirroring which means two hard disks do the same thing in case one breaks down. Some form of fault tolerance should be included to ensure the easy recovery of damaged files.

13.8 INSTALLING AND USING A LAN

Having decided to implement a LAN and selected the appropriate topology and supplier it is then necessary to prepare the site location and users in advance.

13.8.1 WIRING

The method used to transmit data around a network can be either baseband or broadband.

- Baseband generally assumes that only a single channel is available for signal transmission. Furthermore the signal will be simplex or half duplex. This means that only one signal may be passed down the line at one time. In the case of simplex the signal is unidirectional whereas half duplex allows signals to go in both directions, but not at the same time. This form of transmission is cheap and easy to install. It is often used in conjunction with twisted pair cabling.

- Broadband can have multiple channels and allows any form of transmission protocol, namely simplex, half duplex or full duplex. This means that several signals can be simultaneously sent along the cable in either direction without conflicting. The advantage to the user is that the system will be high capacity and will allow for more flexible configurations. In the network environment, broadband usually implies the use of coaxial cable, or in some cases fibre optic.

The three main types of cabling used in PC networks are:

– Coaxial cable

– Twisted pair

– Fibre optics.

Coaxial cable is the type of wire used for television aerials. It is circular with a central core of copper. This is a solid wire which is able to pass a single signal. The copper wire is surrounded first in a plastic insulator and then covered in braided wire which passes the earth signal and works as a screen. A PVC covering provides the outer sheath. Coaxial cable is particularly good for sending high frequency signals over long distances. It is, however relatively expensive, retailing in the UK at between 17-30p per metre. Ethernet cable is usually coaxial

Twisted pair is, as its name suggests, two or more wires twisted together and held in a PVC sheath. The number of wires in the cable can vary, but one will normally carry the earth signal and each of the others can carry a single signal. As this cable is generally not protected with the braiding found on coaxial cable it is subject to electronic interference or 'noise' which can effect the transmission of data. It is however a cheap option, retailing in the UK at between 6-20p per metre and is widely used in the LAN environment, particularly where distances between PCs is relatively short.

The fastest, but most expensive wiring option is fibre optics. A fibre optic cable is capable of sending a large number of signals down a single glass fibre light guide by utilising a large number of different frequencies. Because the data is sent in the form of light as opposed to electricity there can be no electronic noise from external devices, and thus this is a very fast and reliable form of wiring. Primarily due to its cost it is not yet widely used in the LAN environment and retails in the UK for around 58p per metre.

The supplier of a LAN will normally advise on the type of wiring that should be used and it is advisable to install the wires around the building prior to the PCs being installed or joined to the LAN.

It is important not to underestimate the costs involved in installing the cabling. Even for a moderate network with eight users the installation of cabling can cost several hundred pounds.

13.8.2 SOFTWARE

Network software can be divided into two parts. One part controls activities such as passwords, printers, file transfers, mail etc., and is referred to as the network operating system. The second part is a small driver program which provides a standard look to the differing hardware cards. It differs with each setup, but not for the operating system or hardware. This driver program takes two forms. The fastest and most efficient is a driver that has been specially written and is provided with the operating system for the particular variety of hardware card installed. It will only work with the assigned card. The second method is to use a standard driver called NetBIOS. This is supplied by the hardware manufacturer and provides a standard programming interface. The operating system deals with the hardware via the NetBIOS layer. Although standard, this method is slower. Almost all hardware cards and network operating systems support NetBIOS which means in theory anything can run with anything else.

Most general purpose applications, such as word processors, spreadsheets and databases, can run on a range of networks because they use the NetBIOS interface to talk to the network. The basic PC hardware should also be able to support NetBIOS.

Before the network will operate successfully it is necessary to correctly configure both the systems and the application software. This involves installing each workstations software, setting up the user accounts and setting up the drive mappings.

The workstation software is resident on the individual PCs all the time and takes care of tasks such as translating screen commands from a wordprocessor, searching a remote disk drive etc.

User accounts consist of a record with information about when the user was last connected to the network, their rights to look at various files, which printer can be used etc. Each user will have a user name and password and with the aid of an audit trail it is possible to see who has been doing what, when and for how long.

A very important task is drive mapping which involves specifying the total number of accessible disk drives. Typically this is achieved through the use of the LASTDRIVE command which is inserted into the CONFIG.SYS file. If, for example LASTDRIVE has been set to K it would mean that a user would be able to directly access another users drive. Problems can occur with some systems which restrict the LASTDRIVE command to within the confines of a particular PC as opposed to across the network.

Figure 13.7 shows the breakdown of memory usage for a PC connected to an EtherNet LAN running an application program.

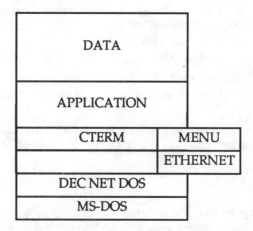

Figure 13.7   Memory usage for a PC on an Ethernet LAN

13.8.3   THE USERS

If a LAN is installed into a situation whereby the users are already established personal computer users, then attaching their PCs to a LAN should be done in as transparent a way as possible. Accessing programs or data from a file server should appear to be no different to accessing information from a standalone system. Indeed it is perfectly possible to install almost any applications software on a file server and for any one user to be able to access that software and run it. A problem only arises if two users wish to run the same package and use the same data file at the same time. It is for this reason the special network versions of software are required. These versions include file locking procedures which involves only allowing one person to open and change a file. If a second user wishes to open the same file they will normally be warned that it is already open and that it may be read by the second user, but may not be changed. In the case of some database applications this can be very limiting and thus a method of record locking as opposed to file locking may be employed. This will allow the same file to be opened and changed by multiple users, but the same record may not be changed at the same time by more than one person.

If the LAN is to be the introduction to personal computing for those who will use it, then the learning curve should be the same as for using a standalone system. One of the greatest benefits in this area is the fact that if a decision is made to draw all applications from a file server on the network, everyone on the LAN will be using the same version of the same software package.

13.8.4 SECURITY

Because the key aspect of computing through a LAN is sharing, the issue of security is a most important one. Users will normally be supplied with a user name and a password that must be entered every time the network is accessed. In addition the network manager will be able to link a user's identity to all or some of the programs and data on the LAN, thus controlling what a particular user is able to use. In addition the ability to update or change files on the LAN can be restricted.

13.9 POSSIBLE LAN INSTALLATION PROBLEMS

The technology surrounding LANs is still unfamiliar to the majority of users. Therefore it is often found that many more problems occur during the installation of a LAN than with any other system. The following outlines some of the more common problems together with suggested remedies.

13.9.1 HIGH SPEED PROBLEMS

Some network designers do not plan for their product to be used in PCs with high clock speeds. For example, some network software will not work on fast machines such as the 80486 based 50MHz PCs as they lose internal synchronisation. There are also some network cards with ROM chips that will not work for the same reason.

This can be a particular problem when considering which PC should be used as a server, as it is normally desirable to have as fast a machine as is available. It is not possible to overcome this problem once the card has been purchased, so it is essential to obtain written guarantees of compatibility when there is a possibility of high-speed machines being used.

13.9.2 IRQ CONFLICTS

IRQ is the technical terminology for an interrupt request. These are special signal lines on the motherboard of the PC that allow add-in cards, peripherals and other devices to communicate with the CPU. However there are only a limited number of IRQ lines in a standard PC, most of which are used by devices in the standard system such as serial ports, hard disk controllers etc. Any additional hardware that is added will also require the use of at least one IRQ line. If there are none available then the device cannot be used without first removing an existing card to free an IRQ line. AT machines have more IRQ lines than standard PCs, although most hardware is not designed to make full use of them. It is therefore necessary to buy a more expensive adapter card to gain the benefit of the additional IRQs.

Note that micro-channel architecture machines such as the higher end IBM PS/2s do not suffer from this problem as they use a totally different system.

13.9.3 MEMORY ADDRESS CONFLICTS

All add-in devices, including network adapters, require memory locations to transfer data to the CPU. Before the advent of advanced video displays there was sufficient free space in the memory of the system to allow this to take place with ease. However, new VGA adapters etc sometimes claim these areas of free space for their own use, meaning that they are no longer available for the network adapter to use. To remedy this situation, it may be possible to change the addresses used by the network adapter. This information can be obtained from the manufacturer of the card. An alternative solution is to use PCs with less advanced displays, as this will liberate more memory.

13.9.4 CABLE TERMINATORS

Network cables used in most station-to-station wiring schemes are almost always terminated with a resistor. This helps to stop electronic echoes from travelling back along the cable, thus reducing interference problems. The problem is that different LANs use different termination schemes.

Sometimes the last adapter card automatically terminates the cable, whilst in other cases it is necessary to install a small carbon resistor between two screws on the appropriate network card. Other systems require the use of a special plug which has a resistor built in to it.

It is always wise to assume that a terminator is required at each end of the wiring system. The exact details of how it works, what it is and how it is installed can be obtained from the manufacturer, if these terminators are not used then the problems can be very difficult to diagnose as they will almost certainly be very intermittent.

13.9.5 CONFIG.SYS PROBLEMS

Network software is often very sensitive to the way in which the system is configured. These choices are made by the CONFIG.SYS file, a special file required by DOS to indicate how it should allocate memory and which devices it should expect to find connected. Some software packages automatically create or modify CONFIG.SYS when they are installed. If this happens, then it may cause the network to stop working properly. Therefore if the network ceases to function properly after installing a new software package, the first thing to check is the CONFIG.SYS file.

Network software is not copy protected in the normal sense of the phrase, as it can be copied any number of times, and all copies will work normally. However, several companies have introduced schemes to prevent the license being abused. These schemes work by checking to see lf two nodes on the network have the same serial number. If so, then the product will not work, often producing a cryptic error code or message.

In normal use this situation will not occur. However, if network files are accidentally transferred along with other data, then problems may become obvious. An example of a system using this method is TOPS.

There is no way to remedy this problem other than by deleting the offending files. It is far better to prevent this problem rather than trying to cure it once it occurs, and the best way to do this is to educate users into organising their work hierarchically, so that when copying data there is no possibility of copying the network files at the same time.

13.10 LAN DIAGNOSTICS AND MAINTENANCE

The issues of network maintenance and diagnostics are usually thought to be low on the list of priorities where small networks are concerned. However, without appropriate maintenance and diagnostics, network performance may quickly degrade, leading to slower response time for users, possible errors in data transmission, minimal cost effectiveness, and in some extreme cases, total network failure.

Maintenance does not only involve fixing things when they go wrong; it also concerns issues such as network downtime, loadings, performance and cost effectiveness. Diagnostics provide the tools for monitoring the network, to ensure that it is maintained to a suitable standard.

So it can be seen that far from being sundry issues, maintenance and diagnostics are essential for the continued reliable service that the company expects from the network.

13.11 DIAGNOSTICS

There are several distinct levels of diagnostics, from simple on-chip test routines that are executed automatically on start-up, through to sophisticated software packages that test every element of the network. On small networks with two or three PCs sharing a disk and a printer, it may complicate matters to have more than the most basic diagnostic procedures. Any problems that occur will usually be noticeable almost immediately. However as the network grows, so does the need for monitoring it and diagnosing the problems. Thus diagnostics are a mandatory part of all large networks.

As mentioned above, there are several distinct levels of diagnostics. These may be categorised into three classes:

- Hardware level
- User level
- Network level.

13.11.1 HARDWARE LEVEL

Most networks usually have low-level, self-test routines that are executed automatically when the network is powered up. These almost always cover the network interface card, and in many cases also check the cable and hardware configuration. This is the most basic of testing, and effectively acts as an extension of the host PCs POST. Failures that are diagnosed at this level are hardware originated, including such things as:

- Component failure in main PC

- Component failure on interface card
- Interface card not connected into the network
- One or more cables broken or disconnected between host PC and rest of network.

If a new workstation or server is added to the network, then the diagnostics will often report any configuration problems that are present. These may include:

- Incorrect positioning of one or more jumpers on interface card
- Conflict between interface card and other subsystems trying to use the same interrupt or memory location.

More advanced diagnostics may perform *loop-backs*. This involves electrically isolating the network interface card from the rest of the network, and then sending a test signal which is "looped back" to the same card. This allows the card to verify that a valid signal is being sent and received. Other self tests may be used to verify that different devices can communicate, by sending pre-determined test patterns over the network. This low-level testing of the network takes place very quickly, and allows the network configuration to be established before any actual data traffic begins to flow.

Any errors that are discovered by these self-tests are normally reported on the monitor, in the form of a simple message or code number. The user is then expected to contact the support centre or system vendor and repeat the message. They will then be told which component is malfunctioning, or will be guided through more advanced diagnostics by an experienced technician.

13.11.2   USER LEVEL

The hardware level diagnostics will usually determine whether there are any fundamental problems with the network that will prevent it from operating. Assuming that no errors are reported, the workstation will continue to work normally, allowing all network operations to be carried on.

Many networks will now allow further diagnostic tests to be performed by running appropriate software. In the majority of cases, detailed tests are available only to the network manager, as most users have no need to know this information. However, there will almost certainly be some form of further diagnostics available to everyone. This may take the form of a more comprehensive loop-back procedure, or a more sophisticated test routine for use between two nodes. There may be additional facilities to provide information on the current status of the network, including the number of nodes currently operational, the current loading and the volume of traffic.

One of the most important points to remember when considering any of these user-level diagnostics is the format in which the results will be produced. If the utilities produce reams and reams of data then they will hardly ever be used as they will appear to be more trouble than they are worth. On the other hand, if they do not provide a useful and informative diagnosis of the data, then the same problems will arise as users will believe that there is no benefit to be derived by running them. Thus user diagnostics should be chosen with great care, with due thought given to the above problems.

13.11.3   NETWORK LEVEL

Network level diagnostics are the most in-depth of all. There are a great variety of diagnostics available that fall into this category, both from network vendors, and third-party companies. These provide much of the necessary monitoring information that is not provided by the system itself, allowing the network to be properly maintained.

The information provided by these diagnostics needs to go into greater detail than any of the previous categories. Generally, the information falls into three groups:

- Status
- Utilisation
- Performance data.

13.11.3.1   Status information

Status information summarises the operation of the network. These parameters are collected over time and show how the network has performed historically. Three of the major parameters are error rates, time-outs and connection quality:

- The error rate is the number of transmission failures or corrupted data packet receptions that have occurred in the course of a particular operation.

- A time-out is when an expected event does not occur within the expected time. This is an important measurement, often indicating when a configuration is only marginally coping with a particular load, or that the hardware is failing.

- By testing the quality of the connection between two nodes, it is possible to determine whether poor performance is due to heavy traffic, or whether the number of retries due to faulty connections is wasting time and bandwidth. The connection quality is obviously related to the error rate, but it is a particularly vital measure of performance, and should always be seen as a unique network measurement.

13.11.3.2   Utilisation

Utilisation measures the peak loading of the network and the level of services that can be delivered. The peak loading does not refer to a one time maximum loading that occurs, but rather the regular periods of highest activity. These may occur on a multiple-hour cycle, a daily or weekly cycle, or even a monthly or yearly basis. The utilisation measurement can be used to ascertain whether a redistribution of existing resources will satisfy an expansion need, or whether it is necessary to invest in additional hardware. The two most important areas of measurement are as follows:

- *Configuration efficiency*; poor performance is often caused by an inadequately configured system. One of the most common problems arises when insufficient RAM is allocated for disk caching - this will often lead to disk thrashing and poor response times.

- *Equipment availability*; the ratio of the amount of time that any particular device is operational to the amount of time that it is out of service is known as its duty cycle. A low duty cycle indicates that the unit is not providing a dependable service. The availability records will show where the problem lies.

13.11.3.3   Performance data

The performance data measures the systems capability to perform its functions. Raw performance data is often massive and unintelligible, therefore the measurements are summarisations of the raw data. Even so, the presentation of the measurements is crucial to revealing the underlying information.

Some networks support centralised or distributed statistics gathering. This may be designed into the network, or may be available as an add-on product from a third-party. In general, the more open the architecture of the network, the more advanced will be the level of diagnostics available for it. In many cases the network vendors are unable to meet the entire range of user needs. In such cases, third party diagnostics are invaluable in assisting the construction of sophisticated networks.

There are many different measures of performance, a selection of which may be used in any one diagnostic program. The following three are considered to be among the most important:

–   The response time of the system is perhaps the most critical issue. This is often the only effect of the network that is directly felt by the user, and as such tends to be the measure by which the success of the network is calculated. The important measurement is not the average response time, but rather the worst-case response.

–   Traffic volumes reveal how data is flowing around the network. Monitoring traffic volumes can produce surprising results; for instance, a word processing program may be considered to be a low-volume traffic generator. However, if it is used for a variety of applications from letters and memos to electronic mail, then the loading will be quite considerable. Traffic monitoring enables these factors to be observed and measured.

   One common method of traffic monitoring is transaction counting. A transaction may be defined in several different ways, but common events that are used are I/O requests and disk accesses. Many networks provide a primitive method of traffic monitoring by displaying the number of transactions per second. More advanced diagnostics allow this information to be recorded and compiled for later analysis.

–   An audit trail records who used the network, how long it was in use and what files were accessed. This information can then be used to supply data for billing etc, or for network security. Audit trails may be implemented in the network operating system, in the existing hardware, in a dedicated device attached to the network or in the applications software.

   One of the most secure ways of keeping an audit trail is through the use of a WORM (Write Once Read Many times) drive, as it can only be written once. This has the additional advantage that if the network hard disk fails, the audit trail can be used in conjunction with a backup of the firm's data to recreate the lost information, by adding one transaction at a time to the original data.

13.11.4   THE IMPORTANCE OF INFORMATION

From a day-to-day point of view, the most important of the diagnostics services is the supply of status information. This allows the network manager to determine who is using the resources and to what extent, as well as many other important factors regarding network utilisation.

For example, a typical status report from a disk server should include a list of files currently being accessed, the location of the user of each file, and whether each file is locked or available to others. Other useful information that may be provided in status reports from other devices such as workstations includes each user's current error status, their charge information and their input/output rate.

The last parameter, I/O rate, is particularly useful as it allows the loading characteristics of users and their software requirements to be measured. The rate may also indicate attempted security violations; a common method of cracking network security is to log on under a known ID, and then randomly try passwords. This is made easier by the fact that lists are published containing the 1000 most often used passwords. The status report can be monitored to prevent a user from attempting to log on more than a certain number of times. If this number is exceeded then the user name is denied access until reset by the system manager.

Status information should also be available to the manager about any queueing systems that may be supported, such as queueing for files or printer access. The manager should be able to alter the order of entries in the queue as well as checking the data.

In some networks a status list is kept with up-to-date information about the status of every device that is logged on. If a device fails or goes off-line, this fact is noted in the list. Every device on the network should have immediate access to this list, or alternatively the network operating system should have an alert generator which automatically notifies the network manager, and perhaps one or more other users, when a fault occurs. A typical situation of when an alert may be used in preference to a status list is in the case of a printer that has gone off-line or run out of paper. The alert would be sent to all users of the appropriate printer, telling them not to send any data to the device.

There will be some situations where a failure will go unnoticed. If a network node never transmits, then its failure will only become apparent when it does not respond to a message. Some diagnostics cause regular messages to be sent to every node on the network, telling them to respond. This will automatically detect any failed node, but will impose an additional load on the network. In many cases these *are you awake ?* messages are an unnecessary burden, although for certain devices they are essential (eg print server, modem server etc.).

Future planning of the network is also simplified by having appropriate status information to hand. For example, a network may have a total of 200 devices connected, although it is only estimated that 20 will be in use at any one time. Periodically the status information should be examined, to see if it shows that this number is being exceeded. If so, then another server or a different cabling system may be necessary to cope with the additional load.

13.11.5 USING THIRD-PARTY DIAGNOSTICS

If the network vendor does not offer suitable diagnostics of their own, then it is likely that a third-party supplier will be able to provide a solution. There are many companies specialising in providing add-ons for networks. The products range from simple inexpensive software utilities to sophisticated hardware devices costing more than many entire networks.

There are two basic approaches: hardware and software.

The hardware approach relies on adding electronic systems that capture network data as it flows and analyse its structure and content. Hardware systems are usually sophisticated and expensive, and often require highly trained personnel to interpret the results. However, they are excellent tools for identifying and remedying obscure or complex problems.

The software approach requires the network hardware to already have the appropriate interfaces available. The diagnostics software intercepts transmissions and receptions and analyses the data for error conditions, quality and performance parameters. The analysed data may then typically be displayed using proprietary software such as a spreadsheet or database.

The hardware approach is typically 10 times more expensive than the software method, but does allow the fine detail of the network traffic to be observed and analysed. However the software approach allows the data to be produced in a more presentable form, providing interfaces to many common software packages.

Two examples of diagnostics systems will be examined to show the facilities offered. The first of these is the built in diagnostics monitor that is supplied with Novell NetWare. The second example looks at the 82586 integrated circuit, a third-party device that is designed to work with CSMA-CD networks such as EtherNet.

13.11.5.1   NetWare

The diagnostics system is invoked by entering the command *MONITOR* on any file server. A file server will typically be an 80286 or 80386 based computer with a keyboard and display.

This causes the display to show a grid of six cells, each indicating a single workstation on the network. If there are more than six workstations on the network then the screen can be scrolled to show additional cells. In the top left of each cell is shown the station number, and the names of the last five files opened by the workstation are shown in the main area of the cell, together with the type of access.

The monitor also displays the percentage of server utilisation. This value is updated every second, and shows the percentage of the file-server processor time that was taken up by network requests during the previous second. It is easy to ascertain whether the file server is becoming overloaded by looking at this figure, for example a utilisation figure of 70–80 percent indicates that the server may well be causing a bottleneck, and that significant performance improvements may be made by adding a more powerful machine or a second server.

NetWare uses a technique known as cache buffering to improve the efficiency of the network. This works as follows.

Disk read requests are for one or more specific sectors. If there are several sectors, they are often sequential. When the system receives a request to read a particular sector, it guesses that another request will be received to read the next one or more sectors and so reads several into memory although it only transmits the requested one immediately. The other sectors are held in an area of RAM known as the cache buffer. If the expected requests come in later, the sectors held in memory can be delivered much more quickly than if they had to be read from disk.

When a write request occurs the data is written into a new sector in the cache buffer, where it is held until the system has time to write it to disk. If the sector to be written is already in the buffer, then the system uses the existing copy, thus ensuring that only one version of each sector exists in the buffer at any one time.

These techniques mean that the system does not have to spend an excessive amount of time reading and writing disk information. However the pitfall of this method is that there will usually be some data held in memory that has not been written to disk. Therefore if the network is shut down the data will be lost. It is therefore necessary to ensure that all buffered data is written to disk using specific network commands before the network is closed down.

Information concerning the above caching techniques is summarised on the monitor display in the form of the number of disk I/O requests pending. This value indicates the number of cache buffers that have been changed in the servers memory without having been written to disk. This figure is a good measure of the amount of work that the server is doing.

13.11.5.2 The 82586 Chip

Recent developments in network technology have lead to efficient diagnostic co-processors becoming available for network hardware. A typical example of this is the Intel 82586 chip. This device is designed to work with contention networks (Carrier Sense Multiple Access with Collision Detection or CSMA-CD), such as Ethernet. The chip has built in diagnostics and management functions, and sends status information on every message handled to the CPU. The chip also counts the number of collisions and message errors, which is a good indicator of the overall condition of the network.

Systematic diagnostics can be implemented for individual workstations, or for the network as a whole. The chip can be put into loop-back mode to determine whether a problem lies within a workstation or whether it is external. The chip also has the capability for isolating problems between PCs.

Breaks or shorts in the network cabling can be diagnosed by the device. Additionally the chip can estimate the distance of the short from the workstation using a technique known as *time domain reflectometry (TDR)*. A diagnose command in the chip allows a self-test routine to be performed to check the main CPU.

The network software is supplied with routing information regarding the network's health. This includes details about how many collisions are experienced before the message gets through, and how many packets are received with errors. Statistics are recorded for individual packets, and the chip keeps three or four key parameters in memory, in whole representing the condition of the network.

13.12 THE NETWORK MANAGER

The network manager or administrator is a person assigned to be responsible for the day-to-day running of the system, ensuring that new workstations are configured correctly, applications software is kept up-to-date, files are backed up and other administrative duties are performed. The network manager is also the connection between the diagnostics procedures and the maintenance that is required.

In many cases, the network manager need not be a trained technician or programmer, rather it is more important that they have a good knowledge of the network, the operating system, the utilities, and in particular, the way in which it is used in the firm. Thus the network manager should be able to interpret the data supplied by the diagnostics to determine where in the system a problem lies, whether it is in software (eg the operating system) or hardware.

The manager forms an integral part of the diagnostics, and should be able to quickly note slower response times, increased error rates or other problem indicators. If the diagnostics for a system are not particularly sophisticated, then it will be necessary for the manager to play a greater role in diagnosis, requiring an intuitive understanding of the operation of the network.

The manager is also responsible for the periodic monitoring of the network. This will involve collating the various performance and utilisation figures discussed previously, and then using this data to determine how well the network is functioning. Records should be kept by hour, day and month of the more important figures which will indicate peak loading times. If the network is seen to be overloaded, then it may well be possible for the network manager to shift some of the work load rather than simply investing in new hardware.

Planning for network growth is another important duty for the manager. Performance measurements indicate how efficiently the network is working. If the performance is beginning to fall off, then it will be possible to see this from the recorded data. Thus the network manager will be able to anticipate the need for further expansion and make arrangement for appropriate hardware and software to be modified or added before the problems are felt by the other users of the network.

13.13 MAINTENANCE

The aim of maintenance is to ensure that the system is operated on a reliable, cost-effective basis, and that performance meets the required specifications. However, in many organisations maintenance is only considered as an afterthought, on the basis that it is not cost-effective. If there is a major system failure leading to the loss of valuable data, then the true value of maintenance becomes obvious. The cost of downtime for the network may be several times more than appropriate preventative measures, and there will certainly be a great amount of upheaval.

Once it is possible to quantify the cost of network failure, or even the cost of a degradation in performance, then there is a basis on which the costs of prevention and cure can be judged.

The maintenance services available for networks fall broadly into two categories; *support*, including network systems support and applications support, and *repair*, including on and off-site repair services and preventative maintenance.

13.13.1 SUPPORT SERVICES

Support services are available from many different sources. The original network vendor is usually considered to supply the best support services, but products from third-party manufacturers should also be investigated.

Products are often classed as integrating or non-integrating. An integrating product either creates a system or enables one to operate fully, a non-integrating product is just a component of a system. It is as well to remember this differentiation, as the warranties supplied with devices are often dependent upon this factor. For example, some manufacturers disclaim responsibility for providing support for non-integrating products, as there is no guarantee that they will be used in an environment that the supplier is familiar with. Integrating products, on the other hand, tend to create their own environments, and as long as the other components of the system are of approved types then support will usually be available.

In practice, it is essential to determine compatibility before installing any new devices. This information can be obtained from the manufacturers. It is also wise to confirm that the supplier will offer technical backup if the device is used in the chosen environment, as many manufacturers offer no free support service.

If it becomes necessary to pay for support advice, then there are many firms specialising in problem solving and general maintenance advice. Before embarking on a contract with the chosen consultant, contact should be made with some of their existing clients to determine the quality and reliability of their service. Once support has been arranged, notes should be kept of all contacts made with the service organisation and work carried out, so that references are available in case of dispute.

The staff responsible for contacting the support service should follow a set procedure if problems occur. This includes noting all symptoms that are displayed, likely causes (recently moved workstation, rerouted cable etc) and what was happening when the fault appeared. This will speed up the process of fault location, and builds a more professional relationship with the support organisation. All problems should be documented fully, including all symptoms etc. as reported to the support personnel, as well as the actions taken and the degree of success that they achieved. If the problem occurs in the future, a large portion of the fault diagnosis procedure has already been accomplished, meaning that repairs can be started as soon as possible.

Applications support is as important as network systems support. Many software developers only warrant their product under a certain operating system, such as PC-DOS or MS-DOS, and not under a network system. Thus it is important to find out whether the required package is compatible with the network before purchasing and installing. Unfortunately few third-party companies offer more than basic support for applications, so the services offered by the software developer and supplier may have to suffice.

13.13.2 REPAIR SERVICES

Repair services are often offered in conjunction with support services by the vendor or the support consultants. This may take the form of a joint venture by the vendor or consultants with a hardware orientated service company.

Repairs may be conducted either on or off-site. Off-site repairs can be cost-effective if the downtime for the equipment is not critical. However, turnaround time for off-site repairs can be lengthy, as much as weeks or even months in some extreme cases. On-site repairs are obviously much quicker but they do involve considerably greater costs, as there is not only the cost of the work, but often a standard call-out charge as well.

Repair costs can be controlled by contracting an organisation on a fixed-fee basis. This means that a set fee will be payable on a regular basis regardless of the amount of work required. Obviously if there are few repairs required then this will be an expensive method. However, the advantage is that there will not be an unexpected bill for an excessive amount if, for example, 30 PCs fail in a week.

Preventative maintenance is usually only applicable to mechanical devices such as printers and plotters etc. Some companies run routine tests on other components, such as cabling, floppy disks etc, as well as carrying out visual inspections on the network. This is of benefit mainly to large networks, as they are normally sufficiently complex to ensure that something is going wrong somewhere on a regular basis.

13.13.3 THE VALUE OF MAINTENANCE

Maintenance is an essential part of the operation of any network. the lack of a suitable maintenance plan is often found to be the cause of avoidable, and perhaps costly, problems. It is important to consider the cost of each form of maintenance, and evaluate the benefits to be gained. The high-integrity systems that comprise modern networks rely not only on good design and construction, but also on good servicing.

13.14 SUMMARY

LANs seem set to become a part of everyday office life, offering benefits in terms of increased information flow, increased productivity and efficiency, and reduced costs. However, the implementation of a LAN is not a trivial matter, and it is important to approach the project with caution. Incorrect choices of hardware or software can lead to costly changes in the long run.

Before making the decision whether or not to install a LAN it is important to bear in mind the overheads in terms of workstation memory, the general degradation in performance that almost invariably occurs until the network is optimised, and not least of all, the cost of the network. Despite these factors, the benefits of networking can be substantial.

When implementing the chosen system, it is essential to plan thoroughly, and obtain as much information as possible from manufacturers. Only in this way will it be possible to minimise the problems that will almost certainly occur.

Finally, it will be necessary to monitor network performance, add new workstations and possibly upgrade certain components. These issues are realyy a part of the larger topic of LAN maintenance and diagnostics. Maintenance and diagnostics are often overlooked during system planning and implementation. However, far from being unnecessary complications to the network, they are essential to its continued operations, improving the day-to-day reliability, performance and cost-effectiveness of the system.

14 The Computer Virus

14.1 WHAT IS A COMPUTER VIRUS?

A computer virus may be defined as a piece of software which infects programs, data or disks and has the ability to reproduce itself in the same or in some other form. It is therefore a program and not a strain of biological bacteria.

The origin of the computer virus is said to have been the result of an experiment conducted by Dr Fred Cohen. He presented the virus as a computer security threat at a conference in November 1983. He suggested that for a virus to exist and become infectious it needs three basic properties.

14.1.1 A PERSON TO DESIGN AND CODE IT

A virus cannot create itself and must be originated by a computer programmer. Programmers of viruses have become known as *virus perpetrators* or *data invaders*.

14.1.2 A SUITABLE ENVIRONMENT TO REPRODUCE AND SPREAD

The portability of data on personal computers has provided the ideal conditions for hosting and breeding viruses

14.1.3 AN OPPORTUNITY OF WHICH IT CAN TAKE ADVANTAGE

A virus must be given the opportunity to run in order to reproduce and thus propagate. It must be able to spread in order to grow. It is for this reason that virus infections often come from tempting free software or from appealing games and other pirated packages.

The main characteristics of a virus can be seen as follows:

- They are hidden so as to avoid detection and destruction, often sitting in a computer in a benign state for some time.

- They are self-replicating so as to ensure the continued and contagious infection of computer resources.

- They interfere with normal computer operations in a number of different ways, including deleting files, corrupting screen displays, corrupting data, slowing down the operation of a system, displaying messages and creating errors.

It has recently been suggested that the computer virus may be considered as a living entity, as it fulfils the four primary requirements of life, namely:

- It can reproduce itself

219

- It can move around within its environment
- It can affect and change its environment
- Separate virus programs will often group to form a population.

An additional requirement which is sometimes stated is that the lifeform should be able to mutate, to alter itself to take advantage of changing circumstances. At present, this condition does not appear to have been met by the computer virus, although some mutated viruses have been produced by programmers. However, it is generally agreed that this phase is not far off.

A virus operates at two levels. First, it must have some way of replicating and secondly, it may contain code to perform damaging or annoying routines. For example, the Italian or Ping-Pong virus replicates by copying itself to the boot sector of any write-enabled diskette that is used in an infected machine. Every half hour, the virus routine triggers and causes a ball to bounce around the screen, sometimes messing up the display. Viruses are sometimes detected because repetitive infection over a period of time will reduce system performance, or because the virus routine triggers and the effects are noticed by the user.

14.2   TYPES OF VIRUS

Over the last couple of years since the subject of computer virus became of popular interest they have been divided into two main categories; parasitic viruses and boot sector viruses.

14.2.1   THE PARASITIC VIRUS

A parasitic virus is carried by an executable application program and is copied into other applications as they are run. The virus code attaches itself to the application's program code so that it is activated every time the program is loaded. A parasitic virus can be resident or non-resident. A resident virus makes itself memory resident and then infects other program files. When the infected application is exited, the virus remains in memory to continue replicating. A non-resident parasitic virus will infect programs in much the same way, however, it will not remain in memory when the infected application is exited.

14.2.2   THE BOOT SECTOR VIRUS

A boot sector virus is quite different in that it modifies the boot sector of a hard disk and in effect become part of the computer's operating system. It is spread when a program or data file is copied from an infected hard disk to a floppy or to another hard disk. The most common methodology here is to copy boot sector 0 of a hard disk to an unused sector on the disk and then to overwrite boot sector 0 with the virus code. Whenever the disk is subsequently booted the virus code will be executed and loaded into memory. The virus code will then load the original boot sector from its new position on the disk and passes control to it, thus hiding the presence of a virus from the user.

14.2.3   DESIGN ELEMENTS OF A VIRUS

There are a number of design elements that can go into the creation of a virus and some of the more common terms applied to such elements are described below. Both parasitic and boot sector viruses can make use of these techniques.

14.2.3.1 Trojan horse

The term Trojan Horse describes a program which pretends to be something harmless, and indeed often useful, such as a shareware utility, a program compiler, password checker etc, but which contains a hidden and harmful function. A Trojan Horse can only be transferred to another machine if the actual programs it is on is copied to another system, but it cannot actually reproduce itself. A Trojan Horse is therefore not strictly a virus, but in fact most viruses use Trojan Horses as the primary carrier.

14.2.3.2 Logic bomb

This is code within a program that is triggered by certain events. A program containing a logic bomb will appear to be completely normal until a set of conditions is met, at which point it will start to cause damage. Situations that may trigger the logic bomb include:

- disk usage exceeding a limit, such as 75 percent full
- number of users on a network exceeding a limit
- taking a certain path through the use of an application.

14.2.3.3 Time bomb

This is actually a type of logic bomb which is triggered by time. It is code within a program that checks the date and time and when certain criteria are met performs unexpected and often damaging functions. For example Friday 13th and April Fools Day are suspected targets for time bomb programs. A time bomb can also be linked to a logic bomb to give greater sophistication.

14.2.3.4 Trap door

This is a legitimate term used to describe the ability to get into the code of a computer operating system or application program. Typically a trap door will be built into software to help developers get into the code without having to go through tedious access controls each time. Such a trap door would, of course, not be included in the software's design specifications and consequently may be forgotten. The result is that commercial software could be inadvertently released with the trap door still present, or it could be left in deliberately by a potential data invader who will attack at a later date.

14.2.3.5 Worm

A worm is a single entity that burrows through a computer or computer network, but does not continually replicate to produce a mass of infected programs. The term should not be confused with the new type of storage media referred to as WORM, meaning Write Once Read Many times. For most practical purposes the effects of a Worm and a virus are much the same in that they do damage. However a virus replicates and typically causes damage quickly whereas a worm slowly eats its way through the system.

14.3 METHODS OF INFECTION

In the personal computer environment the most common, if somewhat crude, way a virus shows itself is by deleting the contents of the hard disk, usually after infecting the users floppy disks so as to ensure the spread of the infection.

A more subtle approach is to selectively alter data and this has been widely reported in the banking industry in particular. An example of such a program, which is sometimes referred to as a virus, but which is really just a defrauding technique, is the Salami Technique which slices off cents from an account and adds them to the account of the perpetrator; or the French Round-Off which takes fractions of cents less than 0.005 in interest computations and adds them to the account of the perpetrator.

The degree of sophistication in the design of a virus is often evidenced by the sort of damage it does. Destroying an entire hard disk is not at all subtle and the effects will be noticed immediately by the user. After detection, destruction of a virus is considerably easier. Selective alteration of data may only be noticed periodically - at the time of an audit for example, and by then it may then be extremely difficult or even impossible to correct the situation. The effects of the cleverest viruses may be so well hidden in the normal day-to-day course of business that the virus may, even after months of damage, still not have come to light.

Before it can do damage a virus must be run. Typically infection of a program file will take place in advance and the damage will be done when the infected program is run. When a system disk is infected the virus will run the next time the computer system is restarted. When executed a virus may show itself immediately by displaying a message or by obviously damaging a file or the disk. Alternatively it may wait, using a logic and/or time bomb to trigger the action.

14.3.1 PC INFECTION

Virus infection on a PC can take a number of different forms. Boot sector viruses inhabit the system areas, whilst the following five DOS files are immediate targets for file viruses:

- The two boot files (described as hidden files when CHKDSK is typed)
- COMMAND.COM (the command processor)
- AUTOEXEC.BAT (the batch file executed on booting the system)
- CONFIG.SYS (the file that defines the configuration setup for the computer).

In addition all program files are possible targets. This includes files with extensions of:

- EXE
- COM
- SYS
- DRV
- OVR
- OVL
- BIN

A simple virus will copy itself into its chosen file, thus overwriting the original contents of the file. This however is reasonably easy to detect and so a more subtle approach is to use spare space at the end of a file, usually between the end-of-file and end-of-disk sector markers. At the time of implanting itself on the disk the virus will code a pointer to the end-of-file marker in another program, thus ensuring that the virus will be replicated when that program is run at a later date.

Another method, often employed on PCs is for the virus to create and occupy false bad sectors. Bad sectors are areas on the disk which have been identified as unusable by the operating system and are thus bypassed by data when it is written to disk. A virus can be placed on the disk and then all but a small part of its code can be marked as bad sectors. A small controlling part of the virus will be located in a program and then when the host program is run it will invoke the code in the main body of the virus located on so called bad sectors. This means that it is possible to hide all but a tiny portion of the virus code.

Once executed, the most common technique employed by viruses to ensure continued replication and infection is for the virus to become memory resident. This means that it stays in the main memory of the PC during its operation. The key to memory resident viruses is the way in which interrupts are used. An interrupt is a mechanism whereby the computer's processor is interrupted from its normal course of action to perform a particular task. For example, when a key is typed at the keyboard, processing will stop while the key is stored in the keyboard buffer. Interrupts are taking place all the time, and allow the processor to perform at maximum efficiency, processing the user program and data most of the time and only dealing with housekeeping type tasks when required.

The application program actually initiates the interrupt by looking at the appropriate interrupt vector. This is a memory location which stores the address of the interrupt routine. The system will then go to this routine and perform the required task before returning control to the application program. Figure 14.1 shows this diagrammatically.

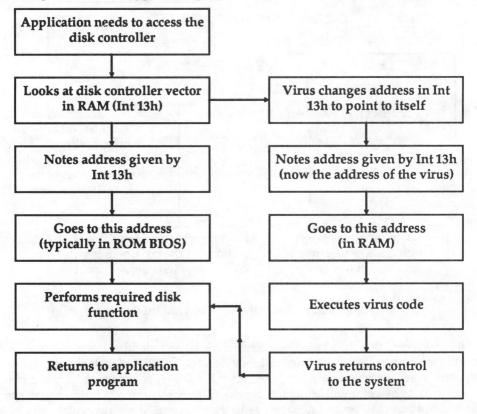

Figure 14.1   Flowchart showing how a virus uses interrupts

A virus may alter one or more of the interrupt vectors, causing the system to go to an address containing the main body of the virus instead of the required interrupt routine. For example, by changing the address in the flowchart, instead of performing a normal disk access routine, a virus can take control and corrupt the disk data. In order for the virus to remain active while other programs are run it will often use the Terminate Stay Resident (TSR) interrupt. This interrupt is normally used by programs which remain active and available for use in RAM whilst another program is run, for example Sidekick. In a virus situation the virus program uses this interrupt to ensure that it remains in memory after the program it is attached to is exited. This means that the viral code will still be executed when another application program is running. Only when the computer is switched off will infection cease. However, the virus will probably have also written itself to each application program it infected and so when the computer is next used the virus is still active.

14.4   RECOGNISING A VIRUS

The symptoms of a virus infection can show itself in many different ways. Figure 14.2 shows some of the tell tale signs in the PC-DOS environment.

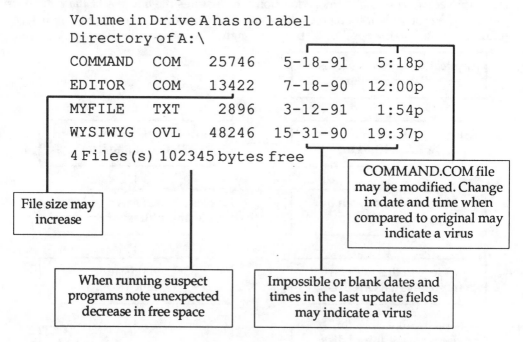

Figure 14.2   Tell-tale signs of viral infection

If it is suspected that the virus is located on the boot sector of the disk, a utility such as Norton may be used to rewrite the boot sector on the infected disk. It should be noted that some game programs use the boot sector for copy protection code. Since many viruses in the boot sector will by default overwrite the copy protection, a games program that will not run may be an indication as to the presence of a virus which may have already infected the system.

14.5   SOME POPULAR VIRUS PROGRAMS AND THEIR EFFECTS

There are literally hundreds, if not thousands, of documented viruses circulating around the world. There are however a core of more common ones, a brief description of which follows.

14.5.1   THE BRAIN VIRUS

The Brain virus originated in Pakistan and affects the IBM PC/XT/AT/PS2 and compatible computers. It only affects floppy disks and is located on the boot sector which is, in effect, the first part of DOS to be loaded. It is about 4100 bytes in length, but only half the code as actually used.

The virus creates three successive clusters of the virus code and flags the six disk sectors that it has used as bad sectors. The virus code then makes a copy of the FAT, changes the FAT code numbers and then destroys the original FAT and bootstrap sectors. The virus alters the memory size by changing the address on interrupt vector A2 HEX (18) in order to disguise the presence of the virus in memory. The virus then substitutes the floppy disk interrupt (vector 13 HEX) with its own address so that when the application program calls to the floppy disk the virus address is accessed and the contents of the disk are destroyed. When new floppy disks are used in the same working session the virus copies itself onto spare space within files on the disk and thus continues to replicate from the newly infected diskette.

If the floppy disk has no volume label, the virus creates one containing the word 'Brain'.

This virus is sometimes referred to as the Pakistan Brain as it originally spread to universities in the UK and USA from Pakistan. It was thought to have come from exchange students who bought pirated and infected software from Pakistan.

As can be seen from Figure 14.3 the code contains the name, address and telephone number of the authors in Lahore who suggest that any victim of the virus contact them for the vaccine.

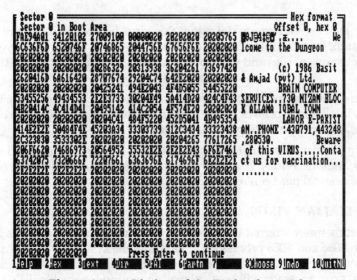

Figure 14.3   Listing of the Brain virus code

The Brain virus spread to the University of Delaware where employees of 480 of the Fortune 500 company headquarters attended computer classes. The students were allowed to do college homework on the company computers during lunch breaks and it is said to be as a result of this that the virus spread rapidly to various corporate computer systems. It has also been reported in a number of other US universities as well as in corporate computers in Australia, UK, Israel, West Germany and Switzerland.

Unfortunately the Brain virus has more recently been reported in several mutated forms, one of which being the introduction of random errors on hard disk files.

14.5.2   THE JERUSALEM VIRUS

Sometimes referred to as the Hebrew University or Friday 13th, this time bomb virus was originally set to activate on Friday 13 May 1988 which happens to be the 40th anniversary of the last free Palestinian entity before the creation of Israel on 14 May 1948!

The virus was written by a Palestinian student as an act of "hi-tech sabotage" and was discovered because of a bug in the virus code itself. It began to treat previously infected programs as uninfected and copied itself twice onto the disks. This caused an obvious increase in the use of available memory and enabled the virus to be detected.

The virus operates in two stages. First, when an infected EXE or COM file is executed the first time after booting the virus copies itself into RAM as a TSR. Secondly, once the memory is infected, any time an EXE file is run, the virus code is copied to the end of that file. When a COM file is run, the virus code is copied to the beginning of the file. The virus is also sometimes referred to as the 1808 or 1813 virus because of the lengths by which it increases the size of EXE and COM files respectively. As an indication of infection the virus writes the string MsDos to the end of a COM file.

Being a parasitic virus, this virus makes its presence known by increasing the size of program files. It also moves a small section of the display up, 30 minutes after infection and slows the operation of the machine down from this point until it is rendered virtually unusable. As soon as reinfection has taken place the previous host file is deleted from the disk.

Staff at the Hebrew University claim that this virus had been so virulent that several years of research, financial information and student files have been destroyed. They also think that thousands of files and years of research were wiped out before the virus was discovered.

The Hebrew University computers are networked to computer systems in the Israeli Military and Intelligence centres and it is possible that the virus could have spread to these systems, adversely affecting Israels national security.

Having lain dormant for sometime after detection, the virus reappeared on Friday 13 January 1989, the first Friday 13th after 13 May 1988. In this version the bug that was present in the original has been removed.

14.5.3   THE ITALIAN VIRUS

This virus is sometimes referred to as the Ping Pong virus and only effects floppy disks working with 8086 and 8088 processors. It monitors the system clock and can reside on any disk, bootable or data. If an attempt is made to boot up with an infected non-bootable disk the usual error message will be displayed to request a bootable disk, but infection will already have taken place as the virus is in RAM. It will then copy itself onto any unprotected floppy introduced into the system during that working session.

The virus uses the time of day register in the system clock. The computer clock ticks at a rate of 18.2 times per second or 65,200 times per hour. As part of the infection process when the register goes above 14 bits, an oval bouncing ball activates and bounces around the screen. When the ball encounters a character, it will deflect off of it, but will also remove it in the process.

14.5.4 MACINTOSH VIRUSES

Virus attacks are by no means restricted to the IBM-PC compatible market. For sometime the Apple Macintosh has been a target for a number of destructive viruses. The following are some of the more common.

14.5.4.1 Scores virus

This parasitic virus increases application file size by 7000 bytes and is RAM based. It attacks only EDS application software which contains the unique programming signatures of ERIC or VULT. These are programs which control MAC word processors and spreadsheets. The virus is not difficult to detect as it changes the shape of the notepad and scrapbook icons displaying them as "dog-eared".

The Scores virus is thought to have attacked a number of US federal agencies, although some suspected victims have been reluctant to confirm the virus' presence.

14.5.4.2 Freehand virus

This relatively harmless virus first appeared to Macintosh users in the US, Canada, Italy, Belgium and France on 2 March 1988 which was the first birthday of the Mac II computer. When users booted their systems the message in Figure 14.4 was displayed.

Richard Brandow, Publisher of MacMag, and its entire staff would like to take this opportunity to convey their Universal Message of World Peace to all Macintosh users around the world

---

Figure 14.4   Message produced by the Freehand virus

The virus did not destroy data or programs, but some users complained that it caused the system to crash and that some programs would not run with the virus present in the computer.

Mr Brandow, referred to in the diagram above, said that he wrote the virus to show how easy it was to infect the Mac. He is said to belong to a religious group called the "Church of the Sub-Genius" and wrote the virus to spread the message of goodwill.

Importation of the virus to the Macintosh was through an infected game supplied from a Compuserve network bulletin board and also through a training disk for the drawing application package Freehand supplied by the well-known software house Aldus. The Freehand package was infected when Marc Canter, President of MacroMind Inc., was given a copy of an infected game program in Canada called Mr Potato Head. MacroMind make training diskettes for Aldus. Canter loaded the game program causing the computer to be infected and then went on to work with Freehand. As a result he infected a floppy disk containing Freehand that was delivered to Aldus and was subsequently sold to customers.

14.5.4.3   nVIR

This virus places nVIR resources in the system file which contains all applications and the main operating system. The system file is mainly a series of initialising resources. As the virus is initiated a beep is heard when an application is opened and if using MacinTalk "Don't Panic" is broadcast. Files then start to disappear. nVIR is very virulent and can infect all programs within an infected system in minutes. It was originally distributed at MACWORLD EXPO in San Francisco by two one-person companies on demo diskettes.

14.6   VIRUSES IN THE NETWORK ENVIRONMENT

There are many types and sizes of networks ranging from relatively small Local Area Networks (LANS) to large sophisticated configurations spanning long distances referred to as Wide Area Networks (WANs).

A typical LAN is an office based system serving a number of PCs, Macintoshes or stand-alone workstations. In addition to each user's machine there is usually a file server which may be a PC dedicated to providing information services on the network. It is clear therefore that a virus has the opportunity to attack a number of personal computers as well as the file server and so the LAN environment provides a free rein to attach all machines in the LAN community. How much damage a virus can ultimately do is largely a function of the controls applied to the LAN.

Whilst the general nature of LANs is one of open architecture which could be seen to encourage attack, network software such as Novell's NetWare and SFT NetWare has a good set of security features which can reduce the risk. When selecting the type of network to install in conjunction with virus attack, a hierarchical system provides more possibility for control. For example, a star network requires any two PCs that wish to transfer information to pass through the file server in the centre of the network. This means that virus controls only need to check between the file server and one PC and there is no immediate way to spread to other PCs on the network. On a bus or ring network it can be the responsibility of each node of the network to establish the bona fides of the other nodes with which it wishes to transfer information and thus there is greater scope for a virus attach.

In addition to password and login controls, the file server may have a good set of file access controls, giving access only to limited, defined sets of data. By reducing the scope for data access means that a virus has to do more work in order to exploit any trap doors in order to be effective.

14.6.1   ELECTRONIC MAIL SYSTEMS

Both dedicated electronic mail systems and applications available on networks are particularly susceptible to virus attack, due primarily to the free and open environment which support them. Electronic mail may sometimes come from any source worldwide and it is unreasonable to expect users to necessarily know the source of a message. Therefore protection is generally provided by placing the electronic mail system in an entirely separate environment to all other applications. When mail arrives for a user it will be written to his/her mail folder, thus restricting the possibility of attach to the electronic mail sub-system and the mail folder. This does, however still leave two areas of weakness. First, a user must get into the mail system and so it cannot be entirely isolated within the computer, thus exposing the user/mail interface to possible attack. For example, a virus program may be copied into a user's mail folder without him/her knowing and on opening the file to discover the contents damage can be done and infection can be spread. Secondly there could be a flaw in the mail system itself which allows a virus writer to break out of the restrictions applied to the system and wreak havoc on the rest of the system.

14.6.2   THE CHRISTMAS VIRUS

This is a popular example of a network virus that hit IBM's worldwide MVS computer network on 11 December 1987. The virus was in the electronic mail system as a Christmas card and as can be seen in Figure 14.5 contained a picture of a Christmas tree composed of rows of asterisks.

When a user typed "Christmas" the virus code was triggered and copies of the virus program were sent to every name and address on the user's mail directory file. The recipients, when they read the message and typed "Christmas" caused the virus to duplicate and be sent to all the names and addresses on their respective distribution lists. This resulted in a worldwide network lock up and affected IBM offices across the US and around the world. The virus affected 250,000 users and resulted in two hours of E-Mail down time. It was eventually traced to a West German law student at the University of Clausthal-Zellerfield who had created it as a seasonal prank. He had wanted to send Christmas greetings to his friends within the University, but did not realise that the University E-Mail system was part of EARN - the European Academic Research Network - which in turn connects with BITNET in North America, which is the gateway to the IBM E-Mail network, VNet. Fortunately for IBM the Christmas virus did not destroy any programs or data. However it is on record as having replicated one million times in a few days. If the downtime per user was two hours and there were initially 50,000 users, and the cost of downtime was $20 per hour, the damage in financial terms would be $2 million. Assuming the same figures for EARN and BITNET, the total loss could be around $6 million which goes to prove just how costly a virus attack can be.

14.7   PREVENTING AND CURING A VIRUS ATTACK

Prevention is better than cure with electronic diseases in the same way as with biological ones, so it is wise to take steps to safeguard computers from infection in the first place.

The most fundamental precaution is to limit physical access to a machine so that unauthorised users cannot tamper with the system. In the case of floppy disks the simplest form of protection is to place write protect tabs on all disks so that any attempt

```
/**********************/
/*    LET THIS EXEC   */
/*        RUN         */
/*        AND         */
/*      ENJOY         */
/*     YOURSELF!      */
/**********************/
```

```
SAY '                         *                    '
SAY '                        ***                   '
SAY '                       *****                  '
SAY '                      *******                 '
SAY '                     *********                '
SAY '                   *************               '
SAY '                      *******                 '
SAY '                    ***********                '
SAY '                   ***************         A'
SAY '                 *******************       VERY'
SAY '                  **********              HAPPY'
SAY '                 ***************          CHRISTMAS'
SAY '               *******************        AND MY'
SAY '             ***********************      BEST WISHES'
SAY '                *************             FOR THE NEXT'
SAY '               *****************          YEAR'
SAY '             ***********************        '
SAY '           ***************************      '
SAY '                 *******                    '
SAY '                 *******                    '
SAY '                 *******                    '
```

```
/* browsing this file is no fun at all
   just type CHRISTMAS from cmd */
```

Figure 14.5   The Christmas virus message screen

by a virus to write to the disk would result in an error message. Only when data is to be expressly written to the floppy should the write protect tab be removed. It should be remembered however that even the simple act of inserting a floppy disk and getting a directory listing can be enough to infect a machine. Whilst write protect facilities are generally not available for hard disks, hardware products have started to appear on the market offering users the ability to write protect hard disks, but as they are expensive they are not likely to become widely used. Software products to write protect hard disks are also available, but these of course also render themselves vulnerable to virus attack. In the network environment, the use of diskless or hard disk only systems is becoming popular, as control of software is then restricted to the file server and network administrators.

Programs that prevent virus attack are usually TSR programs that monitor systems activity and watch out for characteristic viral replication activities. They check all disk reads and writes and generate a warning message when potential viral activities are attempted. This includes actions such as writes to executable programs, systems device drivers and boot blocks. The problem with these programs is that they are generally not able to distinguish between valid write requests and an invalid request. The result can be a large number of messages leading users to eventually ignore the warnings, with the risk that a genuine virus attempt to overwrite a disk file would also be ignored. This type of protection has the advantage of stopping viruses before they get the chance to enter a system, but as time goes on so virus programs become more sophisticated and new versions are written to overcome the protection programs.

Another approach are anti-viral programs that help identify already infected systems. These must first be installed on a clean system or be run from a "safe" floppy disk. They work by periodically checking key information such as date stamps, file sizes and check-sums on the system disks looking for changes that would indicate a virus has infected the system.

Both the above types of program are generically referred to as vaccines. Suppliers of vaccine software admit that their products are only effective against known viruses and will most likely lag one step behind the most recent virus strain. Not only are newer versions of a virus likely to be more resistant to vaccines, they are also likely to be more difficult to trace due to increased complexity.

Although names have been given to some of the more popular viruses, it is quite likely that different program structures exist for different versions of a virus and thus anyone with the appropriate technical expertise could take a copy of say the Brain virus and modify the code so that existing anti-Brain virus software would be useless.

The results of an evaluation show that very few anti-viral products on the market actually offer a comprehensive level of protection. About 40 percent will only report on virus damage to programs or data files after the event, Furthermore, those viruses that do not create detectable files such as the Pakistan Brain, are only detected by a few.

The following are examples of a few anti-viral products currently available.

14.7.1 ASP

This is a menu driven program that uses checksums to detect the spread of viruses and restricts access to the machine by fencing it off with a password and pass number. A simple install command copies ASP to the hard disk. A checksum for the ASP disk is also transferred as part of this process, to check that the act of installation has not infected the ASP program itself. After installation it is necessary to delete the ASP checksum in order that all the COM and EXE files on the hard disk can be registered. The system works by presenting a menu of all the programs in the current directory. The user runs a program by selecting from the directory at which point ASP checks the program checksum with the one stored and if it has altered a prompt will be displayed requesting whether the program should be run, whether the checksum table should be updated or whether the operation should be rejected.

After running the program a further test can be performed so that if a TSR virus has been installed, the amount of free memory will have been reduced and ASP notes and reports such a change. A further check looks at the table of interrupt vectors. If the vectors have changed they can be corrected at this stage, but otherwise ASP will report that the system is still suspect. It will also check the boot block.

14.7.2 DR SOLOMON'S ANTI-VIRUS TOOLKIT

This popular suite of anti-virus programs accurately identifies whether a virus is present, and in many cases can report which one is the culprit.

The package contains a number of different programs to deal with different aspects of viruses. For example FINDVIRU locates the common viruses by identifying the viral signatures in programs. SHERLOCK, HOLMES and WATSON identify changes made to software and the operating system. WATSON creates a fingerprint file which is used to provide a list of files. SHERLOCK uses the list to calculate checksums for the files and for the relevant DOS interrupts and HOLMES can check whether files or interrupts have changed. To help detect viruses like BRAIN which use false bad sectors there is a program called KILLBAD which contains a series of inoculation routines to fool viruses into thinking that the programs being run have already been infected.

A number of utilities programs are included in the package including a low level disk read routine and an undelete program. Two hard disk protection programs called NOHARD 1 and NOHARD 2 ensure that the disk acts as if it were write protected.

The packages cited here are only two examples of the hundreds of anti-virus programs that have now invaded the market. The table in Figure 14.6 cross-references the main features of five popular products in the UK.

	Disktrap	Dr Solomons Anti-Virus ToolKit	Flushot	Immunise	Viruspro
OPERATIONAL FEATURES					
Uses checksums	N	N	Y	Y	Y
Uses cyclic redundancy checking	N	N	Y	N	N
Uses non-CRC proprietary signature	N	Y	Y	Y	Y
Requires list of files, directories	N	N	Y	N	N
Operates on boot up	N	Y	Y	Y	N
Offers password protection	N	N	N	Y	Y
Maintains operational log	N	Y	N	N	N
PROTECTION FEATURES					
Uses signature methodology	N	Y	Y	Y	Y
Uses encrypted checksums	N	Y	Y	Y	N
Uses other checks	Y	Y	N	Y	Y
Monitors DOS interrupts	Y	Y	Y	N	Y
Monitors vector interrupt table	Y	Y	N	N	N
Protects critical system area	N	Y	Y	Y	N
Protects boot sector	Y	Y	Y	Y	N
Protects COMMAND.COM	N	Y	Y	Y	N
Protects hidden system files	N	Y	Y	Y	N
Protects FAT	N	Y	Y	N	N
Protects partition table	Y	Y	Y	N	N
Protects RAM	N	N	Y	N	N
Can restore CMOS	N	N	Y	N	N
Protects logical drives beyond C:	Y	Y	Y	Y	N
DETECTION FEATURES					
Detects at boot-up	N	Y	Y	Y	N
Detects on demand	N	Y	N	Y	Y
Detects before program execution	N	Y	Y	Y	N
Notifies when a program goes TSR	N	N	Y	N	N
Flags new programs	N	N	N	Y	Y
Flags programs with changed signatures	N	Y	Y	Y	Y
Uses integrity statistics	N	Y	Y	N	Y
Uses write traps and format traps	Y	Y	Y	N	N
Uses read traps	N	Y	Y	N	N
Uses program integrity checks	N	Y	Y	Y	Y
Uses memory integrity checks	N	N	Y	N	N
Uses critical-area integrity checks	N	Y	Y	Y	Y

Figure 14.6   The main anti-viral products

14.8   PC VIRUS COUNTERMEASURES

The following recommendations, should if followed, minimise the risk of becoming a victim of a virus epidemic. Of course, in a realistic situation it is not always possible, or indeed practical, to follow all these steps to the letter. They do however draw attention to the danger areas.

- **Use standalone PCs**

  As mentioned previously networks leave themselves open to easier infection than a standalone PC, the security for which can be more easily monitored.

- **Avoid the use of modems**

  As viruses can be passed through electronic mail, bulletin boards and other communications software the avoidance of modems will make this sort of infection more difficult.

- **Ensure that your computer and software are only used by you**

  This is often a very hard condition to meet and the term 'you' will invariable mean you and your secretary/partner/clerk etc. However, try to minimise the number of people using a particular computer.

- **Prevent others from accessing your computer and software**

  The use of passwords and user identification can make it more difficult for unauthorised personnel to access a computer. Although these steps are common-place in the networking environment they can be applied to standalone systems as well.

- **Avoid sharing programs or files with others**

  There is a tendency, particularly if a new software package is being evaluated, to install a system on one machine and then to make a copy and pass onto another machine which can give a free ride to a virus. It can be even more difficult where data in concerned as many firms depend on the regular movement of data on floppy disks from office to office.

- **Never use unauthorised copies of proprietary software or operating systems**

  Many viruses are carried on pirated versions of well-known software products and so users should always ensure that they are using a genuine copy of all packages on the PC.

- **Only use public domain or shareware software from recognised sources**

  As public domain software is so easily copied and sent from user to user it provides a good vehicle for the transportation of viruses. The shareware market has grown a lot over the past few years offering a wide range of good quality utilities and software packages at very low prices, and many catalogues and clubs providing this service declare that software from them has been tested with a particular anti-virus package. However, it is still advisable to re-test ALL software before installing on a user's machine.

- **If infected with a virus ensure all infected software, including backup copies, are purged of the virus**

  All too often a virus is eradicated from a system, only to mysteriously return some time later because the user reinstated their system from backups that were already infected. It is also important to inform any other users who could possibly have become infected as a result of using data from an infected machine.

  Despite the improvement in vaccine and anti-virus techniques in recent years, the only way to be absolutely sure that a system is free of viruses is to reformat the hard disk at low level. Every backup disk must then be tested to ensure that the virus is not re-introduced as the system is reinstalled. Also make sure that the version of DOS used on floppy to boot the system is clear of viruses.

- **Ensure employees use only designated standalone PCs to perform homework**

  With all the controls possible applied to in-company machines it is equally important to control home computers that personnel might be using which could be infected without their knowing. As games software is a common carrier of viruses the home computer can be a major threat.

- **Avoid using non-certified vaccine software**

  As mentioned above there are now hundreds of anti-virus software packages and some of these are not as reputable as they might be, containing lethal viruses themselves. Beware particularly of free software offered in the classified ads section of magazines or distributed as free gifts.

- **Write protect critical or sensitive files**

  The simplest form of virus protection on floppy disks is to place a write protect tab on the disk. As any virus has to get onto a disk in order to do damage, this simple precaution is almost failsafe.

  Hard disks can be write protected through the use of special utilities or hardware modifications. However, it should be remembered that any software measure that is taken can be circumvented by a virus.

- **Maintain up-to-date program and file information (date, size) for master, working and backup copies**

  As many viruses display themselves by incrementing the size of program files precautions such as this can help in the detection process if infection is suspected.

14.9 HOW MUCH SHOULD YOU WORRY?

Donn Parker of the Stanford Research Institute in California says that "computer viruses are the current crimoid". They have, without doubt, captured the imagination of the press and the resulting myriad of articles have brought the problem to the attention of many computer users.

It does, however, appear that the publicity exaggerates the problem to quite a high degree in that the incidence of virus infection is actually quite low, and for most organisations is far from being a day-to-day occurrence. The problem does seem to be largely confined to the PC environment and as a result the majority of PC users are taking precautions to avoid exposure to viruses. The result of the increasing use of routine precautions makes it harder for viruses to spread, and new viruses or strains are detected sooner than they used to be.

The inconvenience and indirect cost factors of a virus attack should not be underestimated. Even if a relatively harmless virus invades an organisation the time involved in clearing all affected disks, performing low level formats on hard disks and then reinstating clean versions of all software packages can be considerable. The resulting downtime and loss of productivity to users can add up to a substantial bill.

15 Troubleshooting Case Situations

15.1 PROBLEM SITUATIONS

It is important as a troubleshooter to be in a position to assist with problems that occur in a wide range of situations, when different software is in use, on different PC configurations, and with a range of expertise among users.

This chapter gives 40 typical case situations that a troubleshooter might have to face, and readers can use these to see how they would go about tackling such problems. Suggested solutions follow (see Section 15.2).

1   You are called to a department where Lotus is being used on a new machine which has just been purchased. The new machine is an IBM PC/AT compatible. They have attempted to produce some graphs, but are getting no image on the screen. They are using a Lotus from a floppy disk which has been available to the department for the last 6 months and has been used successfully on other machines.

2   You are called to a department where a machine has been switched on and a loud bang like a rifle shot was heard. What has most likely happened and what can be done about it?

3   A user has come to you complaining that the keyboard keeps sticking. How would you go about establishing the most likely cause of this. What steps are required to rectify the problem and what advice would you give in order to prevent a reoccurrence?

4   You are asked to install an external 3½ inch disk drive into an AT compatible computer. What steps are required and what problems may be encountered?

5   You want to install a new printer which requires a serial interface. What steps are required and what problems may be encountered?

6   A user comes to you complaining that they are experiencing an intermittent fault with a floppy disk drive on their machine. The fault presents itself by displaying the message Abort, Retry, Ignore on the screen when the disk is being read.

7   A user comes to you saying that they have accidentally entered DEL *.* and responded to the Y/N prompt with Y. Subsequently, it was realised that the directory cleared with this instruction contained valuable data for which there was not an up-to-date security copy. They want to know if there is any way of retrieving the data from the disk. How can you help them?

8   A user comes to you saying that they have tried to copy a file from a floppy disk back onto the hard disk and that the file cannot now be read. The version of the file on the floppy disk was originally taken from the hard disk using the BACKUP command. What is the most likely problem and what advice can you give the user?

9   You have to send some important data disks in the post to another office. What precautions should you take?

10 A user has come to you saying that their printer is not working. What steps would you take to ascertain the most likely cause of the problem?

11 A user has switched on his computer but is getting no response from the monitor. What steps can you ask the user to perform that might solve the problem and if none of these work what else might be problem be?

12 A user reports an error message that is displayed on the screen when the computer is switched on. This message takes the form of a number such as 2004 201. You identify the error as a memory problem, but how do you go about establishing which chip has failed and what steps must be taken to replace the faulty chip?

13 When using an applications package such as dBase III+, dBase IV or WordStar 5, the system supplies an error message such as cannot save or cannot open file. What is the most likely problem?

14 A regular personal computer user tells you that the response time on his/her system has been gradually slowing down for the last few months. It now takes ages for the system to load or save on the disk. What is the most likely problem?

15 The typing pool has a network of 20 IBM PC compatible machines. They are placed in the centre of a large room in which there are also three laser printers and three fast dot matrix printers. In the room there are also two photocopiers, a telex and a fax machine. Each desk has a telephone. The room has a thick piled nylon carpet and is centrally heated. A typist reports occasional corruption of her data. What issues should be considered?

16 A user calls you to look at a system that has been producing data files with randomly corrupted records. Also, some of the standard application programs crash for no apparent reason. In the same department there is another system which periodically generates corrupted screens. What are the most likely problems?

17 When a user switches on his machine it is absolutely dead. What are the main possible causes of this problem?

18 When the computer is switched on the user finds that the keyboard does not respond in any way. What are the possible problems?

19 When the computer is switched on the system begins to boot, but it hangs before the POST has finished. What is a likely cause of this?

20 A user with a new machine complains that the @ symbol does not function and that when pressed the double quotes (") appear on the screen. What can be done to rectify this situation?

21 An experienced PC user comes to you with a problem involving a batch file they have written. It is intended to copy data from a hard drive to a floppy disk. However, the results are erratic, with the copy occasionally taking place, but every

now and then the system will print garbage on the screen and then hang. To add to the confusion, it appears to do this more often when the batch file is executed after leaving Lotus with the /System command, although it has been known to occur at other times. What steps would you take to remedy the problem?

22 Several users in one of the departmental offices complain of problems when starting up their computers, lack of speed when using software and general difficulties. It is known that certain system disks have been corrupted when the computer is booted up with them, as well as memory problems being encountered with proprietary software packages. What would you suspect to be the likely cause of these problems?

23 Network users complain that they cannot use all of the facilities offered by some software. They find that if their PCs are disconnected from the network and used as standalone machines then they have no problems, but as soon as the network software is loaded then the trouble starts. As an example, a program called PC/Focus should be able to run in either enhanced or standard mode. However, when connected to the network it will only operate in standard mode, limiting its functionality. What ways would you recommend to the users to overcome these problems. Would you consider them to be hardware or software originated, and how can you confirm your suspicions?

24 While using Lotus 1-2-3, you try to retrieve a file from disk, only to be confronted with the MEM indicator. The file has been successfully loaded on previous occasions. What steps can be taken to remedy the situation?

25 As manager of a systems department you have a variety of XT and AT type machines at your disposal. However, in moving office, many of the keyboards have been swapped over, causing the machines to hang on start-up. How can you determine which keyboards belong to which machines?

26 A user comes to you complaining that they cannot execute their newly installed WordStar program. On entering WS at the prompt to run the software, the message BAD COMMAND OR FILENAME is displayed. What do you tell them to do?

27 Three typists are all using WordPerfect V5.0. Each has their own machine, onto which the software has been installed. All three machines are PC compatibles. When information is written to a floppy by machine A, it can be read by machine B but not machine C. However. machine C can read and write data that it generates itself. What are the likely problems, and how can you pinpoint which machine is the primary cause?

28 The CGA monitor on one particular PC tends to go blank at odd moments. Sometimes it is blank when the machine is switched on, other times it goes blank when the machine has been running for some time. It can take up to five minutes for the picture to reappear, although a knock on the side sometimes fixes it. What do you suspect to be the cause of the problem, and can you do anything the fix it?

29 A member of staff regularly complains of floppy disk problems, including system disks that won't boot up, read errors for data disks, or software that won't execute from the floppy disk. You have had the drives on the PC aligned and checked, and they appear to be in A1 condition. What do you think is the most likely cause of these problems?

30   You have used the BACKUP command from DOS to transfer files onto a 3½ inch floppy disk. However, the files cannot be RESTOREd onto another machine. If the COPY command is used instead of BACKUP and RESTORE then there is no problem. What is the reason?

31   There is an intermittent fault on one of the AT type machines in your department, which shows itself as a refusal to execute the SETUP procedure properly, or simply forgetting all of its settings when it is switched off. It appears to manifest itself more often if the machine is left switched-off for a period of an hour or so before switching on again. What do you think is the most likely cause?

32   A user complains that their system will not print. They have been successfully printing before switching on the machine this morning, but can get no response from the printer now. What do you check to determine the cause of the problem?

33   Several different PCs with CGA displays have *fuzzy* displays, with a *snowy* picture. What is the most likely cause, and what is the correct remedy?

34   On booting up one of the computer systems, an error message is displayed - "Non system disk or Disk error". If a different system diskette is used the error still appears. Which components are likely to be at fault, and how do you change them?

35   A hard disk machine repeatedly indicates that there are bad sectors on its disk. You have tried re-formatting it but the problems persist. What is the next step necessary to remedy the situation?

36   Some of the PCs in your office are mounted into consoles, with the PC at desk level, the monitor on top of it and then a shelf above the monitor to support the printer. What problems would you expect from this arrangement?

37   A colleague rushes up to you saying that he has tried to cancel a drawing sent to a plotter, but although the PC seems to have stopped, the plotter is still going. He estimates that it will take over 45 minutes to complete the plot. Why is the system behaving like this, and what can you do to stop the plotter?

38   One of the PCs that you deal with has developed a fault. Occasionally when it is first switched on, it completes the POST and starts to load DOS for approximately five seconds. It then beeps very quietly and freezes. If it is reset it boots up perfectly. What do you suspect to be the cause of the problem and how do you remedy it?

39   An experienced PC user has a particularly high specification PC, with an 80386 processor, expanded and extended memory, a maths co-processor and a very fast disk drive. They are using the latest software which can make full use of extended memory, and are also implementing a virtual disk. They also require certain utilities such as SideKick to be in memory. However, at certain times, especially when calling up SideKick, the system will freeze, requiring a cold start before it will do anything. There is no memory problem as the applications software is mainly using extended memory, and reports that there is over 200K of main memory available. What do you suspect to be the cause of the problem?

40   As an experienced user of PCs, you have been approached by a colleague who wants to use a Yen symbol (¥) in WordStar. However, this is not directly available on the keyboard, although it appears in the ASCII tables that are supplied in the DOS handbook. Do you think that he can produce this character, and if so how do you suggest he obtains it in his document?

15.2 SUGGESTED SOLUTIONS

The following sections give guidelines as to how these case situations can be tackled by the troubleshooter. They are not exhaustive but should give sufficient information to help the troubleshooter apply the methodology to similar problems should they arise.

1 This problem could be due either to the hardware or the software. In terms of the hardware the new computer may not have a suitable graphics adapter card installed. This is however unlikely with a new machine. More likely is that the graphics card has not been correctly installed in terms of setting the necessary dip switchers or jumpers. With regards the software, the installation may be incorrect in terms of the type of screen that is being used. If the new computer has an EGA or VGA screen and the currently used systems are CGA then the graphics may not work without re-installation of the Lotus software.

   Finally the problem could be one of user ignorance; if an attempt is made to view a Lotus graph without having specified a graph type, the system will beep and give a blank display.

2 It is most likely that there has been a short circuit and the transformer in the power supply has blown. It is not feasible for a troubleshooter to attempt to repair a power supply. In fact it would be dangerous for anyone other than a professional engineer to do this. There is only one course of action available which is to replace the power supply. It is especially important to ensure that a compatible power supply is replaced into the computer, using the wrong voltage power supply could be very dangerous. It might be worth checking to see whether the power supply output might need increasing due to the number of installed peripherals.

3 Keys sticking on the keyboard are usually due to dirt getting under the key contacts. Perhaps the most troublesome type of dirt is cigarette ash which leaves a residue of tar behind that quickly becomes sticky. Enquire whether the user smokes and what sort of environment is the keyboard used in - is it on the factory floor, does the user eat and/or drink by the computer, is the system in a damp environment. To fix the problem it is necessary to dismantle the keyboard and clean each key component with a spirit cleaner, ensuring that all parts are completely dry before re-assembly - this can most easily be done with a hair dryer. To prevent the problem arising again ensure that smoke, food and drink are kept well away from the computer - these items can damage other computer components just as easily. If the problem has been due to the working environment of the keyboard, covering the entire keypad with a transparent plastic protection will help prevent dust from getting behind the keys.

4 Most peripheral components, including an external disk drive require a card to be placed in one of the option slots on the computer motherboard. In addition to this it may be necessary to adjust dip switches or jumpers, both on the main system board and on the new option card. Once the new drive has been physically installed it is then necessary to inform the operating system that there is an additional disk drive on the system and this is done by installing one or more disk driver programs. The driver programs will have been supplied on a floppy disk with the new disk drive and it must be copied onto the main disk containing the DOS file CONFIG.SYS. The CONFIG.SYS file is executed every time the computer is switched on and as the name suggests it sets the configuration for the system.

5   A printer with a serial interface requires a serial card to have been installed in one of the option slots on the system board. This type of card is referred to as a communications card or RS232, and in order for the computer to know that data to be printed must be directed through this card, it is necessary to set a number of parameters in the AUTOEXEC.BAT file. The manual for the particular printer will give precise instructions as to the settings required, but the following is typical:

   MODE COM1:9600,N,8,2

where COM1 is the name of the port that the data is to be sent to, 9600 represents the baud rate, N means that parity is set to none, 8 refers to the number of databits and 2 to the number of stopbits. Databits are the number of electrical signals required to define a character and stopbits are the number of electrical signals that mark the end of a character.

This mode command sets the communications protocol necessary for the installed serial printer. If the serial printer is the primary printing device the LPT1 mode command must be directed to the 1st communications port which is referenced as COM1. This must be a second line of code in the AUTOEXEC.BAT file.

   MODE LPT1:=COM1

6   Intermittent disk faults are the most difficult to troubleshoot, especially if they occur on a hard disk. However, if from the users report it appears that the same message is always displayed on the screen when the disk fails it narrows down the possibilities. The most likely cause of the problem is a dirty drive head. It is believed that 80 percent of disk problems are due to dirty drive heads and that the majority of users never routinely clean them. The cleaning of disk drive heads requires a special disk which is made of an absorbent cleaning material. A small amount of spirit cleaner is applied to the disk cleaner which is then inserted and spun round in the disk drive. This activity should be done routinely after every 10 or so hours of disk use. If this does not solve the problem it might still be that the disk head is dirty, but that it needs to be manually cleaned by first dismantling the disk drive to gain access to the head. Although this can be done by the troubleshooter, it is preferable for a technician to be called. Other possible causes of the problem are that the alignment of the disk drive could be out or that the speed of disk revolution in the disk drive is too slow or too fast. The speed of the disk drive can be checked by running the diagnostics software and if the speed is reported to be outside the tolerance range the troubleshooter can adjust the potentiometer at the back of the disk drive using a jewellers screwdriver. If however it is thought that the head alignment might be out then a technician must be called as special monitoring equipment is required to test and reset the drive.

7   Providing the user has not saved any new material to disk after entering DEL *.* it is usually possible to retrieve the data from disk using one of the many utility programs available on the market. Some of the better known products are Norton Utilities or PC Tools. In fact most public domain utility software provide programs for the recovery of data lost in this way. The reason that recovery is straightforward is that when the DOS DEL command is used, it does not actually erase the data from the disk, but rather cancels the filenames from the directory, freeing up the space for use by other files. It is therefore important that the computer is not used between performing the erroneous DEL and recovering the files.

8 The clue to the users problem here is that the copy of the file on floppy disk was originally copied from the hard disk with the BACKUP command. This command allows a selection or all of the files on a hard disk to be copied onto floppy disks in such a way that the system controls how much information will fit onto each disk. A special identifier file is included on the directory of each floppy disk and it is important that files are returned to the hard disk through the use of the RESTORE command which will look for the BACKUP identifier. As the user had attempted to use the COPY command he/she was not able to gain access to the file.

9 Sending floppy disks through the post should not be a problem providing they are securely packaged. It is advisable to first wrap the disk in silver paper as this will reduce the danger to the information on the disk if it is exposed to electro-magnetic fields. The disk must then be placed in a rigid container so that it is not easily bent. The envelope or packaging should be clearly marked DO NOT BEND and MAGNETIC MATERIAL – AVOID MAGNETIC FIELDS. In addition, a security backup copy of the disk should be made before it is sent.

10 Traditionally a printer is the part of a computer configuration with the most moving parts and as such is perhaps the most likely item to suffer component failure. It is normally not recommended that the troubleshooter get involved with the repair of printers other than unjamming paper, replacing ribbons, and general cleaning. However, there are a number of checks that should be performed before calling a technician as printer failure can also be due to a number of basic problems. First check that the cabling between the printer and the computer is correctly attached. If it is correctly attached change the cable for another one to see if it is the cable that is faulty. If this does not improve the situation then either the interface card or the printer is at fault. The next step, if possible, is to attach another printer to the computer. If this printer does not work then it would appear to be the interface card that is faulty. Check to see that it is correctly seated in the slot on the motherboard. If it appears to be correctly seated, try it in another slot. Also check that the chips on the interface card have not worked loose.

11 If when the computer is switched on the monitor does not come on first listen and look at the computer to see if the system has been successfully powered up. Then check that the cabling to the monitor is correct and in particular that the monitor interface cable is plugged into the correct monitor port on the computer. Some monitors have independent on/off switches which can be left on all the time as the power is controlled by switching the computer on and off. It may be that this switch has inadvertently been turned off. In addition the contrast and/or brightness switches may have been turned so far down that no image is being displayed. The monitor control card may not be correctly seated in the slot, or some of the chips may have worked themselves loose. If the monitor continues not to function then an integrated circuit on the monitor control card may have failed and this must be replaced. Of course, it is possible, although very rare, that the tube itself could have failed and if this is the case it must be attended to by a technician. A troubleshooter should never attempt to open up a monitor.

12 The number reported by the system identifies the location of the faulty chip. It is necessary to open up the system box in order to expose the banks of RAM chips on the system board. If for example the error message was 2004 201, it is the 201 that suggests the problem is memory chip. The 2004 locates the chip on the bank of RAM

chips. The 20 means that the chip is on the second bank and the 04 means it is the fourth chip along the bank from the left. As the numbering system varies from PC to AT systems, the technical manual may be necessary in order to correctly interpret the failed chip.

13 Cannot save or cannot open file errors usually occur when the CONFIG.SYS file has not been written so as to accommodate the requirements of the software in use. It is a useful rule to set the command FILES=20 in the CONFIG.SYS file. This commands controls the total number of files that can be open at a time. These include DOS files, drivers, program files and data files.

14 The response of the system in retrieving or saving data can deteriorate when the hard disk begins to fill. This problem occurs because data becomes scattered over non contiguous sectors on the drive. The main way of rectifying this is to use an optimising utility which rearranges the data on the hard disk in a contiguous manner. This procedure can be time consuming on a badly fragmented disk, and it is important to ensure that there is a full backup before commencing the optimising routine.

15 A concentration of a large number of computers, photocopiers and telephones in the same room can produce electro-magnetic fields which in turn can cause data corruption. The combination of nylon carpet and central heating can cause static to build-up which results in sparks jumping from users hands to the equipment and the disks. This can cause data loss, corruption and power failure. Anti static mats should be placed beneath each computer to discharge the static, and the furnishings in the room should be improved.

16 These are the classic symptoms of a virus. A computer virus is a program that invades a computer by attaching itself to a program, which when executed allows the virus to load itself into memory. The virus can then either attack the system areas of the disk, or attach itself to other programs as they are executed. In addition to ensuring it spreads, the virus can destroy data in memory or on the disk. This destruction is often intermittent and subtle, as it is the aim of the virus writer to ensure their programs are not discovered until considerable havoc has been wreaked. It is important to adopt routine anti-virus checks on computers, and to ensure users are aware of the risks, especially when introducing new software onto the computer.

17 There are a number of different circumstances which will lead to the machine being absolutely dead on switching on, most of which lead to some form of power problem. These range from problems such as the machine having been plugged out to a fuse in the building having blown or a fuse in the plug or a fuse in the machine itself having failed. Alternatively, the actual power supply unit could have failed. It is important to ensure that the system is completely dead, and that no lights show when powering up. If there are lights then power must be reaching the system and the failure could be chip related. Note that if the fan on the power supply is not heard then there is no point in looking for integrated circuit failure on the motherboard and the problem must be in some way power related.

18 The keyboard can fail for several reasons. It can be due to the fact that the keyboard is not plugged in, and if this is the case the POST should give an appropriate error message on the screen. However, with a number of systems this message only

flashes briefly on the screen and the user may not notice it. If the keyboard is switchable between XT and AT systems, it will not function with the switch wrongly set. The keyboard may also fail if one of the components on the printed circuit board in the keyboard fails. The remedial action should be to swap the keyboard for another compatible one. This will prove whether it is the keyboard or the computer that is at fault.

19   If the system begins to boot, but fails before the POST has finished then a component on the motherboard is likely to have failed. The first step in this circumstance is to check all the connections, and that none of the components or chips have worked themselves loose. As the POST is controlled by the ROM BIOS, this is a possible source of the fault. In some cases it may be possible to change this, but it is more likely that the system will have to be sent away for repair.

20   There are minimal layout differences between the American and British keyboards, one of which is that the location of the @ symbol and the double quotes are interposed. The effect of this is that on pressing @ double quotes appear on the screen and vice versa. The problem is easily remedied by incorporating the command KEYBUK into the AUTOEXEC.BAT file.

21   The problem is a software one. It is due to the imbalance between DOS and other applications programs. The fault is enhanced when Lotus is exited using /System as this does not clear the program from the memory but rather just temporarily halts execution. Thus the software is using some of the available file handles and buffers, and is consuming most of the available memory. The remedy is to check the CONFIG.SYS and AUTOEXEC.BAT files. The statements FILES=n and BUFFERS=m must be included in CONFIG.SYS with the values of m and n correctly set for the software in use. Most software currently requires files set to 20 or more, and buffers set to 15 or more. The AUTOEXEC.BAT file should also have any non-essential TSR programs removed from it. This includes things like SideKick and other memory-resident utilities that are not often used by the operator.

22   These are classic virus symptoms. The virus was probably initiated on one PC, and then spread to the others when data was transferred via floppy disk. There are two possible courses of action. Either an anti-viral software package can be used to vaccinate the PC, or the hard disks of all machines can be low-level formatted to eradicate the virus code. In either case, all floppy disks used to boot up the PCs should be re-formatted with a known-to-be-uninfected system. Any applications software packages should be reinstalled from the master disks. It is important that no infected software is run on the vaccinated systems or the problem will recur. Security measures should be enforced on the systems to ensure that no infected software or data is imported from any other source in the future.

23   The problems are caused by the LAN software. This is using up some of the PC memory, so that the applications software cannot be executed properly. Without the LAN software, the PC operates correctly. The remedy to these problems involves expense. Either a different software package can be purchased which is more compatible with the network, or alternatively additional memory can be acquired together with the appropriate expanded memory driver.

24   The file is too large for the system to load into its available workspace. Since the file has been successfully loaded previously, then it can be assumed that something

has happened to change the amount of available memory. The most likely cause is a TSR program, such as a memory resident utility. Another possible reason is the presence of Lotus add-ins such as Cell Works or Allways. Add-ins can consume large amounts of memory, and this leads to problems when working with large files. All TSRs and add-ins should be removed from memory, and then the File Retrieve attempted again. Once retrieved, it is advisable to separate the file into smaller parts (if possible) so that the problem will not occur again.

25   There are several ways to determine whether a keyboard is for a PC/XT or a PC/AT machine. First, AT type keyboards normally have more keys, and they tend to have twelve or more function keys as opposed to the XT's ten. Secondly, they may have additional keys such as the one marked [Sys Rq] and one the marked [Alt Gr]. Certain keyboards are switchable between AT and XT. This is achieved by moving a small switch, found on the side or underneath of the keyboard, to the desired setting.

26   The problem has probably arisen due to the fact that the directory containing the Wordstar system files was not current at the time when the command was issued. The user should therefore either change to the wordstar directory prior to entering WS with the CD command, or alternatively add the wordstar directory to the DOS path, by placing the PATH=C:\WS5 command in the AUTOEXEC.BAT file. If these measures do not work, then it will be necessary to re-install the software, as the problem is due to mistakes in the installation procedure.

27   There are two likely causes. Either the software is failing to read the files correctly, or the hardware is producing errors. To determine which problem it is, use a different software package on the machines, and see whether files saved to the floppy can be read back on each machine. If all three machines can read each other's files, then it must be a problem with the WordPerfect software, and it should be reinstalled. It is possible that if the system had been upgraded from version 4.0 to version 5.1, some of the version 4.0 files are still present in the appropriate directory of machine C.

However, if the problem persists, then it is more than likely due to the disk drive speed or alignment being out of the specified tolerance range on one of the systems. As data can be transferred between machines A and B, but not C, it is likely that C is the problem system. It is quite common to find that a system with the drive speed or alignment on the edge of the tolerance range can read and write data to disks that it has formatted. It is only when disks formatted on another system are introduced that the problem exhibits. If this is the problem, then it is also likely that disks used on machine C would not work on machines A and B.

28   The success of the knock on the side technique to fix the problem suggests that there is possibly a loose connection inside the monitor. Alternatively, some systems have a special time-out feature, which switches off the monitor if there is no change to the picture for a set time. This prevents an image being permanently burned into the phosphorus on the screen, and is not a fault at all. Loose connections in a monitor are not repairable by the troubleshooter, as these devices must never be opened or repaired by untrained personnel as they contain lethal voltages, even for several hours after they have been switched off and unplugged. Therefore the only remedy is to have the monitor serviced by the local repair centre.

29   As all of the problems are oriented towards floppy disks it is fairly safe to assume that there is some problem in their handling, especially as the hardware appears to be OK. It is more than likely that the read errors etc are due to the floppies being mis-treated, either by being bent, heated or by having their surfaces contaminated with fingerprints. The floppy disk care guidelines should be explained to the user in question. If the problem is not due to the handling, then the only other cause is a faulty disk controller which can be diagnosed and replaced.

30   The only reason that RESTORE will not recover files is if a different version of DOS is being used on the second machine. The BACKUP and RESTORE commands are a matched pair, and as such the same version must be used for both backing up and restoring the data. Since copy does not encrypt the files, then any version of DOS can be used at either end of the process.

31   This is a fairly rare fault, and is due to the battery used for the backed up RAM going flat. This RAM is used to store a variety of general settings, such as the current date and time, the country code and the system configuration. If the battery goes flat, then the settings are lost. With certain systems, the SETUP procedure will not execute properly if the battery is flat. Note that in general, these batteries are either rechargeable, in which case they should never go flat if the system is regularly used, or they are long-life lithium batteries, with a life expectancy of over five years. If the battery goes flat in less time than this then it may be that there is a fault in the system causing a greater than normal power drain.

32   The answer to this is to run through a checklist of standard faults:

   • Check printer cable is connected at both ends
   • Check printer has power, is on-line, has enough paper and is correctly loaded
   • Check software is being correctly used (ie correct printer driver is in use).

If this does not highlight the cause of the problem, then:

   • Replace printer cable with a different one and try again
   • Switch off printer, leave for 10 minutes then switch on and try again. This clears the buffer of data from any previous jobs.
   • Reboot computer and restart software.

If the problem is still not solved then it is likely to be due to a hardware fault in either the PC or the printer itself. If there is another printer available that would work with the existing interface card, then it can be connected to see whether the fault is with the printer or the PC. If it is with the PC, it is likely to be the interface card or the system board. As the printer was functioning previously, it is unlikely to be incorrectly set switches, and so other than trying another interface card there is little else the troubleshooter can do. If the problem is isolated to either the card, cable or printer and a suitable substitution is made, ensure that the user is aware of the order in which computer components should be switched on. The general rule is that peripherals should be powered on before the system unit; it is possible, if unlikely, that failure to observe this rule can cause peripheral components to fail.

If the problem is due to the failure of the printer, it will be necessary to have the unit repaired by a qualified engineer as there is nothing the troubleshooter can do to remedy such faults.

33   The most likely cause is incorrect installation of the software. Any display system must have the correct software drivers loaded before it will work correctly. This is because certain displays take the data signals directly from the software, whilst others require it to be routed through the BIOS. Thus, the driver determines which way the signals should be transmitted to the display card. The remedy to the problem is to reinstall the software, and select the correct display.

Although less likely, it is possible that the interface card is sending a bad signal to the monitor, or that the monitor itself is faulty. Swapping out these components should isolate the source of the problem.

> ### WARNING
>
> *If the monitor is suspected to be the cause of the problem, never attempt to open it up. Other than adjusting external switches, and checking external connections, all repairs must be left to a qualified technician.*

34   Although the question reports that two system disks have been tried in the system, it is advisable not to entirely trust the word of the user and the troubleshooter should test the system again with a reliable system disk. If the same message is displayed, then there are three components that are likely to have caused this problem. First, the disk drive itself may be at fault, either through its adjustments being incorrect (alignment or speed) or by one or more of its internal components failing. Secondly, the disk drive controller may be faulty. Thirdly, the motherboard components may be at fault.

If there are two floppy disks on the system the cables can be swapped and the system booted from the other drive. If this works, the fault is with the disk drive. If the bootup procedure still fails then the next area to check is the cable and controller card. If, after swapping these components, the problem persists, it is most likely to be due to motherboard problems and an engineer should be called.

35   If the high-level format does not remove the problem of bad sectors, then the disk must be low-level formatted. It is essential that a full backup of all data and programs be made before proceeding. A low level formatting program can then be used to format the disk, and mark any bad sectors so that they are not used by DOS. The low level formatting programs are not supplied with all versions of DOS, so it may be necessary to contact the supplier of the system as it is important to use a program that is compatible with the disk drive in use. If the problems persists after low-level formatting, then the disk is at fault and should be replaced to ensure that no data is lost.

36   This layout of the system is particularly likely to cause problems, due to the proximity of the various pieces of equipment. First, when the printer is operating it may cause interference on the screen of the monitor. Whilst this is not generally dangerous, it is annoying. Secondly, the high voltage signals in the monitor may well interfere with the signals that are sent to the printer, especially if a parallel interface is used, as the cable will have to run immediately behind the monitor. This may at times cause information to be garbled when printed, or occasionally cause the printer to hang, possibly crashing the system. There is also a greater likelihood of heat related problems as the stacked systems do not always allow

adequate ventilation around the various peripherals. In addition, vibrations from the printer can lead to chip creep. In general, the different system components should not be stacked in this way, and a reasonable distance should be left between them. Cable should be routed sensibly, with thought to possible interference. Note that PCs are internally screened against electrical interference and so are less susceptible to it than cable etc.

37   All printers and plotters have some form of buffer that is used to store the information from the computer before it is printed. This is due to the fact that printers and plotters can only reproduce the data at a much slower rate than the computer can transmit it to them. The more advanced devices have larger buffers, and so can store more information. Thus when the command was issued, a large amount of data was transmitted to the plotter and stored in its buffer. When the command was cancelled, the PC stopped transmitting, but the plotter still has a full buffer which it will continue to process. The only way to stop the plotter will be to switch it off and leave it for a couple of minutes or so. If this means that control software has to be loaded into it when it is started up again, then it may be better to let it finish plotting rather than switching it off. It can be seen from this example that it is important to ensure that the data is correct before actually printing or plotting it.

38   This is obviously an intermittent fault, and is almost certainly due to a component on the motherboard failing. It would be useful to try and ascertain how far through the POST the system got before failing. Had anything been displayed on the screen? Had the disk drive light flashed on? If the drive light did come on, then it is possible that the problem is connected with the disk drive. However more likely culprits are the BIOS chips, the clock circuitry and, in particular, one of the crystals. You could try to diagnose the problem yourself, and in many cases this may work. However, as the problem is intermittent, it may not show up again for some time. Thus you would be well advised in this case to refer the equipment to a trained technician, who will have the equipment to recreate the fault and thus have a better chance of diagnosing the problem.

39   This problem is again due to the TSR programs that are in use, although not because of the amount of memory that they consume. In this case, the problem lies in the fact that there are so many different TSRs loaded. There will be one for the virtual disk, one for expanded memory management, one for keyboard control (this is a DOS TSR) and also there are the utility TSRs such as SideKick. The problem occurs when calling up the utilities because they are all probably trying to use the same signal lines. Invoking the utility has the effect of overloading these signal lines, thus causing the system to crash. The only way to guarantee that the problem does not occur is to use fewer TSRs. For example, the virtual disk is perhaps not essential. It may also be possible to remove the DOS keyboard control TSR, which will have the effect of making the keyboard work as if it were American (eg [Shift]+[2] gives @ instead of "). In some cases, it may be sufficient to change the order in which the TSRs are loaded into memory, but as there may be many possible combinations, this trial and error approach can be time consuming.

40   The answer to this problem lies in the use of a special keyboard shortcut that enables the generation of any ASCII character simply from its code. For example, the Yen sign (¥) has an ASCII code of 157. To obtain the character on the screen, hold down

the [Alt] key and enter the numbers 1, 5 and 7 on the numeric keypad to the right of the keyboard. On releasing the [Alt] key after entering the code the character appears on the screen. This method works in most software packages, and allows the user to produce a wide range of special symbols and characters, such as ¥ Ç Æ § ¶ © ® ™.

Note, however, that these characters will not necessarily appear on the printer when the document is printed. They will only correspond to the screen if the appropriate character set has been selected on the printer using the DIP switches inside the device, or if appropriate fonts are installed.

15.3 SUMMARY

This chapter has served to illustrate some of the more common problems that occur, together with a few that are less common. It can be seen that in some cases the symptoms of the faults are not necessarily obvious, but indicate at first sight that the problem lies elsewhere. This is particularly noticeable with problems involving software incompatibilities, where error messages and other symptoms often indicate that the problems are hardware orientated.

With these points in mind, it is only by considering the situation as a whole that a solution will be found. Therefore it is always wise to only make a decision as to the cause of the problem when the full complement of information, error messages and symptoms are available for inspection.

16 How to Introduce PC Support into Your Organisation Effectively

16.1 THE IMPORTANCE OF PC SUPPORT

In the previous chapters focus has been placed on the issues of troubleshooting and how to prepare PC systems for new peripherals or new software. Troubleshooting is in fact a form of first aid and can actually be seen as part of a greater issue of PC support which includes the preparation of systems for additional applications. Therefore in this final chapter the issues of PC support are directly emphasised as a way of minimising problems and maximising user self help.

In order to ensure that the firm obtains maximum benefits from the concepts of PC support it is necessary to prepare the organisation in a number of ways. The following is an eight-step approach:

1 Create a PC support organisation

The main form of PC support organisation is the information centre. Information centres are set up for the purposes of assisting users obtain the best value from their systems. In larger firms the information centre will include a help desk which will act as a frontline troubleshooter. Help desks will often give advice on the phone and thus help individual users find faults and make minor repairs. Similarly help desk staff may assist users install hardware or software. In small firms an individual may be designated to be both the information centre and the help desk.

2 User training

To attempt to minimise the number of calls which the help desk will receive appropriate training should be given to users. Users should attend a training course in hardware and software configuration as well as basic troubleshooting techniques. In addition users may be given checklists which they can use to do preliminary diagnostic work to see if they are experiencing very trivial faults before they call for assistance from the help desk.

3 Departmental gurus

In larger firms a technique that is frequently used is the appointment of departmental gurus. A departmental guru is an individual who has a particular interest and aptitude in personal computing and who is prepared to assist his/her colleagues with minor problems as they arrive. Departmental gurus take some of the pressure off the help desk.

4 PC registers

In order to assist users, gurus and help desk staff it is important that the exact nature of a configuration and the software in use be known. Therefore PC hardware and software asset registers must be established and continually updated by the support centre. In addition to the asset register, information on who has access to each machine should be held.

5 Tools and equipment

The troubleshooter must have a basic set of tools and equipment to hand in order to perform routine tasks. These include a toolkit of screwdrivers, chip extractors etc, as well as software utilities, books and manuals. Particularly in larger organisations, a "spares kit" should be available with items ranging from cables to spare disk drives, controllers or even entire systems.

6 Insurance and warranty

It is possible that the firm's insurance may not cover accidents to either the staff or the equipment when users attempt to make repairs. Clearly there is a risk to both individuals and the equipment and although this book has continually emphasised ways in which to reduce the risk, accidents still sometimes occur. Therefore it is important to ensure that the firms' insurance covers both staff and equipment adequately.

Similarly to the issue of insurance is the question of hardware and software warranties which may be nullified if equipment is not handled in the correct manner. Therefore if the equipment is under warranty ensure that nothing is done to put this is jeopardy.

7 Access to software

It is clearly important to ensure that employees use only registered copies of software on their systems. For users to continue to be productive, necessary software and updates must be made available as and when required.

8 Commitment from management

In order for the previous six issues to be fully addressed as well as funded it is important to obtain the commitment of senior management to the use of personal computers in the firm. Without this the PC support function will not be properly staffed or funded.

16.2 SUMMARY

The philosophy that has underpinned all the discussion in this book is that users and internal support staff can save the firm considerable time and cost in undertaking routine hardware and software support and maintenance for themselves. However this always involves some degree of risk and it is essential that all those concerned always act with considerable care as a reckless approach to personal computers can not only damage the equipment but cause harm to life and limb.

Appendix 1
Glossary

Adapter	A printed-circuit card on board used to connect peripheral equipment such as disk drives and display monitors to the IBM PC.
Address Bus	The collection of tracks on the motherboard that carry the address information between the CPU and memory or external storage devices. On the original IBM PC there were 20 individual tracks, whilst the AT has 24. Systems based on the 80386 and 80486 processors have 32. The number of tracks is often referred to as the bit rating of the bus, thus it may be a 20-bit, 24-bit or 32-bit address bus.
Address	A value representing a unique location in IBM PC memory.
ANSI **American National** **Standards Institute**	Organisation that sets standards on a wide range of issues from cable specifications to screen customisations. DOS offers the ANSI.SYS device driver to makes the screen and keyboard compatible with the standards established for terminals by the American National Standards Institute.
API **Application Program** **Interface**	The API provides a channel or linkage point between an application and the underlying software which might be an operating system or communications software. Standards organisations are currently promoting APIs as the most strategic route to portability and compatibility.
Architecture	The architecture of the system describes its overall design philosophy. PCs are often described as having an 8-bit, 16-bit or 32-bit architecture, which relates to the size of the data bus on the motherboard.
ASCII **American Standard Code** **For Information** **Interchange**	A code representing the 128 different character symbols that can be generated from a 7-bit value, although not all of these characters are printable. The ASCII character set has been expanded to 256 characters for use in the IBM PC, and is now standard for all PC compatibles. Thus 1 byte can represents any single ASCII character.

AT
Advanced Technology

First 80286 personal computer from IBM

Baud

A unit of measurement for the speed of digital communications; for practical purposes one baud equates approximately to one bit per second.

BIOS
Basic Input/Output
System

A collection of special routines that are stored in a special ROM chip in the IBM PC and compatibles. These routines control all standard input and output functions involving the keyboard, display unit, disk drives and interface ports, and start the computer up when it is switched on or reset.

BIT
BInary digiT

A bit is the smallest unit of information storage, and can have a value of 0 or 1. Bits are grouped into larger units called Bytes and Words.

Boot

A term applied to the process of loading and starting an operating system. The boot process is initiated by the BIOS of the computer system. The terms was used in the early days of computing to describe the startup process for mainframe computers, which were said to pull themselves up by their 'bootstrap.'

bps
Bits Per Second

A measurement of speed, most often used to quantify the rate of data transfer between two devices such as the microprocessor and the disk drive logic. This should always be represented in lower case.

Buffer

A storage location in an electronic chip that is used to temporarily hold data during electronic communication between two devices that are operating different speeds. Buffers exist in the PC for communicating with the keyboard, the disks and the interface ports.

Bus

A communication circuit in a computer. The IBM PC has a data bus, a control bus and an address bus. Other systems may have additional buses for other purposes. The bus allows multiple BITs of information to be communicated simultaneously, thus enhancing the speed of the system.

Byte

A byte is a group of eight bits, and is the standard unit of storage in a computer system. A byte can represent any decimal value between 0 and 255, or any ASCII character.

CGA
Colour Graphics Adapter

Usually in the form of a peripheral card, produces a screen resolution of 320 x 200 pixels in four colours or 640x200 pixels in two colours selected from a palette of 16 colours.

Channel

A pathway for input or output of information. The expansion slots are called the PC's I/O channel, and the circuitry allowing the CPU to communicate with the disk drive is known as the disk channel.

Chip	A slang term for an integrated circuit. Derived from *Silicon Chip*, which describes the material from which such devices are constructed.
Clock	In computer terminology the term clock refers to two things: first, a circuit that sends a consistent, periodic signal that is used to step logic information through a computer circuit, and secondly, the logic in the computer that keeps track of the current date and time.
Cold Boot	The process of switching the machine on, and starting operations by initialising the start-up conditions. The cold boot process assumes no previous activity in the computer and sets all the registers in the machine accordingly.
Control Bus	The circuit along which control signals are transmitted. The control bus passes through the major integrated circuits that are installed on the motherboard.
cps **Cycles Per Second** **or Characters Per Second**	Measurements of speeds. Cycles per second is the same as frequency, thus 10cps = 10Hz. Characters per second is a measure of printer speed, often used with dot matrix printers which may have speeds of 25cps, 100cps or greater. Should always be represented in lower case.
CPU **Central Processing Unit**	Refers to the microprocessor, which is the heart of the computer, and its immediate supporting circuitry. This device fetches, decodes, and executes instructions and controls the overall activity of the computer.
CRT **Cathode Ray Tube**	The display screen used in computer systems for viewing data and graphics. CRT displays are available in many different standards.
Data Bus	The collection of tracks on the motherboard that carry the data between the CPU and memory or other devices. On the original IBM PC there were eight individual tracks, whilst the AT has 16. Systems based on the 80386 and 80486 processors have 32. The number of tracks is often referred to as the bit rating of the bus, thus it may be an 8-bit, 16-bit or 32-bit data bus. The size of the data bus determines the *architecture* of the system.
Diagnostic	An action or program that detects and isolates malfunctions or failures in computer hardware or software.
DIL **Dual In-Line**	Term to describe any device with two rows of connecting pins. Often used interchangeably with DIP.
DIN **Deutsche Industrie Norm**	A German standards organisation. The term is most often encountered in the form of DIN plugs, which are used to connect the keyboard to the system unit.

DIP **Dual Inline Package**	Small semiconductor or switch set formed from a plastic package having two parallel rows of pins for connection to the motherboard.
DIP Switches	Sets of on/off switches used to establish specific device configurations within the system. Each bank of DIP switches usually has eight individual switches.
Disk	A magnetic device for the storage of computer data. PC Disks may be classed as either hard disks or floppy disks, and whilst in principle they are similar, the performance differs greatly between the two..
Display	The device on which visual information is displayed on a screen. Sometimes referred to as the screen, CRT or VDU.
DMA **Direct Memory Access**	A method for transferring data between the disk drive unit and main memory, by-passing the CPU. This significantly enhances the speed of access to disk data, as the CPU is not tied-down to trivial data transfer operations.
DOS **Disk Operating System**	An operating system for the manipulation of disk based information. The most popular form of operating system is MS-DOS from Microsoft. This was produced for the original IBM PC, and is still by far the most used. MS-DOS may also be encountered under the name of PC-DOS as it was licenced to several different manufacturers.
DPI **Dots Per Inch**	Number of dots generated by printers or computer software for every linear inch of paper.
DRAM **Dynamic Random** **Access Memory**	Most of the RAM that is used by the system is dynamic which means it has to be continually refreshed in order to retain information.
Driver	A short routine or program that controls the I/O interaction between two devices (eg between the disk drives and the computer's CPU). The driver is specific to one particular device.
EBCDIC **Extended Binary Coded** **Decimal Interchange Code**	IBM code format used to transfer information, particularly on mainframe and mini computers. It is sometimes necessary to use an EBCDIC to ASCII converter in order to read information from a mainframe into a PC.
EGA **Enhanced Graphics** **Adapter**	Usually in the form of a peripheral card, produces a screen resolution of 640 x 200 pixels or 640 x 350 pixels in 16 colours from a palette of up to 64 colours, depending on the particular card and/or configuration.
EISA **Expanded Industry** **Standard Architecture**	Standard for computer bus architecture developed to compete with and succeed the AT bus. EISA is a 32 bit bus with 32 address lines. Popular with 386 and 486 systems.

EOF **End Of File**	Term used by many programming language to indicate the end of a file.
EPROM **Erasable Programmable** **Read-Only Memory**	A type of ROM that can be reused. It is programmed with a special device called an *EPROM Blower* that applies a specified voltage to a certain pin on the chip when data is written to it. The contents of the chip can be erased by exposing the device to very intense ultra-violet light for 15-20 minutes
ESDI **Enhanced Small** **Device Interface**	Type of disk drive technology that has become popular recently. Competes with SCSI and is especially popular with high capacity drives.
Firmware	Programs and data that are stored in ROMs, PROMs and EPROMs. The BIOS of the computer system is an example of firmware.
Flip-flop	An electronic device that maintains a value of 1 or O until acted on by a signal on a certain input pin. Flip-flops form the basis of all electronic memory, and most computer logic circuitry.
GUI **Graphical User Interface**	Interface using Windows, Icons, Menus and Pull-down Screens (WIMPS). Usually operated partly or entirely through the use of a mouse.
Hardware	The physical components of a computer system, including the system unit, the disk drives, the keyboard, the printer, the monitor and all associated devices and option cards.
Head	The electro-magnetic device that transfers data to and from the disks.
Hz **Hertz**	A unit of frequency, used interchangably with cycles per second. Thus 1cps = 1Hz.
Hexadecimal	The numbering system using base 16, in which the values above 9 become A, B, C, D, E, and F. Each hexadecimal number can be represented as a 4-bit code, and thus two hexadecimal digits can represent any byte value..
IC **Integrated Circuit**	An electronic device created on a small silicon flake. It consists of a large number of logic gates and the paths connecting them, formed by very thin films of metal acting as wires. Each IC can perform one or more predefined operations. Integrated circuits are used extensively in all personal computers.
IEEE **Institute of Electrical and** **Electronic Engineers**	Long established institute whose members are drawn from industry and who attempt to establish industry standards. The IEEE 802 committee has published many definitive documents on local area networks.

Initialise	To set a storage location, counter, or variable to a starting value.
Interface	A boundary shared by two or more devices.
Interface Port	A term used as an overall descriptor for the serial and parallel ports. Whilst these components are used in different ways, from a design point of view they are very similar.
IRQ **Interrupt Request**	Technical term to describe the signal a device sends when is wants attention. Works in conjunction with the interrupt controller on the motherboard.
ISA **Industry Standard** **Architecture**	Term used to describe both the original 8-bit bus used on the PC, and the 16-bit bus used on the AT and compatibles..
ISO **International Standards** **Organisation**	An American based organisation which produces international specifications. Communications has always been an important area for the organisation and they developed a model to define a conceptual architecture of communications systems called the OSI Reference Model.
I/O **Input/output**	The process of entering information into the computer or transferring data from the computer to the outside world; for example, disk drives, keyboards, and display units are input/output devices.
K	Stands for Kilo, and in computer jargon is equal to 1024. Thus 1KB (Kilobyte) is 1024 bytes, which is a standard unit of measure when describing the capacity of memory and storage devices.
Kb **Kilobit**	One kilobit represents 1024 bits, where 1 bit is a 1 or 0 – the fundamental unit of digital data. Note the use of an uppercase K and lowercase b.
KB **Kilobyte**	One kilobyte represents 1024 bytes, where one byte is equal to eight bits and is generally referred to as being equal to a character. Note the use of uppercase K and uppercase B.
KHz **Kilohertz**	One thousand hertz, where hertz is a measure of frequency and one hertz is one cycle every second.
LAN **Local Area Network**	A communication network in which all of the nodes are in close proximity to each other, usually in the same building or group of buildings.
LCD **Liquid Crystal Display**	Type of display popular with laptop computers. Works on the principle of small reflective particles suspended in liquid crystal.
LED **Light Emitting Diode**	Semiconductor that emits light when electricity is passed through it. Common technology for small indicator lights.

Location	A place in memory where information may be stored.
Logic Bomb	A virus which remains inactive until a certain condition is satisfied, such as 90 percent of the memory being used by the operator.
Main Storage	The storage located in the computer for the operating system, programs, and data while they are executing. The main storage in the PC is the RAM memory.
MAN **Metropolitan Area** **Network**	Term used to describe a communications network that is geographically too big to be a LAN. Usually implies computers in different buildings in the same town or district.
Mb **Megabit**	One million bits. Note the use of uppercase M and lowercase b.
MB **Megabyte**	One million bytes. Note the use of uppercase M and uppercase B.
MCA **Micro Channel** **Architecture**	A design concept for computers which allows the number of interconnections between components to be restricted and controlled. The IBM PS/2 range are based on the MCA concept, as is the Olivetti P500.
MCGA **Multi-Colour Graphics** **Adapter**	Graphics adapter found on the IBM PS/2 series of computers. Produces a screen resolution of 320 x 200, 640 x 200 or 640 x 480 pixels in up to four colours from a palette of 16.
Memory	The hardware in or on which programs are stored. There are many different types of memory devices, including RAM and ROM chips, magnetic disks, magnetic tape, bubble memory and optical devices such as WORMS.
MFM **Modified Frequency** **Modulation**	Type of disk drive interface technology. Competes with RLL.
MHz **Megahertz**	A frequency of one million hertz.
Microprocessor	An integrated circuit that executes coded instructions that are entered, integrated, or stored within the device.
Modem **MOdulator/DEModulator**	A device that converts digital information into tones so it can be transmitted and received over communications lines such as telephone lines.
Monitor	(a) A high-resolution display unit used for displaying computer data. Monitors often produce sharper images than a standard television display. (b) A special program that is stored permanently in ROM; it enables interaction between you and the computer.

Motherboard	The large printed-circuit board (system board) in the computer on which most of the electronic devices are mounted. The motherboard is the primary or main board in the computer. All other interfaces receive control signals or information from the motherboard. Sometimes referred to as the system board.
MS-DOS **MicroSoft Disk** **Operating System**	Most popular personal computer operating system. MicroSoft is the name of the software house that wrote the operating system.
MTBF **Mean Time Between** **Failure**	Average period of time between the failure of a component. The term was more prevalent in the days of mini and mainframe computers which could have a MTBF of as little as 30 minutes.
Node	A node is the term applied to any device that is connected to a network that is capable of transmitting or receiving in its own right. Nodes may be personal computers, mini or mainframe computers, printers, terminals, gateways etc.
Noise	The electrical interference that distorts the transmission of data and results in errors in the data. Noise can be caused by the presence of an electrical field such as that generated by electric motors, heaters or TV/Radio in the vicinity of electrical signals.
ns **Nanosecond**	One billionth of a second. Note the use of lowercase n and lowercase s.
Open Architecture	In the context of this book, a term used to refer to the fact that the IBM-PCs technical specification is known to the general public and that the IBM-PC is mostly composed of standard integrated circuits. This approach allows the PC to be expanded and enhanced in many different ways.
Operating System	A collection of system programs that control the operation of a computer system. It also handles the interaction between parts of the computer system.
OSI **Open Systems** **Interconnection**	The ISO's OSI model is a set of guidelines for network design, divided into seven layers (physical, data link, network, transport, session, presentation, application).
Parallel Port	The interface used to transmit data from the computer to a remote device, typically a printer. It is also sometimes referred to as a Centronics Interface.
Peripheral	A device, often sold as part of the computer, that is connected to the computer to enhance its operation. Examples of peripherals include disk drives, display units, printers, and modems.

Pin	Any of the leads on a device, such as chip, that plug into a socket and connect it to a system.
Pixel	A picture element. The smallest unit in a display. Usually, this is a dot on the screen.
PM **Presentation Manager**	Version of the operating system OS/2 which uses a graphical user interface and controls other GUI software such as Lotus 1-2-3/G.
Port	A connection between the CPU and another device, such as an I/O device, which allows data to enter or leave the computer.
POST **Power On Self Test**	A diagnostic program on the BIOS chip which tests the system on start-up.
Power Supply	A component of the PC which acts both as a transformer and as a switching device supplying a variety of suitable voltages to the computer hardware.
PROM **Programmable Read** **Only Memory**	A type of ROM that does not have to have its contents defined when it is first manufactured. PROMs can be programmed in the same way as EPROMs, but they cannot be erased in any way. Most chips in PCs that are described as ROMs are actually PROMs and EPROMs.
PS/2 **Personal System 2**	Recent family of personal computers from IBM, successor to the PC.
RAM **Random Access Memory**	Memory that can be directly read from or written to by the CPU. The contents of this memory is lost once the computer is turned off.
Resolution	The measure of sharpness of a display image. Resolution may be described as high or low, or may be quantified in terms of the number of pixels on the screen.
RLL **Run Length Limited**	Type of disk drive interface technology. Competes with MFM.
ROM **Read-only Memory**	A type of memory chip that can be read from but cannot be written to or altered. ROM provides permanent storage for program instructions.
SAA **Systems Application** **Architecture**	An IBM defined set of standard interfaces and protocols that IBM intend to implement across their product line, thus providing compatibility and connectivity among IBM products.
SCSI **Small Computer** **Systems Interface**	Recent type of disk drive interface technology that became an official ANSI standard in 1986. Competes with ESDI for the control of high-performance hard disk drives.

Serial Port	An interface which transmits data on a one bit at a time basis. It may also be referred to as an RS232 Interface. It is normally used for communications purposes, although some printers must be connected using the serial interface.
Shadow Ram	An area of RAM set aside for use by the system. Sections of the ROM dealing with I/O operations are copied into this area which allows the routines to be executed much more quickly, due to the fact that the time taken to access the RAM is significantly less than that taken to access the ROM.
SIMM **Single Inline** **Memory Module**	Replacement technology for traditional memory chips. A circuit board with a single line of connecting pins plugs into the motherboard. Surface mount chips make up the memory modules. Differs from traditional memory in that it is a pre-defined assembly.
Software	The programs that determine or control the actions of the computer. Software may be oriented towards providing system control, utilities or applications.
Spike	A short, powerful burst of electrical energy that, if not by-passed (or shorted) to ground, can cause damage to electronic components.
SRAM **Static Random** **Access Memory**	A form of RAM that although still volatile, does not require to be continually refreshed in the same way as dynamic RAM.
Surge	A temporary increase in electrical voltage lasting long enough for its effect to be noticed on a meter.
System Board	The main printed circuit board in the systems box containing the microprocessor and other control chips, as well as the ROM and the RAM. Sometimes referred to as the Motherboard.
Time Bomb	A virus which remains inactive until a certain time, such as a specific date and time on the system clock.
TPI **Tracks Per Inch**	The surface of a disk is divided into concentric tracks and TPI defines the tracks per inch radius.
Transient	Brief fluctuations in voltage. Transients can be quite sizable in some situations, and can destroy equipment if no preventative measures are taken.
Trojan Horse	A virus which is disguised to be a useful program, often a utility.
Troubleshoot	To systematically locate a computer hardware failure. Software failures are found by systematic debugging.

TSR
Terminate and Stay
Resident

A terminate and stay resident program is a special form of program which does not remove itself from memory once it has been executed. It simply remains in the background of the computer, ready to be activated by some special event. It is only removed when the computer is switched off or reset.

TTL
Transistor/Transistor Logic

Standard which is met by many electronics devices and integrated circuits.

UPS
Uninterruptable Power
Supply

Power supply with a built-in battery that continues to provide power to equipment after mains power has failed.

VGA
Variable Graphics Array

Usually in the form of a peripheral card, can produce a screen resolution of 640 x 200, 640 x 350 or 640 x 480 pixels in 64 colours from a palette of 256, depending on the particular card and/or configuration.

Virus

A special form of computer program, normally created and executed without the operators knowledge. A virus may be malignant, in which case it intentionally causes damage, or benign, in which case it usually just displays a message. A virus is able to replicate itself and spread to other uninfected systems, often through networks, or un-authorised transfer of programs or data.

VLSI
Very Large-Scale
Integration

Term to describe the complexity of an integrated circuit. Normally implies the device consists of over one million transistors.

WAN
Wide Area Network

A communications network in which the nodes are spread over a wide area. Often WANs have nodes in different cities or even different countries.

Warm Boot

The process of restarting the computer without performing the POST. The warm boot is often initiated through software, or by the user pressing a Reset button.

Word

A group of two bytes. A word comprises 16 bits, and can store any decimal value between 0 and 65335. Many of the operations performed by the microprocessor can work with words as well as bytes, thus speeding up performance.

WORM
Write Once Read
Many times

Term used to describe laser or optical disks, the data on which cannot be erased as it can on traditional magnetic disks. Should always be represented in upper case.

Worm

A rogue piece of software which digs its way into one or more programs, often overwriting data as it goes. Worms are not true viruses as they do not replicate.

WYSBYGI
What You See Before
You Get It

Term invented with the introduction of the graphical user interface software which allows the user to preview the appearance of the printed document on the screen.

WYSINWYG
What You See Is Nearly
What You Get

Most WYSIWYG software packages only show you an approximation of what will be printed.

WYSIWYG
What You See Is
What You Get

Implies that the image on the screen represents exactly what will be printed.

Appendix 2
Bibliography and Reading List

Angermeyer J, Fahringer R, Jaeger K, Shafer D, *The Waite Group's Tricks of the MS-DOS Masters*, Howard W Sams, 1988

Beechhold H F, *The Brady Guide to Microcomputer Troubleshooting & Maintenance*, Prentice Hall Press, 1987

Berliner D, with DeVoney C, *Managing Your Hard Disk*, Que, 1986

Brenner R C, *IBM-PC Troubleshooting and Repair Guide*, Howard W Sams, 1988

Brenner R C, *IBM-PC Advanced Troubleshooting & Repair*, Howard W Sams, 1988

Foster D L, *The Practical Guide to the IBM-PC AT*, Addison-Wesley, 1985

Goldthorpe P, Disk Access, *PC Plus*, June/July 1990

Hordeski M, *The Illustrated Dictionary of Microcomputers, 3rd Edition*, TAB Books, 1990

IBM DOS Manual, IBM

IBM Technical Manual, IBM

IBM Users Manual, IBM

Kamin J, *Expert Advisor DOS, Up to and Including DOS 4.0*, Addison-Wesley, 1989

Norton P, *Inside the IBM-PC*, Prentice Hall Press, 1987

Norton P, *The Peter Norton Programmers Guide to the IBM PC*, MicroSoft Press, 1985

Penfold R A, *How to Expand, Modernise and Repair PCs and Compatibles*, Bernard Babani, April 1990

Rimmer S, *Bit-mapped Graphics*, Windcrest Books, 1990

Sheperd S, Digging Deep into Disks!, *.EXE Magazine*, Process Communications, June 1991

Simrin S, *The Waite Group's MS-DOS Bible*, Howard W Sams, 1989

Somerson P, *PC Magazine DOS Power Tools, 2nd Edition*, Bantam Books, 1990

Stephenson J G, Cahill B, *Microcomputer Troubleshooting and Repair*, Howard W Sams, 1988

Wolverton V, *Running MS-DOS*, MicroSoft Press, 1986

Wolverton V, *Supercharging MS-DOS*, MicroSoft Press, 1986

Appendix 3
Board Layouts

The following diagrams are examples of motherboard layouts for a range of different PCs. The first three boards represent the IBM PC, PC/XT and PC/AT computers whilst the fourth is a typical 80386 system board.

Readers should note that the layout and positioning of components on system boards varies quite considerably from computer to computer, and it is even possible to have two computers from the same manufacturer with apparently identical configurations, that have different system board layouts.

The highlighted and numbered components on these diagrams represent those items that are discussed in Chapter 3.

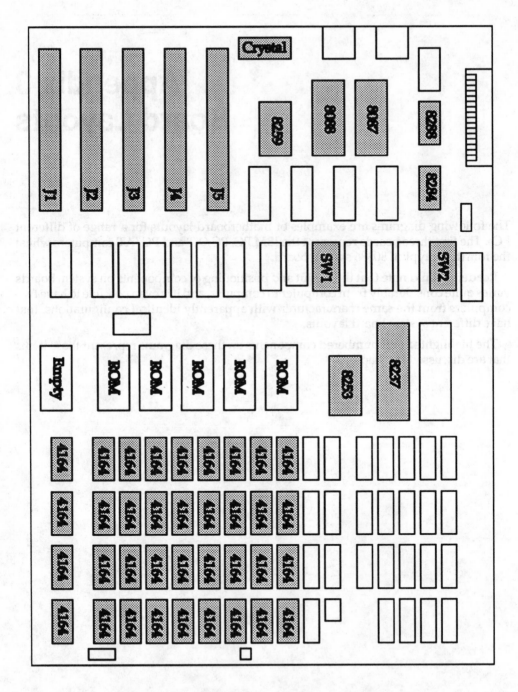

Chip location guide for the IBM-PC systems board

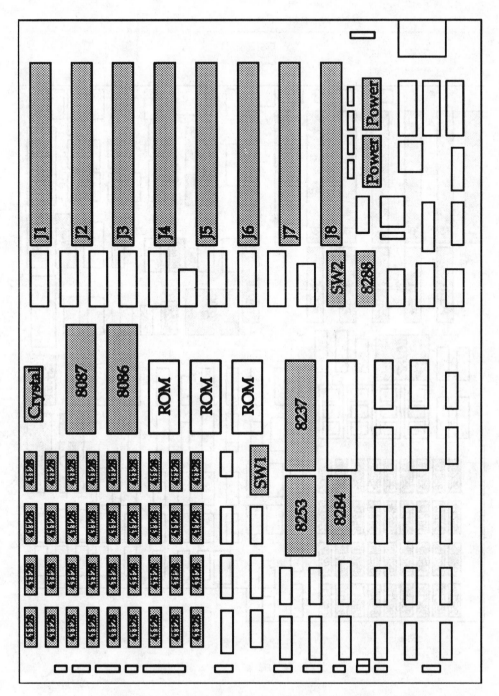

Chip location guide for the IBM-PC XT system board

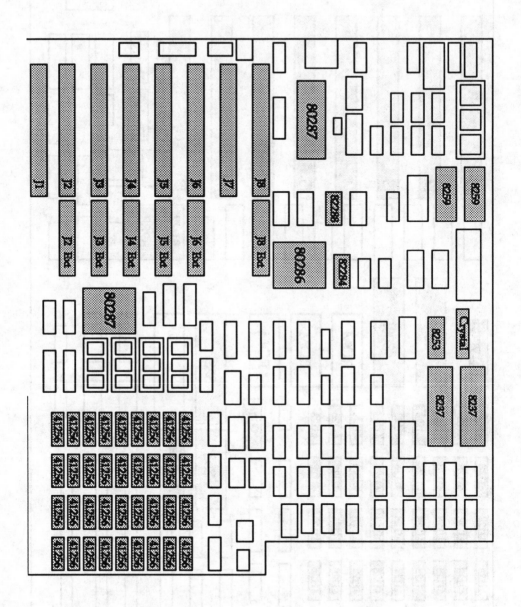

Chip location guide for the IBM-PC AT system board

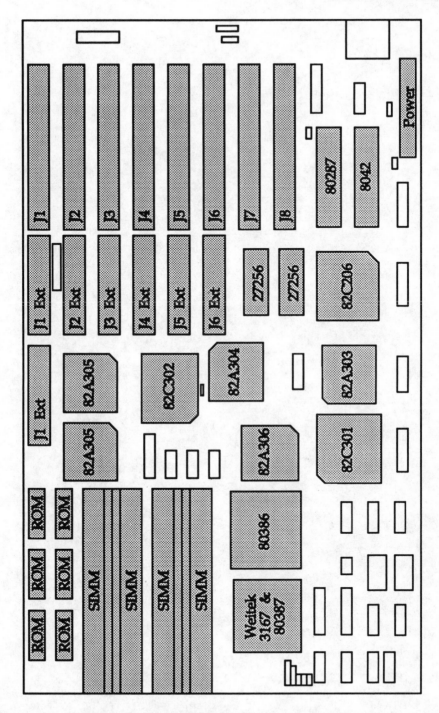

Chip location guide for a typical 80386 based IBM-PC compatible system board

Appendix 4
IBM Error Messages

The following list of error message has been compiled from many sources. The errors listed apply to IBM PC, PC/XT, PC/AT and PS/2 systems, although it is common to find that similar error codes and meanings have been adopted by other manufacturers of compatible systems.

01X	Undetermined problem errors
02x	Power supply errors
1xx	System Board Errors
101	System Board Error; Interrupt failure
102	System Board Error; Timer failure
103	System Board Error; Timer interrupt failure
104	System Board Error; Protected mode failure
105	System Board Error; Last 8042 command not accepted
106	System Board Error; Converting logic test
107	System Board Error; Hot Non Maskable Interrupt test
108	System Board Error; Timer bus test
109	System Board Error; Memory select error
110	PS/2 System Board Error; Parity check error
111	PS/2 Memory adapter error
112	PS/2 MicroChannel arbitration error
113	PS/2 MicroChannel arbitration error
121	Unexpected hardware interrupts occurred
131	PC system board cassette port wrap test failure
161	System Options Not Set – (Run SETUP); Dead battery
162	System Options Not Set – (Run SETUP); CMOS checksum/configuration error
163	Time & Date Not Set – (Run SETUP); Clock not updating

164	Memory Size Error – (Run SETUP); CMOS setting does not match memory
165	PS/2 System options not set
166	PS/2 Micro Channel adapter time-out error
199	User indicated INSTALLED DEVICES list not correct
2xx	Memory (RAM) errors
201	Memory test failure, error location will be displayed in hexadecimal
202	Memory address error, address lines 00–15
203	Memory address error, address lines 16–23
215	PS/2 Motherboard memory failure
216	PS/2 Motherboard memory failure
3xx	Keyboard errors
301	Keyboard did not respond to software reset or a stuck key failure was detected. If a stuck key was detected, the scan code for the key is displayed in hexadecimal
302	System Unit Keylock is Locked
303	Keyboard Or System Unit Error
304	Keyboard Or System Unit Error
305	PS/2 Keyboard fuse (on system board) error
4xx	Monochrome Display Adapter (MDA) errors
4xx	PS/2 System board parallel port errors
401	Monochrome memory test, horizontal sync frequency test, or video test failure
401	PS/2 System board parallel port failure
408	User indicated display attributes failure
416	User indicated character set failure
424	User indicated 80 x 25 mode failure
432	Parallel port test failure; monochrome display adapter
5xx	Colour Graphics Adapter (CGA) errors
501	CGA memory test, horizontal sync frequency test, or video test failure
508	User indicated display attribute failure
516	User indicated character set failure
524	User indicated 80 x 25 mode failure

532	User indicated 40 x 25 mode failure
540	User indicated 320 x 200 graphics mode failure
548	User indicated 640 x 200 graphics mode failure
6xx	Floppy drive/adapter errors
601	Floppy drive/adapter Power On Self Test failure
602	Drive test failure; disk boot record is not valid
606	Disk changeline function failure; drive error
607	Disk is write protected; drive error
608	Bad command; drive error
610	Disk initialisation; track 0 bad
611	Time-out; drive error
612	Bad Controller chip
613	Bad Direct Memory Access; drive error
614	Bad Direct Memory Access; boundary overrun
615	Bad index timing; drive error
616	Drive speed error
621	Bad seek; drive error
622	Bad Cyclic Redundancy Check (CRC); drive error
623	Record not found; drive error
624	Bad address mark; drive error
625	Bad Controller chip; seek error
626	Disk data compare error
7xx	8087, 80287 or 80387 maths co-processor errors
9xx	Parallel printer adapter errors
901	Parallel printer adapter test failure
10xx	Alternate parallel printer adapter errors
1001	Alternate parallel printer adapter test failure
11xx	Asynchronous communications adapter errors
11xx	PS/2 System board async port errors
1101	Asynchronous communications adapter test failure

1102	PS/2 System board async port or serial device error
1106	PS/2 System board async port or serial device error
1107	PS/2 System board async port or serial device error
1108	PS/2 System board async port or serial device error
1109	PS/2 System board async port or serial device error
1112	PS/2 System board async port error
1118	PS/2 System board async port error
1119	PS/2 System board async port error
12xx	Alternate asynchronous communications adapter errors
12xx	PS/2 Dual async adapter error
1201	Alternate asynchronous communications adapter test failure
1202	PS/2 Dual async adapter or serial device error
1206	PS/2 Dual async adapter or serial device error
1207	PS/2 Dual async adapter or serial cable error
1208	PS/2 Dual async adapter or serial device error
1209	PS/2 Dual async adapter or serial device error
1212	PS/2 Dual async adapter or system board error
1218	PS/2 Dual async adapter or system board error
1219	PS/2 Dual async adapter or system board error
1227	PS/2 Dual async adapter or system board error
1233	PS/2 Dual async adapter or system board error
1234	PS/2 Dual async adapter or system board error
13xx	Game control adapter errors
1301	Game control adapter test failure
1302	Joystick test failure
14xx	Matrix printer errors
15xx	Synchronous Data Link Control (SDLC) communications adapter errors
1510	8255 port B failure
1511	8255 port A failure
1512	8255 port C failure
1513	8253 timer 1 did not reach terminal count

1514	8253 timer 1 stuck on
1515	8253 timer 0 did not reach terminal count
1516	8253 timer 0 stuck on
1517	8253 timer 2 did not reach terminal count
1518	8263 timer 2 stuck on
1519	8273 Port B error
1520	8273 Port A error
1521	8273 command/read time-out
1522	Interrupt level 4 failure
1523	Ring Indicate stuck on
1524	Receive clock stuck on
1525	Transmit clock stuck on
1526	Test indicate stuck on
1527	Ring indicate not on
1528	Receive clock not on
1529	Transmit clock not on
1530	Test indicate not on
1531	Data set ready not on
1532	Carrier detect not on
1533	Clear to send not on
1534	Data set ready stuck on
1536	Clear to send stuck on
1537	Level 3 interrupt results error
1538	Receive interrupt results error
1539	Wrap data compare error
1540	Direct Memory Access channel 1 error
1541	Direct Memory Access channel 1 error
1542	Error in 3273 error checking or status reporting
1547	Stray interrupt level 4
1548	Stray interrupt level 3
1549	Interrupt presentation sequence time-out
16xx	Display emulation errors (327x, 5520, 525x)
17xx	Fixed disk errors

1701	Fixed disk POST error
1702	Fixed disk adapter error
1703	Fixed disk drive error
1704	Fixed disk adapter or drive error
1780	Fixed disk 0 failure
1781	Fixed disk 1 failure
1782	Fixed disk controller failure
1790	Fixed disk 0 error
1791	Fixed disk 1 error
18xx	I/O expansion unit errors
1801	I/O expansion unit POST error
1810	Enable/Disable failure
1811	Extender card wrap test failure; disabled
1812	High order address lines failure; disabled
1813	Wait state failure; disabled
1814	Enable/Disable could not be set on
1815	Wait state failure; disabled
1816	Extender card wrap test failure; enabled
1817	High order address lines failure; enabled
1818	Disable not functioning
1819	Wait request switch not set correctly
1820	Receiver card wrap test failure
1821	Receiver high order address lines failure
19xx	3270 PC attachment card errors
20xx	Binary Synchronous Communications (BSC) adapter errors
2010	8255 port A failure
2011	8255 port B failure
2012	8255 port C failure
2013	8253 timer 1 did not reach terminal count
2014	8253 timer 1 stuck on
2015	8253 timer 2 did not reach terminal count or timer 2 stuck on
2017	8251 Data set ready failed to come on

2018	8251 Clear to send not sensed
2019	8251 Data set ready stuck on
2020	8251 Clear to send stuck on
2021	8251 hardware reset failure
2022	8251 software reset failure
2023	8251 software "error reset" failure
2024	8251 transmit ready did not come on
2025	8251 receive ready did not come on
2026	8251 could not force "overrun" error status
2027	Interrupt failure; no timer interrupt
2028	Interrupt failure; transmit, replace card or planar
2029	Interrupt failure; transmit, replace card
2030	Interrupt failure; transmit, replace card or planar
2031	Interrupt failure; transmit, replace card
2033	Ring indicate stuck on
2034	Receive clock stuck on
2035	Transmit clock stuck on
2036	Test indicate stuck on
2037	Ring indicate stuck on
2038	Receive clock not on
2039	Transmit clock not on
2040	Test indicate not on
2041	Data set ready not on
2042	Carrier detect not on
2043	Clear to send not on
2044	Data set ready stuck on
2045	Carrier detect stuck on
2046	Clear to send stuck on
2047	Unexpected transmit interrupt
2048	Unexpected receive interrupt
2049	Transmit data did not equal receive data
2050	8251 detected overrun error
2051	Lost data set ready during data wrap
2052	Receive time-out during data wrap

21xx	Alternate binary synchronous communications adapter errors
2110	8255 port A failure
2111	8255 port B failure
2112	8255 port C failure
2113	8253 timer 1 did not reach terminal count
2114	8253 timer stuck on
2115	8253 timer 2 did not reach terminal count or timer 2 stuck on
2117	8251 Data set ready failed to come on
2118	8251 Clear to send not sensed
2119	8251 Data set ready stuck on
2120	8251 Clear to send stuck on
2121	8251 hardware reset failure
2122	8251 software reset failure
2123	8251 software "error reset" failure
2124	8251 transmit ready did not come on
2125	8251 receive ready did not come on
2126	8251 could not force "overrun" error status
2127	Interrupt failure; no timer interrupt
2128	Interrupt failure; transmit, replace card or planar
2129	Interrupt failure; transmit, replace card
2130	Interrupt failure; transmit, replace card or planar
2131	Interrupt failure; transmit, replace card
2133	Ring indicate stuck on
2134	Receive clock stuck on
2135	Transmit clock stuck on
2136	Test indicate stuck on
2137	Ring indicate stuck on
2138	Receive clock not on
2139	Transmit clock not on
2140	Test indicate not on
2141	Data set ready not on
2142	Carrier detect not on
2143	Clear to send not on
2144	Data set ready stuck on
2145	Carrier detect stuck on

2146	Clear to send stuck on
2147	Unexpected transmit interrupt
2148	Unexpected receive interrupt
2149	Transmit data did not equal receive data
2150	8251 detected overrun error
2151	Lost data set ready during data wrap
2152	Receive time-out during data wrap
22xx	Cluster adapter errors
24xx	Enhanced Graphics Adapter (EGA) errors
24xx	PS/2 System board Video Graphics Array (VGA) errors
26xx	XT/370 errors
27xx	AT/370 errors
28xx	3278/79 emulation adapter errors
29xx	Colour/graphics printer errors
30xx	Primary PC Network adapter errors
3001	Processor test failure
3002	ROM checksum test failure
3003	Unit ID PROM test failure
3004	RAM test failure
3005	Host Interface Controller test failure
3006	+/− 12v test failure
3007	Digital loopback test failure
3008	Host detected Host Interface Controller failure
3009	Sync failure and no Go bit
3010	Go bit and no Command 41
3012	Card not present
3013	Digital failure; fall through
3015	Analogue failure

3041	Hot carrier; not this card
3042	Hot carrier; this card!
31xx	Secondary PC Network adapter errors
3101	Processor test failure
3102	ROM checksum test failure
3103	Unit ID PROM test failure
3104	RAM test failure
3105	Host Interface Controller test failure
3106	+/– 12v test failure
3107	Digital loopback test failure
3108	Host detected Host Interface Controller failure
3109	Sync failure and no Go bit
3110	Host Interface Controller test OK and no Go bit
3111	Go bit and no Command 41
3112	Card not present
3113	Digital failure; fall through
3115	Analogue failure
3141	Hot carrier; not this card
3142	Hot carrier; this card!
	33xx Compact printer errors
36xx	General Purpose Interface Bus (GPIB) adapter errors
38xx	Data acquisition adapter errors
39xx	Professional graphics controller errors
71xx	Voice communications adapter errors
73xx	3.5 inch external diskette drive errors
7306	Disk changeline function failure; drive errors
7307	Disk is write protected; drive error
7308	Bad command; drive error
7310	Disk initialisation failure; track 0 bad

7311	Time-out; drive error
7312	Bad Controller chip
7313	Bad Direct Memory Access; drive error
7314	Bad Direct Memory Access; boundary overrun
7315	Bad index timing; drive error
7316	Drive speed error
7321	Bad seek; drive error
7322	Bad Cyclic Redundancy Check (CRC); drive error
7323	Record not found; drive error
7324	Bad address mark; drive error
7325	Bad Controller chip; seek error
74xx	IBM PS/2 Display adapter (VGA) card) errors
85xx	IBM Expanded Memory Adapter (XMA) errors
86xx	PS/2 Pointing device errors
8601	PS/2 Pointing device error
8602	PS/2 Pointing device error
8603	PS/2 Pointing device error or System board failure
89xx	Music feature card errors
100xx	PS/2 Multiprotocol adapter errors
10002	PS/2 Multiprotocol adapter or serial device error
10006	PS/2 Multiprotocol adapter or serial device error
10007	PS/2 Multiprotocol adapter or communication cable error
10008	PS/2 Multiprotocol adapter or serial device error
10009	PS/2 Multiprotocol adapter or serial device error
10012	PS/2 Multiprotocol adapter or system board error
10018	PS/2 Multiprotocol adapter or system board error
10019	PS/2 Multiprotocol adapter or system board error
10042	PS/2 Multiprotocol adapter or system board error
10056	PS/2 Multiprotocol adapter or system board error

104xx	PS/2 ESDI Fixed disk errors
10480	PS/2 ESDI Fixed disk 0 failure
10481	PS/2 ESDI Fixed disk 1 failure
10482	PS/2 ESDI Fixed disk controller failure
10483	PS/2 ESDI Fixed disk controller failure
10490	PS/2 ESDI Fixed disk 0 error
10491	PS/2 ESDI Fixed disk 1 error

Index

8086	9, 41–42
8088	9, 41–42, 55
80286	9, 41–42, 55
80386	10, 41–42, 57
80486	10, 41–43
Amstrad PC	11
anti-static wristband	30
architecture	124
ASCII	17, 18
ash	107, 110
asset register	24
atmospheric corrosion	114
audit log	185
AUTOEXEC.BAT	70, 132, 135, 142, 158–160
AZERTY	17
bandwidth	19
bank switching	56
BASIC	50
batch files	162–165
Bernoulli Box	16
biometrics	180
BIOS	50, 87, 125
blackouts	111
boot	90
boot sector virus	220
bootstrap	90
Brain virus	225

brownouts   111
bus controller   48
bus network   200

cable terminators   208
Cassette   13
CD ROM   16
CGA   18–19
checklists   66–67
chip   30, 35–36, 39–54, 54–65, 70, 83, 136–141
   extractor   30
   orientation 138, 140
cleaning implements   31
clock   47
   speed   137
coaxial cable   205
cold boot   90
Compaq   11, 22
compatibility   124–125
configuration   7, 24–27, 52–53
CONFIG.SYS   70, 132, 135, 142, 152–158, 206, 208
conflicts
   IRQ   207
   memory address 208
COPY CON: 161
corrosion   107, 114
crystal   51–52

daisywheel printer   20
data
   security   177
   protecting the 179–180
Data Protection act   182
DEBUG   167–175
diagnosing   61–88
diagnostics   31, 70, 92–97, 209–215
DIP switches   36, 52–54, 127, 129–130, 133–134, 141
directories   149–152
disk drives   11, 13–16, 34, 36–37, 70, 75–83

alignment	119
controller	11, 14, 46, 78–80
density	13–14
head cleaning	75–78, 116–118
maintenance	116–120
speed tests	118–119
Disk Optimizer	102–103
disk partitions	146
dismantling	22, 29, 31–38
display unit	17–20, 46, 85
colour	17
monochrome	17
distributed data processing (DDP)	196
DMA	36, 48
dongle	188
DOS	31, 57–59
dot matrix printer	20
Dr Solomon's Anti-Virus Toolkit	31, 231–232
DR-DOS	183
dust	107, 110
dynamic RAM (DRAM)	49, 136–141
EDLIN	161
EGA	18–19
EISA	46, 124
electronic mail (E-MAIL)	196, 229
EMS	56–57
encoding	180
encryption	180, 185
ESDI	14–15
Ethernet	203
execute protection	186
expanded memory	56–59
extended memory	55–59
FAST	179, 187–194
fault log	24, 67–70
faults	61–88
FDISK	146–148

fibre optic   205
file server   197
finger trouble   7
firmware   89
floppy disks   13–14, 16, 75–80, 120–121
FM   14
formatting   146
    high level   148–149
    low level format   146
function keys   16

galvanic corrosion   114
gateway   197
grey scales   19

hard disk   13–16, 36, 80–83
hardware   89
    protecting the   178
    security   177
head cleaning   75–78, 116–118
heat   70–73, 107, 108–109
Hercules   18
high level format   148–149

IBM PC   9, 16, 39, 41–55, 64, 124
    PC compatibles   9–10, 40–54, 124
    PC/XT   9, 40–54
    PC/AT   10, 16, 40–55, 65, 124
    PS/1   10
    PS/2   10, 15, 96–97, 124
IDE   14–16, 83
IEEE   201
ink jet printer   20
integrated circuit (IC)   30, 35–36, 39–54, 54–65, 70, 83, 136–141
    orientation   138, 140
Intel   45, 140
interface connection   125–126
interrupt (IRQ)   47, 126–128, 223
    conflicts   207

ISA	45–46, 124
ISO	201
Italian virus	226
I/O addresses	126–129, 208
I/O devices	21, 46
Jerusalem virus	226
jumpers	36, 53, 127
keyboard	16–17, 85
laptop computer	12, 16–17
laser printer	20
LASTDRIVE	206
LIM	56–57
local area network (LAN)	195
logic bomb	221
logical format	148–149
loop-back cable	31
low level format	146
Macintosh viruses	227–228
magnetism	107, 115
manuals	29.53
maths co-processor	45, 53–54, 136
MCA	46, 124
MCGA	18–19
MDA	18
memory	35, 46, 48–51, 53, 55–59
addresses	128–129, 208
cards	125
speed	49, 137
metal detector	121
MFM	14–15
microprocessor	35, 41–45
moisture	70
monitor	17–20
colour	17
monochrome	17–18

motherboard   11–12, 35, 39–54, 80, 83–84
mouse   21, 46
MS-DOS   9, 55
multi-sync monitor   19

NETBIOS   205
NetWare   214
network   195–218
   components   197–198
   diagnostics   209–215
   maintenance   216–218
   security   207
   server   197
   software   205–206
   standards   201
   topologies   198–200
   viruses   228–229
   wiring   204
Norton Sysinfo   141
Norton Utilities   31, 97–99
notebook computer   12, 16–17

operating system   44
option boards   11, 36–37, 45–46, 70, 83, 123
oscilloscope   30
OSI   201
   7-layer model   202
oxidation   114

page composition language (PCL)   20
Panasonic   11
parallel interface card   125
parasitic virus   220
parking disks   33, 92
partitioning   146–148
partitions   146
PATH   152
PC environment   7
PC Network   201

PCTools   31, 100–102
pliers   30
plotter   21
POST   50, 89–91, 141
Postscript   21
power supply   11–13, 34, 36–37, 73–75
power   107, 111–114
print server   197
printer   20
problem report   67–70
problems   7, 61–88
processor   41–45
programmable timer   47
protecting
    data   179–180
    hardware   178
    software   179

QWERTY   17

RAM   48–50, 55, 64, 136–141
reassembling   38
ring network   198–199
RLL   15
ROM   50–51, 89, 136

scanner   21
screwdrivers   29–30
SCSI   15
secure deletion   186
serial interface cards   125
SETUP   70, 92, 132, 135, 142
SIMM   36, 49, 136–141
SIP   136–141
soft error   109
software   31, 85, 89, 205–206
    protecting the   179
    security   177
soldering iron   30

spare parts   61–63
spike catcher   112
spindle speed   78, 118–119
star network   198
static electricity   30, 107
static RAM (SRAM)   49
SVGA   18–19
SX chips   43
system memory   55–56
system speed   51–52
system unit box   11–13, 24, 33–34

Tandon Data Pac   16
tape streamer   16
test meter   30
TestDrive   103–104, 120
thermal wipeout   109
time bomb   221
time slotting   185
timeout   185
Token Ring   202
tools   29
Toshiba   11–12
transients   111, 112–113
trap door   221
tree network   200
Trojan horse   221
troubleshooting   61–88
TSR   230
twisted pair cable   205

uninterruptable power supply (UPS)   75, 112–113

VGA   18–19
video adapters   125
video RAM   56
virus   219–235
    countermeasures   233–234
    recognition   224

wait state	137
WAN	195
warm boot	90
water	115
Weitek	45, 140
Winchester disk	14
Windows	57–59
wire cutters	30
wire strippers	30
worm	221
XGA	18–19
X-ray	121